The Expanding Universe of English II

Department of English
The University of Tokyo, Komaba

東京大学教養学部英語部会 編

University of Tokyo Press
東京大学出版会

EDWARD STEICHEN. *The Flatiron*, 1905. An example of Pictorialist photography. Gum-bichromate over platinum. Metropolitan Museum of Art, New York.
[SESSION 17] Arresting the Flux of Life

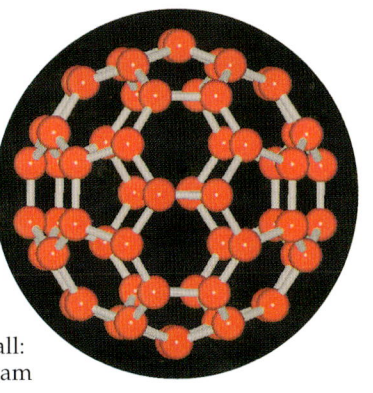

A buckeyball
(a buckminster-fullerene molecule)
[SESSION 22] The Buckeyball: A Diamond Maker's Dream

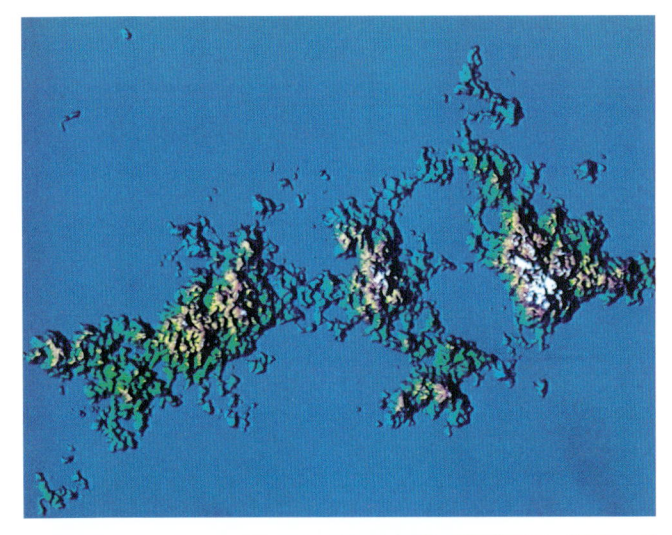

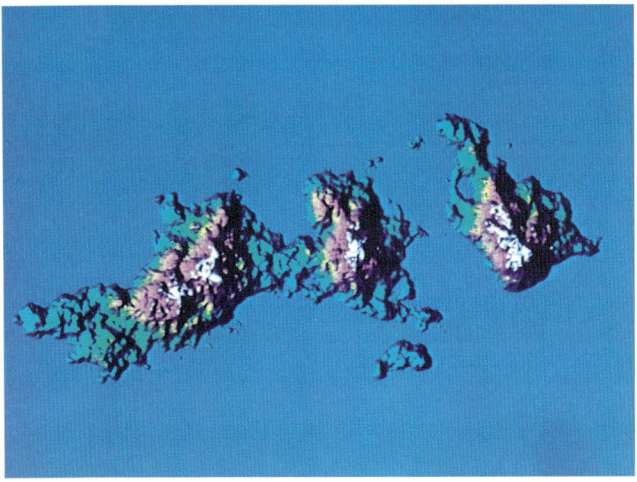

Fractal islands that never were.
[SESSION 14] The Birth of Fractal Geometry

A peasant's daily work through the seasons of the year.
[SESSION 16] **Time in Medieval Europe**

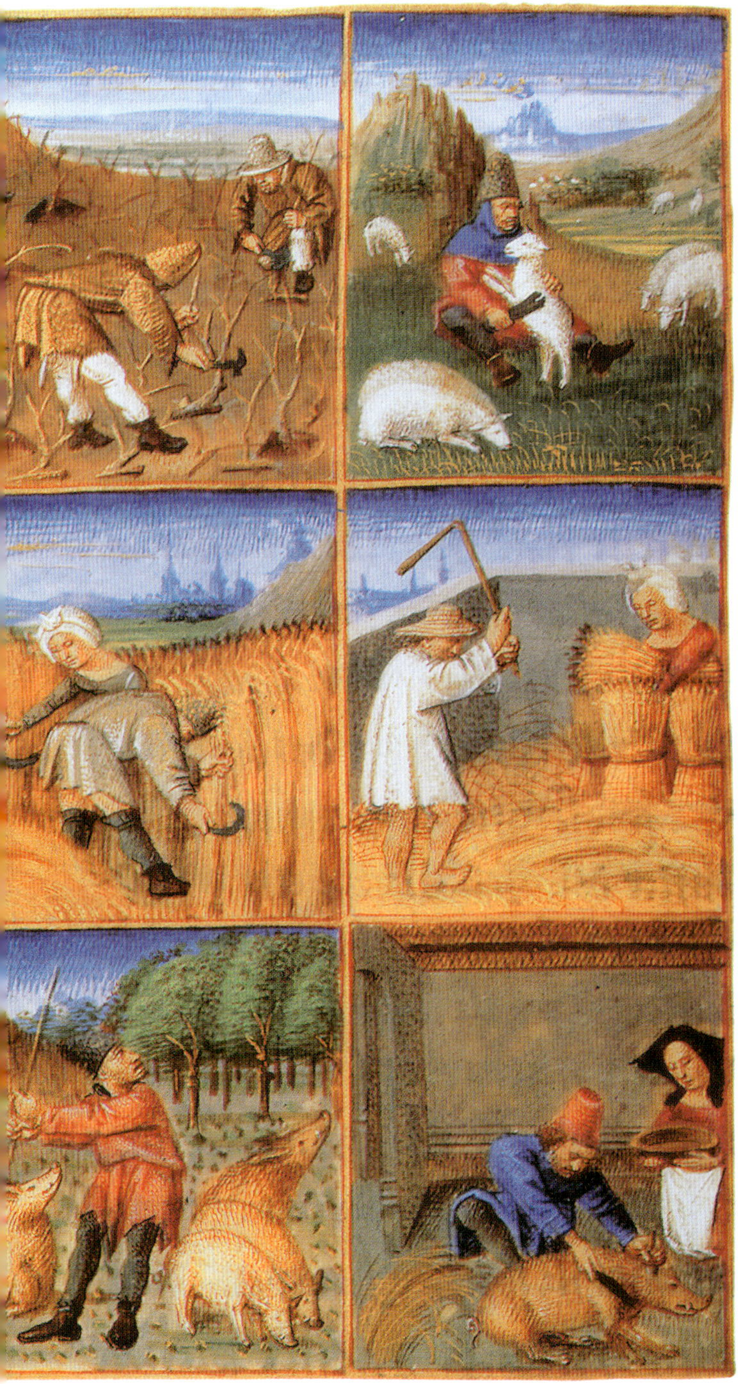

1992 1993

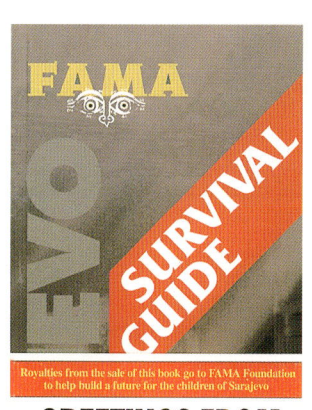

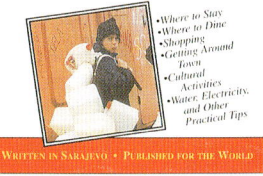

Sarajevo: Survival Guide and "Sarajevo: Survival Map"
[SESSION 13] Sarajevo: Survival Guide 1993

A portrait of Queen Elizabeth I, commemorating the defeat of the Spanish Armada in 1588.

A funeral procession, satirizing the extravagance of the fashionable gallant's wardrobe (*c.* 1625-30).
[SESSION 18] Our Myriad-Dressed Shakespeare

The Expanding Universe of English II

Contents

Preface xii
Acknowledgments xiv

Part I

SESSION 1 Why Do We Laugh?
            V. S. Ramachandran and Sandra Blakeslee 2
SESSION 2 On Jabberwocky   Martin Gardner 12
SESSION 3 The Light of Common Day   Arthur C. Clarke ... 22
SESSION 4 Natural Selection   Lyall Watson 32
SESSION 5 Agriculture's Mixed Blessing
            Jared Diamond 42
SESSION 6 Against Focused Attention
            Mary Catherine Bateson 52
SESSION 7 The Flesh of Language   David Abram 62
SESSION 8 The Fabrication of Race
            Matthew Frye Jacobson 72
SESSION 9 Multiple Personality   Ian Hacking 82
SESSION 10 The Pleasure of Music   Robert Jourdain 92
SESSION 11 None Was for a Party; All Were for the State
            Frank Muir 102

Part II

SESSION 12 The Imam and the Indian   Amitav Ghosh 112
SESSION 13 Sarajevo: Survival Guide 1993   FAMA 128
SESSION 14 The Birth of Fractal Geometry   James Gleick 140
SESSION 15 The Return of Depression Economics
            Paul Krugman 152
SESSION 16 Time in Medieval Europe   David Duncan 162
SESSION 17 Arresting the Flux of Life
            Naomi Rosenblum 172
SESSION 18 Our Myriad-Dressed Shakespeare
            Shoichiro Kawai 186
SESSION 19 The Jurassic According to Hollywood
            Stephen Jay Gould 198
SESSION 20 The New Age of Man   Malcolm Gladwell 208
SESSION 21 The Thrill of Fear   Walter Kendrick 218
SESSION 22 The Buckeyball: A Diamond Maker's Dream
            Robert M. Hazen 228

Preface

　本書は，東京大学教養学部2年生全員を対象した統一授業(英語I)のリーダーである．*The Expanding Universe of English* (1994) の全章が新しくなった．英語学習の刷新を図って7年前にスタートした私たちの授業は，これで1, 2年全セッションの入れ替えを終えたことになる．

　限られた回数の授業で何を読んだらいいのか．私たちの*Universe*シリーズでは，現代の知的話題を盛り込んだ，ナチュラルで活きのいい文章を，できるだけ広い分野から集めてくることを目指してきた．その基本方針は変わっていないが，ただ今回は，「雑多」であることのメリットよりも，各章に内容的なつながりをもたせることの価値を意識した．結果的に(生物・医学以外の)理工学系トピックがやや後退し，代わりに認知科学(心のメカニズム)・現代社会・表象文化史を扱うものが増えた．全体に生態学的・脱欧米中心主義的(ポストコロニアル)な視点が色濃く出たのは，私たち自身の関心がありようが率直に反映した結果だと思う．

　現代のポピュラーな書物から食いつまんで作ったとはいっても，語彙的にも内容的にも，大学教養課程に学ぶ学生にとっては，かなりの難物であることだろう．補注にあたっては，何よりも読者各自が一人で自然に読み下していく助けとなることを心がけた．CDをかけながら読む方もそうでない方も，なるべく段落途中でポーズを入れずに，まずは文章の流れを追ってほしい．そして段落の要点がつかめてから，注で細かな点をカバーし，その上でもう一度同じパラグラフをできるだけ一気に読んでみることをおすすめする．シリーズの伝統にならって，注の中にa / b選択問題を含めたが，これは文意の流れに正しくのっているかどうか自己チェックするためのもので，巻末の答えをそのつど参照する必要はないだろう．(なお，英米で異なる綴りや表記法については基本的に原著に拠った．発音表記は，英米の違いにあまりこだわらず，単純明快であることを旨とした．)

　全章を刷新したと書いたけれども，実は東大の授業では1997年以来*Expanding*の半分の章を入れ替えた『学内版』を使っており．その版で新しくした章のうち7本を本書にも採用している (SESSIONS 5, 6, 9, 13, 18,19 & 21)．

　今回新たにエントリーした15本は，みんなで持ち寄った題材を，編集班(河合祥一

PREFACE

郎，西村義樹，Brendan Wilson & 佐藤)が今年度の英語 I 運営班(大堀壽夫，中澤恒子，坪井栄治郎，小林宜子，寺澤盾，恒吉僚子)からのフィードバックを受けながら選定した．(SESSION 15 のテクストは，慶應義塾大学の大矢玲子氏から提供されたものである)．注つけ作業は，編集班 4 名に，矢口祐人，寺澤，恒吉が加わって書いた第一稿を，英語部会の比較的年長のメンバーが分担して補うという形で進め，最終的な統一(およびテクスト本文の画定)は Wilson と佐藤があたった．『学内版』から引き継いだ 7 課分は，英語 I 発足時より事実上の編集長を務めてきた柴田元幸(現・文学部)に多くを負っている．CD 添付版 CD の収録ディレクターは西村．吹き込み者は私たち英語部会のメンバーおよび非常勤講師である．

英語圏の言語・文学・文化・地域研究の一介の「専門家」にすぎない私たちが，総合大学の学生に「一般教養」を提供するというのは，ずいぶんと背伸びした話である．インターネットの時代に入って広い領域の知識がずいぶん楽に手に入るようになったとはいえ，今回のこの教科書も，部会外の助っ人を必要とした．とりわけ経済関係のことでは，日本政策投資銀行の花崎正晴氏に大変お世話になった．それでもまだ，編者の力不足から，不備が残ったかと思う．題材の新鮮さを売りにしたテクストを作り続けるのは，ある意味で怖い．だが鮮度を失ってしまうことは質の下落を容認することだ．情報化時代の教養教育は，楽しさも大きいとともにつらい面も多い．が，尻込みしてはいられない．

今回も，東京大学出版会の後藤健介氏の，優美にして高品質なサポートを受けることができた．4 ヶ月間に及ぶ，氏のマルチレベルの活躍が，時間に追われた私たちをどれほど助けてくれたことだろう．

2000 年 2 月

編者を代表して——佐藤良明

なお，注の作成にあたっては以下のレファレンスとウェブサイトを活用した．
Microsoft Bookshelf 97, *Microsoft Encarta 97*, *Encyclopedia Americana*, www.britannica.com, www.amazon.com, *The People's Chronology*, *Larousse Biographical Dictionary*, *The Oxford English Dictionary (2nd ed.)*, *Webster's Collegiate Dictionary (10th ed.)*, *Longman Language Activator*, 小学館『ランダムハウス英和大辞典』(第 2 版)，研究社『リーダーズ＋プラス』等．

Acknowledgments

Grateful acknowledgment is made for permission to reprint excerpts and figures from the following publications:

[Texts]
SESSION 1, "Why Do We Laugh?": From *Phantoms in the Brain* by V. S. Ramachandran, M.D., Ph.D. and Sandra Blakeslee. Copyright © 1998 by V. S. Ramachandran and Sandra Blakeslee. Reprinted by Permission of HarperCollins Publishers, Inc. (William Morrow).
SESSION 2, "On Jabberwocky": From *The Annotated Alice* by Martin Gardner (New York: W. W. Norton & Company, Inc.) Copyright © 1970 by Martin Gardner.
SESSION 3, "The Light of Common Day": From *By Space Possessed* by Arthur C. Clarke. Copyright © 1963/1993 by Arthur C. Clarke.
SESSION 4, "Natural Selection": From *Beyond Supernature* by Lyall Watson (London: Hodder and Stoughton). Copyright © by Lyall Watson. Reprinted by permission of David Higham Associates.
SESSION 5, "Agriculture's Mixed Blessing": From *The Third Chimpanzee* by Jared Diamond. Copyright © 1991/1993 by Jared Diamond. Reprinted by permission of Random House U.K. Ltd.
SESSION 6, "Against Focused Attention": From *Peripheral Visions* by Mary Catherine Bateson (New York: Harper-

ACKNOWLEDGMENTS

Collins Publishers, Inc.) Copyright © 1994 by Mary Catherine Bateson. Reprinted by permission of John Brockman Inc.

SESSION 7, "The Flesh of Language": From *The Spell of the Sensuous* by David Abram. Copyright © 1996 by David Abram. Reprinted by permission of Pantheon Books, a division of Random House, Inc.

SESSION 8, "The Fabrication of Race": From *Whiteness of a Different Color* by Matthew Frye Jacobson (Cambridge: Harvard University Press). Copyright © 1998 by Matthew Frye Jacobson.

SESSION 9, "Multiple Personality": From *Rewriting the Soul: Multiple Personality and the Sciences of Memory* by Ian Hacking. Copyright © 1995 by Princeton University Press.

SESSION 10, "The Pleasure of Music": From *Music, the Brain and Ecstasy* by Robert Jourdain. Copyright © 1997 by Robert Jourdain. Reprinted by permission of HarperCollins Publishers, Inc. (William Morrow).

SESSION 11, "None Was for a Party; All Were for the State": From *The Utterly Ultimate 'My Word' Collection* (London: Reed International Books). Copyright © 1991 by Frank Muir.

SESSION 12, "The Imam and the Indian": From *The Granta Book of Travel* (London: Granta Books). Copyright © 1988 by Amitav Ghosh.

SESSION 13, "Sarajevo: Survival Guide 1993": From *Sarajevo: Survival Guide* by FAMA. Copyright © 1993 by FAMA.

SESSION 14, "The Birth of Fractal Geometry": From *Chaos: Making of a New Science* by James Gleik (New York: Penguin Books USA). Copyright © 1987 by James Gleick.

SESSION 15, "The Return of Depression Economics": Reprinted by permission of *Foreign Affairs*, Jan./Feb., 1999. Copyright © 1999 by Paul Krugman, the Council on Foreign Relations, Inc.

SESSION 16, "Time in Medieval Europe": From *Calendar: Humanity's Epic Struggle to Determine a True and Accurate Year* by David Ewing Duncan. Reprinted by permission of

ACKNOWLEDGMENTS

HarperCollins Publishers, Inc. (Avon Books). Copyright © 1998 by David Duncan.

SESSION 17, "Arresting the Flux of Life": From *A World History of Photography*, The Third Edition (New York: Abbeville Press). Copyright © 1997 by Naomi Rosenblum.

SESSION 18, "Our Myriad-Dressed Shakespeare": Copyright © 1997 by Shoichiro Kawai.

SESSION 19, "The Jurassic According to Hollywood": From *Past Imperfect* by Mark C. Carnes (ed.) (New York: Henry Holt and Company, Inc.) Copyright © 1995 by Stephen Jay Gould, Agincourt Press. Reprinted by permission of Henry Holt and Company, Inc.

SESSION 20, "The New Age of Man": Originally published in *The New Yorker* (30 September 1996). Copyright © 1996 by Malcolm Gladwell. Reprinted by permission of the author.

SESSION 21, "The Thrill of Fear": From *The Thrill of Fear: 250 Years of Scary Entertainment* by Walter Kendrick (New York: Grove Weidenfeld). Copyright © 1991 by Walter Kendrick. Reprinted by permission of Grove/Atlantic, Inc.

SESSION 22, "The Buckeyball: A Diamond Maker's Dream": From *The New Alchemists* by Robert M. Hazen (New York: Times Books, Random House, Inc.) Copyright © 1993 by Robert M. Hazen.

[Frontispiece]
SESSION 13, *Sarajevo: Survival Guide* and "Sarajevo: Survival Map": Copyright © 1993 by FAMA.

SESSION 14, "Fractal islands that never were": From *The Fractal Geometry of Nature* by Benoit B. Mandelbrot (New York: W. H. Freeman and Company). Copyright © 1977/1983 by Benoit B. Mandelbrot.

SESSION 16, "A peasant's daily work through the seasons of the year": Archiv für Kunst und Geschichte, Berlin.

SESSION 17, "The Flation" by Edward Steichen, 1905: Metropolitan Museum of Art, New York.

SESSION 18, "A Portrait of Queen Elizabeth I": Bereleigh House, Hampshire. Collection of F. Tyrwhitt-Drake. "A Funeral

ACKNOWLEDGMENTS

Procession": the Bodleian Library. Reprinted from *The Riverside Shakespeare* by G. Blakemore Evans et al. (Boston: Houghton Mifflin Company, 1974).
SESSION 22, "A buckeyball": From *The New Alchemists* by Robert M. Hazen. Copyright © 1993 by Robert M. Hazen, Random House, Inc.

[Plates]
SESSION 1, Cartoons of Rober Crumb: From *The Sad Book: A Collection of Sad Stories* reprinted in *The Complete Crumb Comics*, Volume 4: "Mr. Sixties." Copyright © 1967/1995 by R. Crumb, American Greetings Corporation. Reprinted by permission of Fantagraphics Books.
SESSION 2, The original illustrations "Jabberwocky" and "Humpty Dumpty" by John Tenniel: From *Through the Looking Glass and What Alice Found There* (Lewis Carroll, 1872).
SESSION 3, Illustrations in the notes: From *Science Desk Reference* by The New York Public Library (New York: Stonesong Press, Inc.) Copyright © 1995 by The Stonesong Press, Inc., and The New York Public Library.
SESSION 13, Photographs: From *Sarajevo: Survival Guide*. Copyright © 1993 by FAMA.
SESSION 16, "Hildegard records a vision on a wax tablet with a stylus": From *Liber Divinorum operum*, Codex Latinum 1942 c. I v., Biblioteca Statale Lucca, Italy, courtesy of Benediktinerinnenabtei St. Hildegard, Rüdesheim.
SESSION 17, Edgar Degas, "Diego Martelli", 1879: Oil on canvas. National Gallery of Scotland, Edinburgh, Scotland.
SESSION 22, "Skybreak Dwelling": Reprinted from R. Buckminster Fuller and Robert Marks, 1960/1973, *The Dymaxion World of Buckminster Fuller* (New York: Anchor Books). Copyright © 1973 by R. Buckminster Fuller.

Part I

SESSION 1

Why Do We Laugh?

V. S. Ramachandran and Sandra Blakeslee

IF an alien ethologist were to land on earth and watch us humans, he would be mystified by many aspects of our behavior, but I'll wager that laughter would be very near the top of the list. As he watches people interacting, he notices that every now and then we suddenly stop what we're doing, grimace and make a loud repetitive sound in response to a wide variety of situations. What function could this mysterious behavior possibly serve? Cultural factors undoubtedly influence humor and what people find funny — the English are thought to have a sophisticated sense of humor, whereas Germans or Swiss, it is said, rarely find anything amusing. But even if this is true, might there still be some sort of "deep structure" underlying all humor?

Consider the following two jokes.

A fellow is sitting in a truck stop café in California, having lunch, when suddenly a giant panda bear walks in and orders a burger with fries and a chocolate milkshake. The bear sits down, eats the food, then stands up, shoots several of the other customers and runs out the door. The fellow is astonished, but the waiter seems completely undisturbed. "What the hell is going on?" the customer asks. "Oh, well, there's nothing surprising about that," says the waiter. "Just go look in the dictionary under 'panda.'" So the guy goes to the library, takes out a dictionary and looks up "panda" — a big furry, black and white

WHY DO WE LAUGH?

「紳士は金髪(ブロンド)がお好き」というマリリン・モンロー主演の映画があるが,本論の著者ラマチャンドラン教授は,かつて医学雑誌に「なぜ紳士は金髪が好きか」と題する論文を発表した.①相手が寄生虫に感染していないことが確かめやすい,②出産にとってマイナスとなる老齢の印が見えやすい,③顔面の紅潮や瞳孔拡張など性的興奮のようすが明らか,の3点を骨子に,金髪色白の女性を選ぶことが進化上有利にはたらくことを論じていくものだが,実はその論文,「進化心理学」につきまとう思考のいかがわしさを皮肉るパロディだった.

ここに展開される議論も,ほんの「試論」でしかないが,ひらめきに満ちた論の運びの軽やかさに啓発される読者も少なくないのではないか.著者は切断された手足の感覚が残る「幻影肢」の研究で知られる神経生理学者.1998年の話題の書 *Phantoms in the Brain* からの抜粋である.

[Notes]
[1]   **ethologist:** 動物行動学者
[3]   **I'll wager:** I'll bet
[6]   **grimace** [grímǝs, griméis]: (to make) a twisted expression on the face that usually shows disgust or pain
[15]   **truck stop café:** アメリカの高速道 (interstate highways or freeways) には「トラック専用」とは言えないにせよ,トラック(これがとてつもなくでかい)の運転手を主要客層としたサービスエリアがよくある.café という言葉は,アメリカでは手軽な食堂を指すことが多い.
[17]   **burger with fries:** hamburger (cheeseburger, etc.) with French fries. 日本語の「フライドポテト」に当たるものを北米では (French) fries, イギリス・オーストラリアでは chips という.北米で chips というのは「ポテトチップ」のことで,これをイギリス・オーストラリアでは crisps と呼ぶ.
[22]   **go look:** go and look. cf. *Come see me tomorrow.*

During the chaotic years of the late 1960s, Robert Crumb (1943–   ), an "underground" comic artist, had cult popularity among young and rebellious Americans. These cartoons are from his very early work, *The Sad Book: A Collection of Sad Stories.* © R. Crumb

SESSION 1

animal that lives in the rain forest of China. It eats shoots and leaves.

A magician was working on a cruise ship in the Caribbean. The audience would be different each week, so the magician allowed himself to do the same tricks over and over again. There was only one problem: The captain's parrot saw the shows each week and began to understand how the magician did every trick. Once it understood, it started shouting out in the middle of the show: "Up his sleeve! Up his sleeve!" (when the magician was about to produce a rabbit from a hat), and "Slipped out the back! Slipped out the back!" (when the magician was about to saw his assistant in half). The magician was furious but couldn't do anything; it was, after all, the captain's parrot. One night, the ship's main boiler burst, and the ship was blown into a thousand bits. When morning came, the magician found himself adrift on a piece of wood in the middle of the ocean with the parrot. They glared at each other with hate. Days passed. Neither spoke a word. After a week, the parrot looked the magician straight in the eye and said: "OK, you win. Now tell me — where's the ship?"

Why are these stories funny? And what do they have in common with other jokes? Despite all their surface diversity, most jokes and funny incidents have the following logical structure: Typically you lead the listener along a garden path of expectation, slowly building up tension. At the very end, you introduce an unexpected twist that entails a complete reinterpretation of all the preceding data, and moreover, it's critical that the new interpretation, though wholly unexpected, makes as much "sense" of the entire set of facts as did the originally "expected" interpretation. In this regard, jokes have much in common with scientific creativity, with what Thomas Kuhn calls a "paradigm shift" in response to a single "anomaly." (It's probably not coincidence that many of the most creative scientists have a great sense of humor.) Of course, the anomaly in the joke is the traditional punch line and the joke is "funny" only if

WHY DO WE LAUGH?

[1]   **shoot(s)**: 名詞としては「芽」の意．a bamboo shoot（タケノコ）
[3]   **A magician was …**: このジョークは，実はもともと著者が選んだものがあまりに面白 (?) すぎて授業に支障をきたすだろうという判断から著者の許可を得て編者が差し替えたもの (courtesy Derek Pell).
[9]   **"Up his sleeve!"**: *"Up one's sleeve"* は「何かを隠し持っている」という意味の決まり文句．ここでは帽子から出すと見せて，文字通り袖の中に入れているのだろう．
[22]   **surface diversity**: superficial differences; apparent variety
[26]   **entail(s)**: to result in
[27]   **critical**: essential; important
[31]   **Thomas Kuhn**: アメリカの科学史家 (1922–96)．ヨーロッパ近代科学の言説がどのような知の再編過程の中で生み出されたかを論じる『科学革命の構造』*The Structure of Scientific Revolutions* (1962) は「近代西洋」からの脱却が叫ばれていた 60〜70 年代には広く読まれ「パラダイム・シフト」という言葉を定着させた．
[32]   **paradigm** [pǽrədaim]: a set of accepted concepts
        anomaly [ənáməli]: something abnormal; something that doesn't fit the expected order
[35]   **punch line**: 最後のキメ台詞 ; オチ

FRED "BLAST" GNARR INVENTED THE FIRST EXPLOSIVE KNOWN TO MAN, THOUGH AT THE TIME HE DIDN'T THINK IT WOULD WORK.

© R. Crumb

5

the listener gets the punch line by seeing in a flash of insight how a completely new interpretation of the same set of facts can incorporate the anomalous ending. The longer and more tortuous the garden path of expectation, the "funnier" the punch line when finally delivered.

But although the introduction of a sudden twist at the end is necessary for the genesis of humor, it is certainly not sufficient. Suppose my plane is about to land in San Diego and I fasten my seat belt and get ready for touchdown. The pilot suddenly announces that the "bumps" that he (and I) had earlier dismissed as air turbulence are really due to engine failure and that we need to empty fuel before landing. A paradigm shift has occurred in my mind, but this certainly does not make me laugh. Rather, it makes me orient toward the anomaly and prepare for action to cope with the anomaly. Or consider the time I was staying at some friends' house in Iowa City. They were away and I was alone in unfamiliar surroundings. It was late at night and just as I was about to doze off, I heard a thump downstairs. "Probably the wind," I thought. After a few minutes there was another thud, louder than the one before. Again I "rationalized" it away and went back to sleep. Twenty minutes later I heard an extremely loud, resounding "bang" and leapt out of bed. What was happening? A burglar perhaps? Naturally, with my limbic system activated, I "oriented," grabbed a flashlight and ran down the stairs. Nothing funny so far. Then, suddenly I noticed a large flower vase in pieces on the floor and a large tabby cat right next to it — the obvious culprit! In contrast to the airplane incident, this time I started laughing because I realized that the "anomaly" I had detected and the subsequent paradigm shift were of trivial consequence. All of the facts could now be explained in terms of the cat theory rather than the ominous burglar theory.

On the basis of this example, we can sharpen our definition of humor and laughter. When a person strolls along a garden path of expectation and there is a sudden twist at the end that entails a complete reinterpretation of the same facts *and* the new

WHY DO WE LAUGH?

[3] **incorporate the anomalous ending:** それまでそぐわなかったエンディングをすんなり収める
[4] **tortuous:** twisted; winding
[5] **deliver(ed):**（パンチなどを）放つ． *The boxer delivered a hard right to the jaw.*
[7] **genesis:** creation; arising
[14] **orient toward:** to pay attention to; think about
[18] **thump:**「ドスン」(sound like a heavy blow)
[20] **thud:**「ズシン」(sound like a heavy object falling to the ground)
[21] **"rationalized" it away:** 理由をつけて不安をかき消した．引用符がついているのは，実は rational（合理的）な説明とはいえないため．
[22] **resounding** < resound [rizáund]: 響きわたる
[24] **limbic system:** 脳の内奥にあって互いに関連した，嗅覚，感情，運動などの自律機能を司る部分．合理的な思考を司る部分とちがって，すべての哺乳動物が共通に持っている．
[27] **tabby cat:** 虎斑のネコ
[28] **culprit:** one who is responsible or to blame
[30] **were of trivial consequence:** [a. didn't matter much / b. affected me greatly]
[32] **ominous:** threatening
[36] **and:** この語に強勢を置くことで，2つの条件が両方必要だということが強調される．

© R. Crumb

interpretation has trivial rather than terrifying implications, laughter ensues.

But why laughter? Why this explosive, repetitive sound? To an ethologist, any stereotyped vocalization almost always implies that the organism is trying to *communicate* something to others in the social group. Now what might this be in the case of laughter? I suggest that the main purpose of laughter might be to allow the individual to alert others in the social group (usually kin) that the detected anomaly is trivial, nothing to worry about. The laughing person in effect announces her discovery that there has been a false alarm; that the rest of you chaps need not waste your precious energy and resources responding to a spurious threat. This also explains why laughter is so notoriously contagious, for the value of any such signal would be amplified as it spread through the social group.

This "false alarm theory" of humor may also explain slapstick. You watch a man — preferably one who is portly and self-important — walk down the street when suddenly he slips on a banana peel and falls down. If his head hit the pavement and his skull split open, you would not laugh as you saw blood spill out. But if he got up casually, wiped the remains of the fruit from his face and continued walking, you would probably burst out laughing, thereby letting others standing nearby know that they need not rush to his aid. Of course, when watching Laurel and Hardy or Mr. Bean, we are more willing to tolerate "real" harm or injury to the hapless victim because we are fully aware that it's only a movie.

Although this model accounts for the evolutionary origin of laughter, it by no means explains all the functions of humor among modern humans. Once the mechanism was in place, however, it could easily be exploited for other purposes. (This is common in evolution. Feathers evolved in birds originally to provide insulation but were later adapted for flying.) The ability to reinterpret events in the light of new information may have been refined through the generations to help people playfully juxtapose larger ideas or concepts — that is, to be creative. This capacity for seeing familiar ideas from novel

WHY DO WE LAUGH?

[4] **stereotyped vocalization:** ワンパターンの発声
[10] **her discovery:** Note that it wouldn't be "politically correct" — or "PC" — to always use "he" or "his" to mean "person."
[11] **the rest of you chaps:** the rest of you guys
[12] **waste your precious energy and resources:** "waste your time" と書かずに「エネルギーと資源」と書いているのは，それが進化上の利点であるということを示すため．
[13] **spurious** [spjúːriəs]: false
[14] **is so notoriously contagious:** spreads so easily — with sometimes embarrassing consequences — to other people
[16] **slapstick:**（パイを投げるたぐいの）ドタバタ劇
[17] **portly:** どっしりとした；恰幅のいい
[25] **Laurel and Hardy:** やせたスタン・ローレル (1890–1965) と太っちょのオリヴァー・ハーディ (1892–1957) の喜劇俳優コンビ．短篇デビューは 1917 年，1920 年代の無声映画時代から 40 年代にかけて大活躍．日本でも深夜の BS 放送等でときどきお目にかかることができる．
Mr. Bean: イギリスの喜劇俳優ローワン・アトキンソン扮する，ドジで間抜けで情けないのにプライドだけはある男が主人公の 1990 年代の人気シリーズ．
[26] **hapless:** unfortunate
[33] **insulation:** prevention of the passage of heat (or electricity)
[35] **through the generations:** i.e. as human beings evolved
[36] **playfully juxtapose:**「軽やかにつきあわせる」．creativity と humor が形式的に一致するという考えから引き出された表現．
[37] **novel vantage points:** 新たに得られた，見晴らしのきく地点

© R. Crumb

9

vantage points (an essential element of humor) could be an antidote to conservative thinking and a catalyst to creativity. Laughter and humor may be a dress rehearsal for creativity, and if so, perhaps jokes, puns and other forms of humor should be introduced very early into our elementary schools as part of the formal curriculum.

Although these suggestions may help explain the logical structure of humor, they do not explain why humor itself is sometimes used as a psychological defense mechanism. Is it a coincidence, for example, that a disproportionate number of jokes deal with potentially disturbing topics, such as death or sex? One possibility is that jokes are an attempt to trivialize genuinely disturbing anomalies by pretending they are of no consequence; you distract yourself from your anxiety by setting off your own false alarm mechanism. Thus a trait that evolved to appease others in a social group now becomes internalized to deal with truly stressful situations and may emerge as so-called nervous laughter. Thus even as mysterious a phenomenon as "nervous laughter" begins to make sense in the light of some of the evolutionary ideas discussed here.

WHY DO WE LAUGH?

[2] **antidote:** 緩和剤；解毒剤
       catalyst: 触媒
[3] **Laughter and humor may be a dress rehearsal for creativity:** i.e. laughter and humor may prepare us for creative thinking because both may basically be the same thing. **dress rehearsal:** 衣裳から何からすべて本番と同じにやる，通しの稽古．
[10]   **a disproportionate number of:** an unexpectedly large number of
[14]   **distract yourself from your anxiety:** get yourself to stop worrying
[15]   **set(ting) off:** to release; start
[16]   **appease:** to remove anxiety; soothe
       becomes internalized: 内面化(個人の心的機能に転化)する

The Logics of Laughter

What makes us laugh? There have been three main kinds of explanation in the history of Western thought:

1) We laugh because we have a pleasurable feeling of superiority. The English philosopher **Thomas Hobbes** (1588–1679) defined laughter as a 'sudden glory' arising from the idea of our own superiority. Laughter among children, for example, is often caused by the misfortunes of others.

2) **Francis Hutcheson** (1694–1746) objected to the egoism of Hobbes' account, and proposed instead that we laugh at something incongruous or out of place. When a stout and dignified person slips on a banana skin, according to this view, we laugh because dignity and a sudden fall are incongruous. If our reason for laughing was a Hobbesian feeling of superiority, we would laugh just as much at a thin, meek person's fall.

3) **Immanuel Kant** (1724–1804) proposed a composite theory, when he explained the cause of laughter as a 'strained expectation reduced suddenly to nothing'. This involves incongruity (between what was expected and what really happens), but it also emphasises laughter as relief from some unpleasant strain. According to **Sigmund Freud** (1856–1939), laughter occurs when the strain of controlling our sexual and aggressive urges is suddenly reduced, for example, by jokes with a sexual or violent theme.

Can these Superiority, Incongruity and Relief theories of laughter also help us to explain the pleasure we find in nonsense poetry (such as 'Jabberwocky' in the next session)? **Arthur Schopenhauer** (1788–1860) suggested that nonsense makes us feel superior to reason, or to conventional ideas. Nonsense poetry is also full of incongruous words and happenings, so the incongruity theory is easy to apply. And according to Freud again, nonsense releases us from the strain of being rational.

What kind of theory does Ramachandran propose? And could it help to explain why people enjoy nonsense? (B.W.)

SESSION 2
On Jabberwocky

Martin Gardner

FEW would dispute the fact that *Jabberwocky* is the greatest of all nonsense poems in English. It was so well known to English schoolboys in the late nineteenth century that five of its nonsense words appear casually in the conversation of students in Rudyard Kipling's *Stalky & Co*. Alice herself, in the paragraph following the poem, puts her finger on the secret of the poem's charm: ". . . it seems to fill my head with ideas — only I don't know exactly what they are." Although the strange words have no precise meaning, they chime with subtle overtones:

JABBERWOCKY

'Twas brillig, and the slithy toves
   Did gyre and gimble in the wabe:
All mimsy were the borogoves,
   And the mome raths outgrabe.

"Beware the Jabberwock, my son!
   The jaws that bite, the claws that catch!
Beware the Jubjub bird, and shun
   The frumious Bandersnatch!"

He took his vorpal sword in hand
   Long time the manxome foe he sought —

2冊のアリス本——*Alice's Adventures in Wonderland* (1865) と *Through the Looking Glass* (1872)——に『サイエンティフィック・アメリカン』誌の楽しい数学コラムで知られるマーティン・ガーディナーが詳細な注をつけた *The Annotated Alice* は，1960年の初版以来，愛と博識の結晶として世界の読者にマニアックな文学研究のよろこびを伝えてきた．その中から，あまりにも有名なナンセンス詩 'Jabberwocky' への注の一部を教材用に編集した．使用テキストは 1970年に出た改訂第 2 版．その後も注は増え続け，1999 年には *The Annotated Alice: The Definitive Edition* が出版されている．

[Notes]

[5] **Rudyard Kipling:** ラジャード・キップリング (1865–1936) は *The Jungle Book* (1894) 等，英領時代のインドを舞台にした物語でもよく知られている．***Stalky & Co.*** (1899) はイギリスの寄宿学校を舞台に，いたずら 3 人組の行状を生き生きと描く回想記風物語．"You're a dirty little schoolboy. Besides being frabjously immoral" (cf. p. 15, note [13]) というぐあいに「キャロル語」が登場する．

[6] **puts her finger on the secret of the poem's charm:** i.e. she identifies exactly what makes the poem so charming.

[8] **only I don't know . . . :** [a. though I don't know / b. everyone but me knows]

[9] **they chime with subtle overtones:** 語感の中にこれと断定できない意味あいがこもっている，ということ．**overtone:** implication

[11] **JABBERWOCKY:** jabber = to talk rapidly and indistinctly と jab = to stab の両方がこもる．

[12] **'Twas:** It was. 古い詩だと印象づけるはじまり．以下，第 1 連 (first stanza) にでてくるたくさんの「キャロル語」は後に本文で解説される．

[18] **Jubjub bird:** キャロル作の「スナーク狩り」でも何度か言及される．
shun: to avoid (*normal English*)

[19] **frumious:** "Take the two words 'fuming' and 'furious'. Make up your mind that you will say both words, but leave it unsettled which you will say first. Now open your mouth and speak. . . . If you have that rarest of gifts, a perfectly balanced mind, you will say 'frumious'" — from the preface to Carroll's long poem, *The Hunting of the Snark* (1870). **fuming** and **furious** both mean 'extremely angry'.
Bandersnatch: この「憤々しき」獣も「スナーク狩り」で言及される．

[20] **vorpal:** "Alexander L. Taylor . . . shows how to get 'vorpal' by taking letters alternately from 'verbal' and 'gospel', but there's no evidence that Carroll resorted to such involved techniques" — Gardner's note. 15 頁の試訳「ことたまひたる」は Taylor 説によった．

[21] **manxome:** マン島(アイルランド海上の英領の島)の言語は Manx，マン島の男たちは Manxmen と呼ばれるが，それとは無関係かもしれない．

SESSION 2

Drawing by John Tenniel

So rested he by the Tumtum tree, [1]
   And stood awhile in thought.

And, as in uffish thought he stood,
   The jabberwock, with eyes of flame,
Came whiffling through the tulgey wood, [5]
   And burbled as it came!

One, two! One, two! And through and through
   The vorpal blade went snicker-snack!
He left it dead, and with its head
   He went galumphing back. [10]

"And hast thou slain the Jabberwock?
   Come to my arms, my beamish boy!
O Frabjous day! Callooh! Callay!"
   He chortled in his joy.

ON JABBERWOCKY

[1] **Tumtum:** キャロルの時代，弦の楽器を打ち鳴らす擬声語として使われた言葉．
[3] **uffish:** "a state of mind when the voice is *gruffish*, the manner *roughish*, and the temper *huffish*." — Carroll's own explanation.
[5] **whiffling:** blowing in short puffs (*normal English*)
tulgey [tʌ́ldʒi] **wood:** たぶんもっこり膨れた (bulgy)，薄気味悪い森なのだろう．
[6] **burble(d):** おそらく burst + bubble. "the burbling brook" などという言い方は，古くから英語にあった．
[8] **snicker-snack:** キャロル製擬声語．snip (パチッ)や click (カチッ)の連想あり．
[10] **galumph(ing):** to gallop + triumphant. 「かっぽたけぶ」（勝利の雄叫びをあげながらカッポカッポ早駆けする）?
[11] **hast thou slain . . . ?:** have you killed . . . ?
[12] **beamish:** 実はキャロル語ではない．*The Oxford English Dictionary* (OED) は，"beaming" (shining brightly) の一変形として，1530 年の用例を挙げている．
[13] **Frabjous:** "A nonsense-word invented by Lewis Carroll, apparently intended to suggest 'fair' and 'joyous'" — OED.
Callooh! Callay!: [kəlúː kəléi] ". . . Carroll had in mind two forms of a Greek word, *kalos*, meaning beautiful, good or fair. They would be pronounced as Carroll spells them, and would fit well the meaning of the line" — Gardner's note.
[14] **chortle(d):** 'chuckle' (クックッと 笑う) + 'snort' (豚・馬などが鼻を鳴らす)

邪罵惑鬼　　　　　　　　　　　　　　　　　　　　（佐藤良明 訳）

あぶりの刻に　すらじりトーブら / ぐぬらの丘にぞ　てんぐりどるる
あはれかそけき　ほろどりみどろ / もうまいらーとん　あ、ひゅれぶうる

「息子よ息子　邪罵惑鬼に油断すな /
　　　　そは大顎もて食らいつき　鷲の爪もて飛びかかる
蛇舞蛇舞鳥にも心せよ / うすろしき蛮奪大蛇にゆめ近づくな」

ことたまひたる　剣をとりて / ひとぶく敵追い　幾百里
身を休むるは　ボロロンの樹 / しばし佇み　想いにしずむ

いきどおしさに　胸たぎるとき / ぐろき森抜け　風ひゅーひゅらし
眼火と燃ゆ　惑鬼舞い降り / ぎゃらきその口　ぶうぶく邪罵る

ひーふっ　ひーふっ　さっくりかぱり / ことたまいし刃で　ばらさきむれば
もんぜつたゆる　首をばもぎて / かっぽたけびつ　家路を駆ける．

「邪罵惑鬼を討ちしか　息子. / 勇姿まばふぞ　いざこの胸へ
さてもさやめく　はる華麗かな」/ 歓喜は舞って　笑いぞいびく

あぶりの刻に　すらじりトーブら / ぐぬらの丘にぞ　てんぐりどるる
あはれかそけき　ほろどりみどろ / もうまいらーとん　あ、ひゅれぶうる

SESSION 2

> 'Twas brillig, and the slithy toves [1]
>   Did gyre and gimble in the wabe:
> All mimsy were the borogoves.
> And the mome raths outgrabe.

The opening stanza of *Jabberwocky* first appeared in *Misch-* [5] *Masch*, the last of a series of private little "periodicals" that young Carroll wrote, illustrated and hand-lettered for the amusement of his brothers and sisters. In an issue dated 1855 (Carroll was then twenty-three), under the heading "Stanza of Anglo-Saxon Poetry," the following "curious fragment" [10] appears:

> [ornamental script rendering of the stanza]

Carroll then proceeds to interpret the words as follows.
    BRYLLYG (derived from the verb to BRYL or BROIL): 'the time of broiling dinner. i.e. the close of the afternoon.'
    SLYTHY (compounded of SLIMY and LITHE): 'smooth and [15] active.'
    TOVE: a species of badger. They had smooth white hair, long hind legs, and short horns like a stag; lived chiefly on cheese.
    GYRE: verb (derived from GYAOUR or GIAOUR, 'a dog'). To [20] scratch like a dog.
    GYMBLE (whence GIMBLET): 'to screw out holes in anything.'
    WABE (derived from the verb to SWAB or SOAK): 'the side of a hill' (from its being soaked by the rain).
    MIMSY (whence MIMSERABLE and MISERABLE): 'unhappy.' [25]
    BOROGOVE: an extinct kind of Parrot. They had no wings, beaks turned up, and made their nests under sundials: lived on veal.
    MOME (hence SOLEMOME, SOLEMONE, and SOLEMN): 'grave.'
    RATH: a species of land turtle. Head erect: mouth like a [30] shark: forelegs curved out so that the animal walked on its

ON JABBERWOCKY

[10] **Anglo-Saxon:** Old English（古英語，古期英語）の別称．1150 年ころまでの英語で，アルファベット，語順，発音など，その後の英語と異なる．p. 164 のチョーサーの詩は中(期)英語(*c.* 1150–1500) で書かれている．

[13] **BROIL:** to cook by direct radiant heat

[15] **LITHE** [laɪð]: easily bent; supple

[20] **GYRE** [dʒaɪə]:『鏡の国のアリス』に登場する Humpty Dumpty の解説は，当初のキャロルのものとは異なる．下の Box 参照．

[22] **whence GIMBLET:** from which the word GIMBLET derives. (gimblet = gimlet)

[23] **SWAB:** モップ

[28] **veal:** 仔牛 (calf) の肉

[29] **SOLEMN:** serious, sober, somewhat gloomy. **solemome, solemone** は mimserable や後出の grike, shrike と同じく，説明をそれっぽく聞こえさせるための造語．

[31] **forelegs curved out:** つまり，前足が陸ガメ (tortoise) のようでなく，海ガメ (turtle) のようになっている．

Humpty Dumpty's lecture on 'Jabberwocky'
(*Through the Looking Glass*, Chapter VI)

"To '*gyre*' is to go round and round like a gyroscope. To '*gimble*' is to make a hole like a gimlet."

"And '*the wabe*' is the grass-plot round a sun-dial?" said Alice, surprised at her own ingenuity.

"Of course it is. It's called '*wabe*', you know, because it goes a long way before it, and a long way behind it —"

"And a long way beyond it on each side," Alice added.

"Exactly so. Well then, '*mimsy*' is 'flimsy and miserable' (there's another portmanteau for you). And a '*borogove*' is a thin shabby-looking bird with its feathers sticking out — something like a live mop."

"And the '*mome raths*'?" said Alice. "I'm afraid I'm giving you a great deal of trouble."

"Well, a '*rath*' is a sort of green pig: but '*mome*' I'm not certain about. I think it's short for 'from home' — meaning that they'd lost their way, you know."

"And what does '*outgrabe*' mean?"

"Well, '*outgribing*' is something between bellowing and whistling, with a kind of sneeze in the middle. . . . "

knees: smooth green body: lived on swallows and oysters.

OUTGRABE: past tense of the verb to OUTGRIBE. (It is connected with the old verb to GRIKE, or SHRIKE, from which are derived 'shriek' and 'creak'). 'Squeaked.'

Hence the literal English of the passage is: 'It was evening, and the smooth active badgers were scratching and boring holes in the hill-side; all unhappy were the parrots; and the grave turtles squeaked out.'

There were probably sundials on the top of the hill, and the 'borogoves' were afraid that their nests would be undermined. The hill was probably full of the nests of 'raths', which ran out, squeaking with fear, on hearing the 'toves' scratching outside. This is an obscure, but yet deeply-affecting, relic of ancient Poetry.

There is an obvious similarity between nonsense verse of this sort and an abstract painting. The realistic artist is forced to copy nature, imposing on the copy as much as he can in the way of pleasing forms and colors; but the abstract artist is free to romp with the paint as much as he pleases. In similar fashion the nonsense poet does not have to search for ingenious ways of combining pattern and sense; he simply adopts a policy that is the opposite of the advice given by the Duchess in the previous book. He takes care of the sounds and allows the sense to take care of itself. The words he uses may suggest vague meanings, like an eye here and a foot there in a Picasso abstraction, or they may have no meaning at all — just a play of pleasant sounds like the play of non-objective colors on a canvas.

Carroll was not, of course, the first to use this technique of double-talk in humorous verse. He was preceded by Edward Lear, and it is a curious fact that nowhere in the writings or letters of these two undisputed leaders of English nonsense did either of them refer to the other, nor is there evidence that they ever met. Since the time of Lear and Carroll there have been attempts to produce a more serious poetry of this sort — poems by the Dadaists, the Italian futurists, and Gertrude Stein, for example — but somehow when the technique is taken too

ON JABBERWOCKY

[4] **shriek, creak, squeak:** どれも物がこすれる音だが，shriek はキンキンする (shrill) 叫び声に使われ，creak は物がきしむ感じが強い．ネズミの鳴き声は squeak, カエルは croak を使うのが一般的．

[13] **deeply-affecting:** very moving. 現代ではハイフンはつけないのがふつう．

[19] **romp with the paint:** to paint in a wildly playful manner
In similar fashion: In a similar way

[20] **ingenious** [indʒíːniəs]: clever, skillful

[22] **the advice given by the Duchess:** 『不思議の国のアリス』の第9章で公爵夫人は，"Take care of the sense, and the sounds will take care of themselves" というセリフを口にする．これは "Take care of the pence, and the pounds will take care of themselves" という諺のもじりだが，このもじり自体「音を操作することがおのずと意味深い表現に通じる」というキャロル的命題の見事な例証になっている．

[27] **non-objective:** 具象的でない

[29] **double-talk:** language that mixes sense with nonsense.（ふつうは「どちらともとれる不誠実な発言」の意）
Edward Lear: エドワード・リア (1812–88) の有名な *A Book of Nonsense* (1846) は，こんなふうに始まる．1, 2, 5 行目が韻を踏むこのような 5 行形式の戯れ歌は limerick [límərik] と呼ばれる．

There was an Old Man with a beard,
Who said, "It is just as I feared! —
Two Owls and a Hen,
Four Larks and a Wren,
Have all built their nests in my beard!"

[30] **it is a curious fact . . . :** The curious fact is that evidently Carroll and Lear [a. neither met nor referred to / b. never met though they often referred to] each other.

[35] **the Dadaists , the Italian futurists:** 新世紀の機械文明への強度の信頼を表明するイタリア未来派運動が栄えたのは第一次大戦に先立つ 1910 年代前半のこと．戦後，今度は破壊をスローガンにしたダダイズムが登場する．
Gertrude Stein: (1874?–1946) アメリカの前衛的文人．パリの彼女のサロンに無名時代の Pablo Picasso や Ernest Hemingway らが集まったようすを，金関寿夫『現代芸術のエポック・エロイク』（青土社，1991），映画『月の出を待って』*Waiting for the Moon* (US, 1987) などで知ることができる．

seriously the results seem tiresome. I have yet to meet someone who could recite one of Miss Stein's poetic efforts, but I have known a good many Carrollians who found that they knew *Jabberwocky* by heart without ever having made a conscious effort to memorize it. Ogden Nash produced a fine piece of nonsense in his poem *Geddondillo* ("The Sharrot scudders nights in the quastran now, / The dorlim slinks undeceded in the grost..."), but even here there seems to be a bit too much straining for effect, whereas *Jabberwocky* has a careless lilt and perfection that makes it the unique thing it is.

But what possible value can there be in poetry which does not even try to make sense? One surprising answer comes from Arthur Stanley Eddington, the physicist and astronomer who first confirmed Einstein's General Theory of Relativity. In *New Pathways in Science* he likens the abstract syntactical structure of the poem to that modern branch of mathematics known as group theory. In *The Nature of the Physical World* he points out that the physicist's description of an elementary particle is really a kind of Jabberwocky; words applied to "something unknown" that is "doing we don't know what." Because the description contains numbers, science is able to impose a certain amount of order on the phenomena and to make successful predictions about them.

"By contemplating eight circulating electrons in one atom and seven circulating electrons in another," Eddington writes, "we begin to realize the difference between oxygen and nitrogen. Eight slithy toves gyre and gimble in the oxygen wabe; seven in nitrogen. By admitting a few numbers even 'Jabberwocky' may become scientific. We can now venture on a prediction; if one of its toves escapes, oxygen will be masquerading in a garb properly belonging to nitrogen. In the stars and nebulae we do find such wolves in sheep's clothing which might otherwise have startled us. It would not be a bad reminder of the essential unknownness of the fundamental entities of physics to translate it into 'Jabberwocky'; provided all numbers — all metrical attributes — are unchanged, it does not suffer in the least."

- [1] **I have yet to meet:** I have [a. not yet met / b. already met]
- [6] ***Geddondillo*:** Armageddon (ハルマゲドン) を意識した命名
  sharrot, scudders, quastran, dorlim, undeceded, grost: どの語も英語によくある音の並びでできていることに注意．なお undeceded は undeceased (= undead) + unreceded (= not withdrawn).
- [7] **slink(s):** to move stealthily
- [9] **straining:** (無理を押しての) がんばり．*Don't strain yourself.*
- [10] **lilt:** 声のはずみ，のりのよさ
- [13] **Arthur Stanley Eddington:** アーサー・エディントン (1882–1944)．恒星の組成と進化の研究 *The Internal Constitution of the Stars* (1926) で有名になり，その後一般向け科学書の執筆家としての活動を展開．*The Nature of the Physical World* (1928) は，難解な 20 世紀の科学についての最高の解説書とうたわれた．
- [15] **syntactical structure:** 統語構造
- [17] **group theory:** 群論
- [18] **elementary particle:** 素粒子
- [21] **impose a certain amount of order:** ある程度の秩序をあてがう
- [27] **Eight slithy toves gyre and gimble in the oxygen wabe:** Eddington makes the point here that we don't know what electrons really *are*, nor do we know what they exactly *do*, when we say "eight of them orbit around the oxygen 'nucleus.'"
- [28] **admitting:** letting in; accepting
- [29] **venture on:** to attempt; risk
- [31] **masquerading in a garb properly belonging to nitrogen:**「本来窒素が着るべき衣裳を着て変装する」．窒素原子のモデルは，7 つの陽子と 7 つの中性子からなる原子核のまわりを通常 7 つの電子がまわっているというもの．酸素原子ではそれぞれの数が 8 つになる．
- [32] **nebulae** [nébjəliː, -lai]**:** nebula (星雲) の複数形
  wolves in sheep's clothing:「羊に変装した狼」とは，7 つの電子しかもたない酸素原子のこと．
- [33] **otherwise:** もしそれが変装した酸素原子だと知らなければ
  It would not be a bad reminder:「忘れぬための予防策として悪くないだろう」．実際の主語は "to translate ..."
- [34] **the essential unknownness of the fundamental entities of physics:** 重力，質量，磁性など「物理の世界を構成する基本的存在」の正体がわかっているわけではないということ．
- [35] **provided:** if; as long as
- [36] **all metrical attributes:** 数量的に把握されるもののすべて
  does not suffer in the least: remains as effective as ever

SESSION 3

The Light of Common Day

Arthur C. Clarke

NO man has ever seen the Sun, or ever will. What we call 'sunlight' is only a narrow span of the entire solar spectrum — the immensely broad band of vibrations which the Sun, our nearest star, pours into space. All the colours visible to the eye, from warm red to deepest violet, lie within a single octave of this band — for the waves of violet light have twice the frequency, or 'pitch' if we think in musical terms, of red. On either side of this narrow zone are ranged octave after octave of radiations to which we are totally blind.

However, let us not exaggerate our visual handicap. Though visible light is merely a single octave of the Sun's radiation, this octave contains most of the power; the higher and lower frequencies are relatively feeble. It is, of course, no coincidence that our eyes are adapted to the most intense band of sunlight; if that band had been somewhere else in the spectrum, as is the case with other stars, evolution would have given us eyes appropriately tuned. Nevertheless, the Sun's invisible rays are extremely important. Some of them, indeed, may control our destinies — and even, as we shall see in a moment, our very existence.

The visible spectrum is, quite arbitrarily, divided up into seven primary colours — the famous sequence, red, orange, yellow, green, blue, indigo, violet, if we start from the longest waves and work down to the shortest. Seven main colours in the one octave; but the complete band of solar radiations

THE LIGHT OF COMMON DAY

Arthur C. Clarke (b. 1917) is a popular British science fiction writer whose more than 70 works — among them *Childhood's End* (1953) and *2001: A Space Odyssey* (1968) — are noted for being technologically realistic. He was never able to afford a university education, but worked as an auditor; and at the outbreak of the Second World War went into the Royal Air Force as a radar instructor.

The following passage was taken from an essay written in 1963, but it is still fresh and interesting today. Clarke's prose is so clear and well-crafted that the editors felt it hardly necessary to further clarify the text by writing "notes." Instead we provide some illustrative figures for the reader's assistance.

[Notes]

[7] **twice the frequency, or 'pitch':** a musical note A is one octave higher than a musical note B when A has twice the frequency of B.

[21] **quite arbitrarily:** The answer to the question "How many colors are there in the rainbow?" is quite arbitrary (see p. 63, note [18]) and varies from culture to culture.

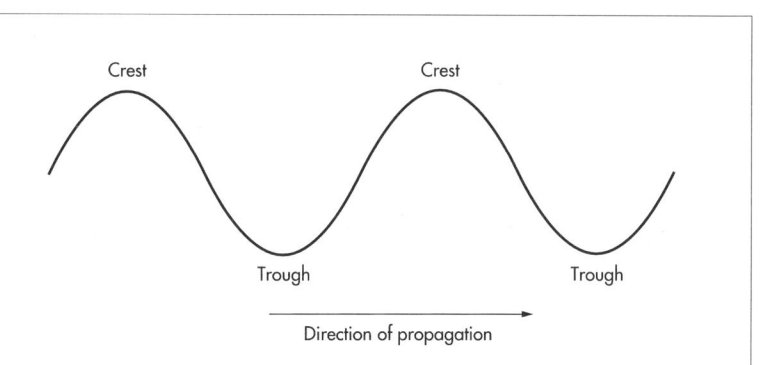

The **wavelength** is the distance between crests, the **frequency** is the number of crests that go by per second, and the **speed** of the wave is the velocity of a single crest.

$$(\text{wavelength}) \times (\text{frequency}) = (\text{speed of the wave})$$

covers at least thirty octaves, or a total frequency range of ten thousand million to one. If we could see the whole of it, therefore, we might expect to discern more than two hundred colours as distinct from each other as orange is from yellow, or green is from blue.

Starting with the Sun's visible rays, let us explore outwards in each direction and see (though that word is hardly applicable) what we can discover. On the long-wave side we come first to the infra-red rays, which can be perceived by our skin but not by our eyes. Infra-red rays are heat radiation; go out of doors on a summer's day, and you can tell where the Sun is even though your eyes may be tightly closed.

Thanks to special photographic films, we have all had glimpses of the world of infra-red. It is an easily recognizable world, though tone values are strangely distorted. Sky and water are black, leaves and grass dazzling white as if covered with snow. It is a world of clear, far horizons, for infra-red rays slice through the normal haze of distance — hence their great value in aerial photography.

Some animals have developed an infra-red sense, to enable them to hunt at night. There is a snake which has two small pits near its nostrils, each holding a directional infra-red detector. These allow it to 'home' upon small, warm animals like mice, and to strike at them even in complete darkness. Only in the last decade have our guided missiles learned the same trick.

Below the infra-red, for several octaves, is a no man's land of radiation about which very little is known. It is hard to generate or to detect waves in this region, and until recently few scientists paid it much attention. But as we press on to more familiar territory, first we encounter the inch-long waves of radar, then the yard-long ones of the shortwave bands, then the hundred-yard waves of the broadcast band.

The Sun's radio output differs profoundly from its visible light, and the difference is not merely one of greater length. Visible sunlight is practically constant in intensity; if there are any fluctuations, they are too slight to be detected. Not only has the Sun shone with unvarying brightness throughout the

THE LIGHT OF COMMON DAY

[23] 'home': to proceed to a source of radiated energy used as a guide. *The infra-red missile homes in on the heat given off from jet engines.*

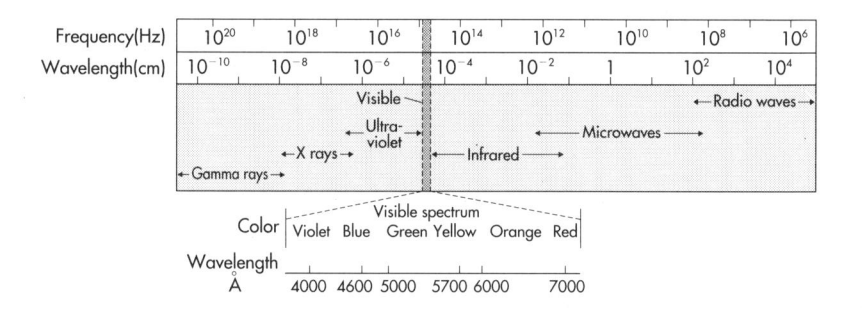

The Electromagnetic Spectrum

On the Radio

The numbers on your radio dial represent frequencies. AM radio operates between about 525 and 1,700 kHz (525,000 and 1,700,000 cycles per second); the FM band extends from about 76 to 108 MHz (76,000,000 to 108,000,000 cycles per second). VHF television channels extend above and below the FM band. UHF channels are higher, at about 470 to 890 MHz.

The speed of light is approximately 300,000 km/s, or 3×10^8 meters per second, so an FM wave of 100 MHz (10^8 cycles) has a wavelength of 3 m. An X ray of 10^{18} cycles has a wavelength of 3×10^{-10} meter (0.3 nanometers). The ratio of those two waves is ten thousand million to one, or 10^{10}: 1. Since 10^{10} is close to 2^{33}, we could say that the X ray's "pitch" is at least 30 octaves higher than that of the FM wave (See text on the opposite page, lines 1–2).

SESSION 3

whole span of human history, but we would probably notice no difference if we could see it through the eyes of one of the great reptiles.

But if you saw only the 'radio' Sun, you would never guess that it was the same object. Most of the time it is very dim — much dimmer, in fact, than many other celestial bodies. To the eye able to see only by radio waves, there would be little difference between day and night; the rising of the Sun would be a minor and inconspicuous event.

From time to time, however, the radio Sun explodes into nova brightness. It may, within *seconds*, flare up to a hundred, a thousand or even a million times its normal brilliance. These colossal outbursts of radio energy do not come from the Sun as a whole, but from small localized areas of the solar disc, often associated with sunspots.

Let us now consider the other end of the spectrum — the rays shorter than visible light. As the blue deepens into indigo and then violet, the human eye soon fails to respond. But there is still 'light' present in solar radiation: the ultraviolet. As in the case of the infra-red, our skins can react to it, often painfully; for ultraviolet rays are the cause of sunburn.

And here is a very strange and little-known fact. Though I have just stated that our eyes do not respond to ultraviolet, the actual situation is a good deal more complicated. (In nature, it usually is.) The sensitive screen at the back of the eye — the retina, which is the precise equivalent of the film in a camera — does react strongly to ultraviolet. If it were the only factor involved, we could see by the invisible ultraviolet rays.

Then why don't we? For a purely technical reason. Though the eye is an evolutionary marvel, it is a very poor piece of optics. To enable it to work properly over the whole range of colours, a good camera has to have four, six or even more lenses, made of different types of glass and assembled with great care into a single unit. The eye has only one lens, and it already has trouble coping with the two-to-one range of wavelengths in the visible spectrum. You can prove this by looking at a bright

THE LIGHT OF COMMON DAY

[3] **the great reptiles:** Dinosaurs dominated the earth for over 150 million years in the Mesozoic era (2–300,000,000 to 70,000,000 years ago).

[10] **explodes into nova brightness:** A nova is a star that suddenly becomes much brighter and then gradually returns to its original brightness over a period of weeks to years.

[15] **sunspots:** The temperature of the spots is lower than that of the surrounding photosphere; thus the spots are, by contrast, darker. Sunspot activity reaches a maximum once every 11 years.

Colorful Skies

One of the major characteristics of the Earth's atmosphere is its color. From the planet's surface, the sky appears to be blue. About 20 miles (32 kilometers) above the surface, the sky is relatively black. The color of the sky on other planets depends on the composition of the atmosphere; on Mars, for example, the sky is pinkish because of the iron particles in its thin atmosphere. But apparently, no other place in the solar system has a blue sky like Earth's.

Our sky is blue because the short blue wavelengths of sunlight scatter in all directions as the light strikes air molecules, other particles, and water and ice from clouds. Sunsets are red because the sunlight is traveling through more of the atmosphere to reach us (see the illustration below); this longer passage scatters all other colors away from the observer except the longer red wavelengths. Reddish sunsets are occasionally enhanced by excessive dust in the atmosphere, such as particles from a recent volcanic eruption. Clouds, haze, and fog are white because the water droplets scatter all wavelengths of the spectrum equally.

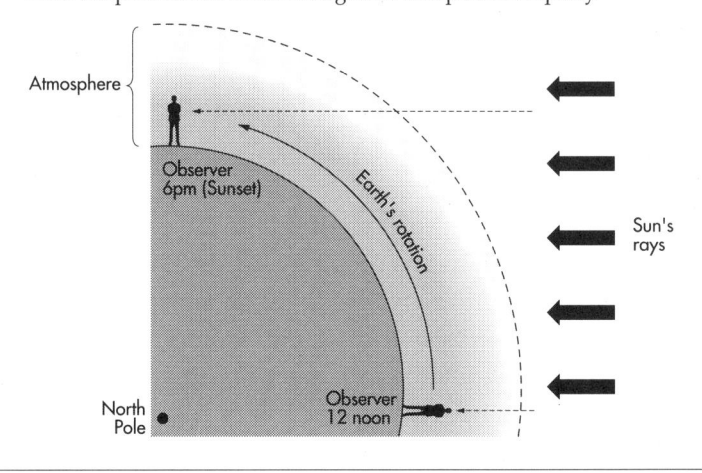

red object on a bright blue background. They won't both be in perfect focus; when you look at one, the other will appear slightly fuzzy.

Objects would be even fuzzier if we could see by ultraviolet as well as by visible light, so the eye deals with this insoluble problem by eliminating it. There is a filter in the front of the eye which blocks the ultraviolet, preventing it from reaching the retina. The haze filter which photographers often employ when using colour film does exactly the same job, and for a somewhat similar reason.

The eye's filter is the lens itself — and here at last is the punch line of this rather long-winded narrative. If you are ever unlucky enough to lose your natural lenses (say through a cataract operation) and have them replaced by artificial lenses of clear glass, you will be able to see quite well in the ultraviolet. Indeed, with a source of ultraviolet illumination, like the so-called 'black light' lamps, you will be able to see perfectly in what is, to the normal person, complete darkness! I hereby donate this valuable information to the CIA, James Bond, or anyone else who is interested.

Normal sunlight, as you can discover during a day at the beach, contains plenty of ultraviolet. It all lies, however, in a narrow band — the single octave just above the visible spectrum in frequency. As we move beyond this to still higher frequencies, the scene suddenly dims and darkens. A being able to see only in the far ultraviolet would be in a very unfortunate position. To him, it would always be night, whether or not the Sun was above the horizon.

What has happened? Doesn't the Sun radiate in the far ultraviolet? Certainly it does, but this radiation is all blocked by the atmosphere, miles above our head. In the far ultraviolet, a few inches of ordinary air are as opaque as a sheet of metal.

If you started off from ground level on a bright, sunny day, this is what you would see. At first, you would be in utter darkness, even though you were looking straight at the Sun. Then, about twenty miles up, you would notice a slow brightening, as you climbed through the opaque fog of the atmosphere.

THE LIGHT OF COMMON DAY

[13]   **cataract:** opacity (⇔ transparency) of the lens of the eye, causing impairment of vision. Most commonly caused by aging.
[32]   **opaque:** ⇔ transparent

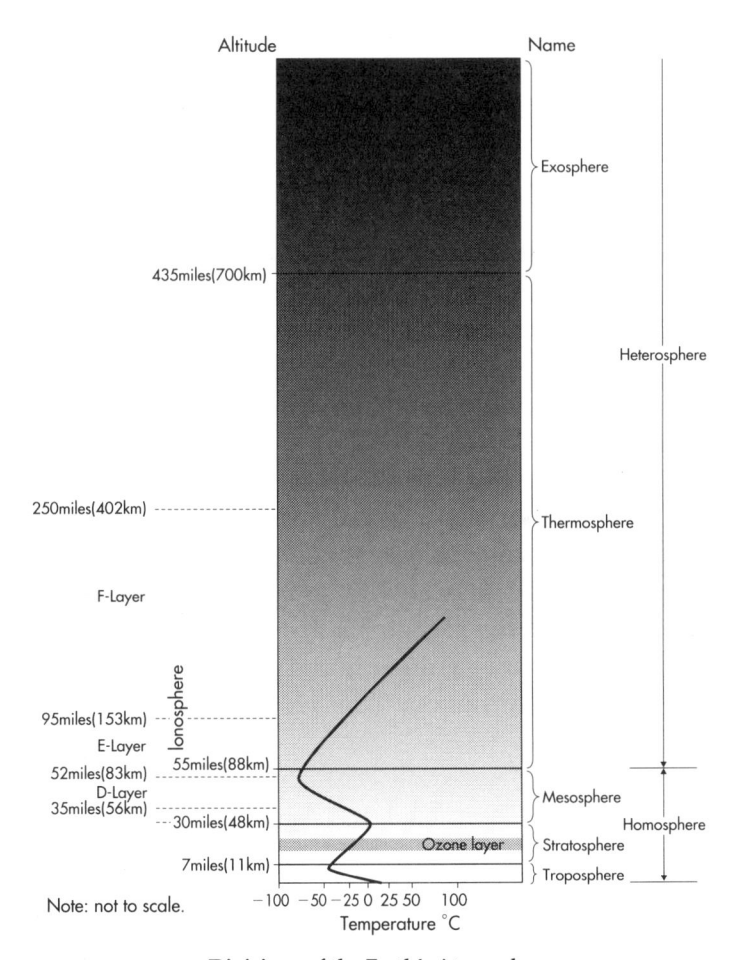

Divisions of the Earth's Atmosphere

Articles in Boxes (on pages 23 and 27) and all illustrations are from The New York Public Library (Patricia Barnes-Svarney, Editorial Director), *Science Desk Reference*, Copyright © 1995 by The Stonesong Press Inc. and The New York Public Library.

Beyond this, between twenty and thirty miles high, the ultraviolet Sun would break through in its awful glory!

I use that word 'awful' with deliberate intent. These rays can kill, and swiftly. They do not bother astronauts, because they can be easily filtered out by special glass. But if they reached the surface of the Earth — if they were not blocked by the upper atmosphere — most existing forms of life would be wiped out. If you regard the existence of this invisible ultraviolet umbrella as in any way providential, you are confusing cause and effect. The screen was not put in the atmosphere to protect terrestrial life: it was put there by life itself, hundreds of millions of years before man appeared on Earth.

The Sun's raw ultraviolet rays, in all probability, did reach the surface of the primeval Earth; the earliest forms of life were adapted to it, perhaps even thrived upon it. In those days, there was no oxygen in the atmosphere; it is a by-product of plant life, and over geological aeons its amount slowly increased, until at last those oxygen-burning creatures called animals had a chance to thrive.

That filter in the sky is made of oxygen — or, rather, the grouping of three oxygen atoms known as ozone. Not until Earth's protective ozone layer was formed, and the short ultraviolet rays were blocked twenty miles up, did the present types of terrestrial life evolve. If there had been no ozone layer, they would doubtless have evolved into different forms. Perhaps we might still be here, but our skins would be very, very black.

THE LIGHT OF COMMON DAY

[9] **providential:** happening through Providence (God's guardianship)
confusing cause and effect: The truth is that life is the cause of the protective umbrella, not that life appeared because of it.

[17] **aeon(s)** [íːən]: the longest division of geologic time, containing two or more eras. In everyday language 'for aeons' means simply 'for a very long time'. Also spelled 'eon'.

The Two Natures of Light

Light remains a central mystery of modern science. It is the earliest and clearest example we have of the wave/particle duality. When light strikes certain substances, electrons are released and this photoelectric effect is used in solar-powered calculators and watches, for example. The number of electrons emitted depends on the intensity of the light. Basically, brighter light means more electrons. But the kinetic energy of the electrons depends on the frequency of the light. Basically, bluer light means more energetic electrons. (In fact, if the light isn't blue enough, then no matter how bright it is, no electrons will be emitted). Einstein argued in 1905 that these results can only be explained if light has a particle nature, that is, if light consists of photons. On the other hand, Thomas Young had already shown in 1801 that two sources of light can interfere, cancelling or adding together like water waves. This seems to rule out any particulate theory of light.

Our best attempt to deal with this problem so far is Bohr's theory of complementarity. In effect, this concedes that the two models of light are incompatible, but takes comfort in the fact that at least light does not show both of its incompatible natures in the same experiment.

SESSION 4

Natural Selection

Lyall Watson

IT is impossible to describe the difference between male [1] and female day-old chicks — and yet there are those who can tell them apart. Most of these experts are Japanese, so I went recently to visit the centre near Osaka where many of the best chicken-sexers are trained. I was hoping, as a biologist, to [5] learn something from them, to uncover the secret cues. But I found no obvious answer. Novices learn by looking over the shoulders of experienced workers, and go on doing so until they acquire the skills, almost by a process of osmosis. The experts themselves cannot explain how they do it. But they do, [10] and so eventually do the trainees, without hesitation and with a success rate of over 99 per cent.

It is clear to me, from what I saw in Japan, that no conscious effort in sexing could ever approach such phenomenal speed and accuracy. Skills of this order seem to be acquired implicitly [15] and unconsciously — and are actually hindered and blocked by any attempt to exercise our ability to reason. They rely instead on the presence and application of what could be called an intuitive edge. Successful chicken-sexing is a little like trying to recall a name or a dream that, for the moment, [20] escapes you. The harder you try, the less successful you are likely to be.

It seems that when faced with particularly subtle tasks, people who feel or intuit their way through them actually have a competitive edge over those who consciously try to think their [25]

NATURAL SELECTION

Natural selection is the central idea of Charles Darwin's **theory of evolution**. Darwin saw that species are not uniform in their **characteristics**, but that there is quite a range of **variations**. He argued that individuals with characteristics that are useful in adjusting to the changing **environment** are indeed more likely to survive. He combined this idea with the widely accepted principle of **inheritance** [passing on of characteristics] and asserted that over long periods of time organisms with advantageous characteristics will eventually become the dominant variation in the population.

Darwin presented this idea in *The Origin of Species* (1859), to a society caught up in the profound changes of emerging capitalism and the Industrial Revolution. To people engaged in their own struggle for survival in a new environment, Darwin's idea of the survival of the fittest must have had special power. At the same time, the phrase came to have a particular moral connotation — as if the weak did not deserve to survive.

Perhaps at the turn of the millennium we are ready to tell ourselves a slightly different story of biological evolution — such as this one by Lyall Watson, a popular British writer on nature topics.

[Notes]
- [5] **chicken-sexers:** people whose job is to tell male chickens from female ones
- [7] **Novice(s)** [nóvis]**:** a beginner
- [9] **osmosis** [ɔzmóusis]**:** a gradual, often unconscious process of absorption. *I learned Spanish by osmosis while living in Madrid for 15 years.*
- [14] **phenomenal:** very unusual and impressive; marvelous; miraculous; sensational. cf. *The Beatles in those days were truly phenomenal.*
- [15] **Skills of this order:** Skills of this class (or grade)
- [16] **hindered and blocked by any attempt to exercise our ability to reason:** i.e. if we begin to reason (= think logically), we are [a. more / b. less] likely to succeed.
- [18] **what could be called an intuitive edge:**「直観の力とでも呼んでよいようなもの」. "what could be called . . ." は名づけにくい(名前のない)ものの呼び名を提案する時の表現. **edge:** 強み (advantage). *Kim's definitely got the edge on you. Don't waste time trying to compete with her.*
- [21] **escapes you:** cf. *His name escapes me. I know it, but I just can't recall it at the moment.*
- [23] **subtle tasks:** jobs that demand extremely fine skills
- [24] **feel or intuit their way through them:** 感覚や直観に頼ってやっていく

way through. Karl Friedrich Gauss is sometimes described, along with Archimedes and Newton, as one of the three greatest mathematicians of all time. He discovered, among many other things, a way of proving that every number can be represented as the product of primes in one and only one way. And the answer came out of the blue. After years of struggle, he recalled in his diary: "Finally two days ago, I succeeded, but not on account of painful efforts. Like a sudden flash of lightning, the riddle happened to be solved."

Much of our success as a species is due to the deliberate and conscious application of explicit knowledge, but there is no denying the power and creativity of the unconscious. We seem to have an ability to know what to do in complicated situations without being able to explain how or why. We act on impulse, on a hunch, making snap decisions that very often turn out to be the most appropriate. And we may not be alone in this. There are signs that other species have similar talents and that intuition and a sense of what is appropriate have played a major role in evolution.

To appreciate the complexities of evolution in action, Fred Hoyle suggests that we consider the problems of a blind man confronted with one of those infuriating multicolored Rubik's Cubes. The man cannot see the results of his manipulations. He has no way of knowing whether he is getting nearer the solution or whether he is scrambling the cube still further. He acts at random and his chance of producing a perfect and simultaneous colour matching for all of the cube's six faces is about 50,000,000,000,000,000,000 to 1.

But suppose that one of those teenage prodigies who can unscramble a cube in less than 23 seconds is available — and agrees to stand behind our beleaguered blind man. At each move of the cube, the young expert remains silent as long as the move is in the right direction. But if a move does not advance the cube towards its solution, he simply and quietly whispers "No", and the blind operator reverses the move just made and tries another one — and goes on doing so until the observer says "Stop". If one minute is allowed for each

NATURAL SELECTION

[1] **Karl Friedrich Gauss:** カール・フリードリッヒ・ガウス (1777–1855)
[2] **Archimedes** [à:kəmíːdiːz]: アルキメデス (287?–212 B.C.)
[5] **product of primes:** 素数の積
[6] **out of the blue:** unexpectedly. cf. *It came to me out of a clear blue sky* (全く突然にひらめいた).
[8] **a sudden flash of lightning:** 日本語の「電光石火」と同じ発想. cf. *a flash of insight* (p. 6, l. 1)
[11] **explicit knowledge:** 明確に意識している知識（⇔ implicit knowledge: 暗黙知）
[14] **act on impulse, on a hunch:** 衝動的, 直観的に行動する. **hunch:** 勘
[15] **snap decision(s):** a decision made on the spot without careful thinking
[16] **we may not be alone in this:** i.e. human beings may not be the only species that has this ability.
[20] **Fred Hoyle:** (1915–2001) English astronomer, best known for developing the steady-state theory, which explains how the universe remains constant in density despite its expansion.
[22] **infuriating:** i.e. infuriatingly difficult.　**infuriate:** to make furious or very angry
[25] **scrambling the cube still further:** ルービック・キューブの解に向かう (unscramble the cube) どころか逆にそこからますます遠ざかる
[26] **his chance:**「確率」を意味する chance は, chances (are) と複数形をとる場合が多い. cf. *The chances are* (= *probably*) *she's still waiting there for you.*
[28] **50,000,000,000,000,000,000:** "fifty quintillion" という読み方もあるが, ふつうは 5×10^{19} として "five times ten to the power of nineteen" と読む.
[29] **prodigies** < prodigy: genius　cf. *child prodigy* (= whiz kid)
[31] **beleaguered:** under attack ; harassed.　*The students were beleaguered by difficult questions.*

successful move and an average of something like 120 moves are needed to reach the solution, even a blind man can do the task in a comparatively short time. The presence of the observer and the use of that one short word "No" at appropriate times, makes all the difference between a directed solution that takes just two hours — and a random one that could take 300 times the age of Earth.

The orthodox view of evolution is a little like this situation with the Rubik's Cube. Mutations, which occur at random and in unpredictable directions, are represented as moves made by a blind man. And natural selection, as it is exercised by the environment, is seen to operate on a mutating species in much the same way as an observer who decides whether or not the moves it makes are good. But the analogy is incomplete and misleading, because even neo-Darwinian evolutionists insist that natural selection is unintelligent — it does not know the solution in advance. All it can do is make limited value judgements about isolated moves.

"Natural selection," in Darwin's own words, "is daily and hourly scrutinising throughout the world, the slightest variations, rejecting those that are bad, preserving and adding up all that are good, silently and insensibly working . . ." The key word here is "insensible". Natural selection is *not* an expert observer. It is a considerable force, but an unintelligent one, in its own way as blind as the operator of the cube or the pattern of mutation. And yet evolution goes on getting things right, guiding mutation in productive directions, making choices that result in the right solutions, producing appropriate changes in an incredibly short time.

But the more closely one looks at what is now described as natural selection, the more it seems to include an essentially artificial component — something that keeps pushing it in a particular direction. It is abundantly clear from the fossil record that when organisms do change, the modifications which occur are of a kind which improve fitness far more often than can be expected from changes taking place on a purely random basis. And, what is even more significant, is the fact that such

NATURAL SELECTION

[8]　**The orthodox view of evolution:**「進化に対する正統的な見解」は，突然変異 (mutation) 等によってランダムに生じる多様性をもつ個体群の上に，高い生存の確率をもった個体をえり抜く過程 (natural selection) が働くという考えを軸にしている．

[15]　**misleading:** giving the wrong idea or impression
　　　neo-Darwinian < neo-Darwinism: a theory of evolution that combines Darwin's mechanisms of natural selection with later findings in modern genetics

[17]　**limited value judgements about isolated moves:** それぞれの個別的な動きの是非だけについての判断

[20]　**scrutinising:** examining in detail

[22]　**The key word here is "insensible":** ダーウィンが "insensibly" という語にこめた意味は，単に「目立たずに」ということであったようだが，ワトソンは独自の解釈によって「知覚能力なしに」の意味にとった．もっとも進化プロセスのことを「盲目の時計職人」(blind watchmaker) になぞらえる言い方は一般的である．

[26]　**getting things right:**「事態を正しく収める」．その具体的内容が続けて3点書かれている．

[32]　**artificial:** ⇔ natural.　a particular direction ⇔ randomness という対照がこれに重なる．つまり完全に natural に事態が進んでいるのならすべては偶然に任され，方向性は生じない．それなのに natural selection と呼ばれているものをよくよく見ると，明らかにそこに何らかの方向性が見て取れる，というのがこの段落のポイント．

[34]　**modifications:** 修正的変化

[35]　**improve fitness far more often than can be expected from changes taking place on a purely random basis:** 純粋にランダムなものとして起こる変化からはまったく期待できないほどの頻度で適合性を増す（環境としっくり噛み合う）．fitness についての筆者の考えは，p. 40, l. 24 以下で述べられる．

SESSION 4

changes quite often occur before the need for them arises.

A good example is the development of the amniotic egg which made it possible for backboned animals to migrate completely from water to land. This was no minor adjustment. The eggs of fish and frogs are simple blobs of jelly that must be kept in water to survive, but reptile and bird eggs have an amnion — a sac filled with fluid that floats each embryo safely in its own private pool and allows the parent responsible to wander Earth at will. And this stunning advance, as big in its way as the appearance of feathers or the development of limbs, was apparently *not* made in response to the pressures produced by a life on dry land. Amniotic eggs in protective shells were, it seems, being laid even by mesosaurs — totally aquatic dinosaurs that never left the water, but carried within them both the genes and the means for doing so. Reptiles and their eggs appear to have been wonderfully pre-adapted for life on land.

There are similar scenarios involved in the transition from walking to climbing. The most alluring of amphibians are the tree frogs — almost five hundred species of pop-eyed, multi-hued clowns and acrobats that hang by their toes from twigs in the rainforest or balance lightly on swaying reeds beside most of the world's great rivers. All these tree frogs have the same kind of feet with terminal suction cups, elongated fingers lined with unusual connective fibre, and an extra segment of cartilage pad shaped like a built-in climbing boot. All of which makes sense for arboreal animals, but it has now been discovered that similar adaptations exist amongst several families of terrestrial frogs which never climb and never have climbed trees. Apart from occasional leaps, for which they are very well designed, these species tend to be confined to the ground, but they have the look and the equipment of frogs that are getting ready to be climbers. They have been armed by evolution for a pre-emptive strike at life in the trees, should such a strategy ever become necessary. They are pre-adapted to a new habitat before its pressures have been brought to bear — and there is nothing in the traditional concept of natural selection which allows them to have such an advantage.

NATURAL SELECTION

[2] **amniotic egg:** 羊膜に包まれた卵(らん). 6行目以下参照.
[3] **backboned animal(s):** 脊椎動物 (= vertebrate, p. 40, l. 18)
[4] **no minor adjustment:** a major adjustment
[5] **blobs of jelly:** ゼリー質の無定型のかたまり
[7] **sac:** 嚢(のう)
[8] **wander Earth at will:** 地上を好きなように動き回る
[12] **protective shell(s):** 言うまでもなく，この固い殻の中に羊水 (amniotic fluid) と卵を包んだ羊膜が収まっている.
[13] **laid:** cf. *That chicken laid five eggs today.*
mesosaur(s) [mésəsɔ̀ː, mézə-]: 南米とアフリカの二畳紀(古生代最後の紀)の地層からのみ化石が発見されている初期爬虫類．二つの大陸が完全に分離する以前の海水に棲息したと考えられている．
aquatic: living in water
[18] **alluring:** attractive
amphibian(s) [æmfíbiən]: 両生動物
[19] **multi-hued** [mʌ̀ltihjúːd, mʌ̀ltai-]: multicoloured
[21] **reed(s):** 葦
[23] **with terminal suction cups:** 先に吸盤のついた
lined with unusual connective fibre: まとわりつく珍奇な繊維で覆われた
[24] **extra segment of cartilage pad:** 軟骨でできた覆い状の節が余分についている
[26] **arboreal** [ɑːbɔ́ːriəl]: living in trees
[27] **terrestrial** [təréstriəl]: living on land
[28] **Apart from occasional leaps:** Except for jumping from time to time
[32] **armed . . . for a pre-emptive strike:**「先制攻撃をかけられるよう武装している」．樹上での生活にあらかじめ適応している (pre-adapted) ことの比喩．すぐ後の strategy（戦略）も戦いの比喩を引き継いでいる．
[33] **should such a strategy ever become necessary:** if the need for arboreal life should ever arise
[34] **habitat:** 棲息地
[35] **have been brought to bear:** have begun to apply
there is nothing . . . which allows them to have such an advantage: i.e. the traditional concept of evolution cannot explain why they should have such an advantage (which is not yet an advantage).

Nothing, that is, unless it is admitted that there are connections between all parts of the environment. The environment as a whole is in some sense intelligent and exercises a degree of pattern and control. Unintelligent selection can only produce random and unintelligent results. But if the system itself has an inherent form, and encourages developments which are appropriate to that form, then fitness for a species or a new mutation begins to mean something more than a slight statistical shift in the odds on its survival.

All that is necessary is that the environment, or some observant part of it, should whisper "No" at the critical moments of poor choice, forestalling whole sequences of unproductive moves. This guidance can be as trivial as the unconscious ability that makes it possible for someone to sex day-old chicks, or as profound as the sequence of specific mutations that led, against all the odds and in an incredibly short space of time, to the production of whole haemoglobin or the perfection of the vertebrate eye.

I suggest that natural selection is subject to such guidance, that it is not altogether neutral or unintelligent, but can respond to a still small voice that, in effect, says, "No, that doesn't feel right. Try again in another way." And goes on nagging just often enough and long enough to make a powerful difference. Biologists talk a lot about survival of the "fittest", using the word more often than not to describe an organism which is big enough, strong enough, smart enough. But it seems to me to be more appropriate to take the word to mean befitted to and not armed against.

It may sound passive and unheroic, lacking in the muscular qualities we have come to associate with the struggle for survival, but true fitness is a very powerful property indeed.

NATURAL SELECTION

[1] **Nothing, that is, ...:**（前文で）"nothing" といったのは，つまり〜
connections between all parts of the environment: 省略した原文で筆者はこの「結びつき」を，より具体的に「情報伝達経路」として捉え，システム全体にかかわる情報が個々の種にも与えられるのではないかという考えを示している．ひらたく言えば，環境全体 (system) が常に種に対してなんらかの「形づけ」を行なっているということ．5〜7行目に書かれている "the system itself has an inherent form, and encourages developments which are appropriate to that form" とは，まさにそのような「形づけ」についての言及である．

[8] **something more than a slight statistical shift in the odds on its survival:**「統計学的に見た生存の確率のわずかな変動以上のもの」．つまり，確率論的思考にそぐわない「パターンへの適合」が起こっているということ．

[10] **observant:** observing; sensing (⇔ insensible, p. 36, l. 23)

[11] **the critical moments of poor choice:** まずい方向へ踏みだそうとする決定的瞬間に

[12] **forestalling whole sequences of unproductive moves:** preventing all (chains of) useless changes before they occur

[16] **against all the odds:**「成功の見込みが非常に少ないにもかかわらず」．ルービック・キューブの例からもわかる通り，確率論的に見ると生物の進化過程は奇跡の連続としかみえない．

[17] **haemoglobin** [hìːməglóubin, hèmə-]: ヘモグロビン． **haemo-** (hemo-): blood

[19] **is subject to:** receives; is (liable to be) controlled by

[20] **not altogether neutral:** [a. not at all neutral / b. not entirely neutral]． cf. *I don't altogether agree with you.*

[21] **still small voice:** 穏やかな小さい声
that doesn't feel right:「それじゃない気がする」．ここで "that isn't right" とか "that doesn't *look* right" と言わずに feel という，より漠然とした表現を使っているのは，自然選択機構がルービック・キューブの例とはちがって暗黙知 (implicit knowledge) に頼っていると著者が見ているからだろう．

[22] **nag(ging):** to say the same thing again and again

[24] **survival of the "fittest":** ちなみに「適者生存」という表現を流行させたのは "social Darwinist" のハーバート・スペンサーであり，ダーウィン自身は『種の起源』第5版 (1869) で初めて使った．

[25] **more often than not:** [a. on rare occasions / b. frequently]

[26] **smart:** [a. intelligent / b. stylish]

[29] **muscular qualities:** i.e. power, size, speed, etc.

SESSION 5

Agriculture's Mixed Blessing

Jared Diamond

WE are accustomed to assuming that the transition from the hunter-gatherer lifestyle to agriculture brought us health, longevity, security, leisure, and great art. While the case for this view *seems* overwhelming, it is hard to prove. How do you actually show that the lives of people ten thousand years ago got better when they abandoned hunting for farming?

The question has become answerable only in recent years, through the newly emerging science of "paleopathology": looking for signs of disease in the remains of ancient peoples. In some lucky situations, the paleopathologist has almost as much material to study as does a pathologist. For example, archaeologists in the deserts of Chile found well-preserved mummies whose medical condition at the time of death could be determined by an autopsy, just as one would do on a fresh corpse in a hospital today.

Usually, though, the only human remains available for paleopathologists to study are skeletons, but they still permit a surprising number of deductions about health. To begin with, a skeleton identifies its owner's sex, and his/her weight and approximate age at the time of death. Thus, with enough skeletons, one can construct mortality tables like those used by life-insurance companies to calculate expected life span and risk of death at any given age. Paleopathologists can also calculate growth rates by measuring bones of people of different ages,

"evolve" という英語に「進」を意味する要素はない．"e-" は "out", "volve" は「回転」を意味するのだから，巻物が解かれてゆく，あるいは渦巻きの内側から新しいパターンが出てくるというイメージで捉えたほうが正確だろう．歴史の過程も同様である．狩猟採集から，農耕中心の生活へと歴史が展開したのは大いなる「進歩」だと私たちはなんとなく思っているが，本当にそれは「進歩」だったのだろうか？ ニューギニアで長年フィールドワークを行なった人類学者による 1991 年の話題作 *The Third Chimpanzee* を手がかりに，この問題について考えてみよう．

[Notes]
[3] **longevity** [lɑndʒévəti]: long life
[4] **case:** 論拠，言い分
[9] **paleopathology** [pèilioupəθálədʒi, pæ̀liou-]: **paleo-:** ancient; **pathology:** (the study of) the causes and effects of illnesses
[10] **remains:** 残余物，亡きがら
[15] **autopsy:** 検屍，解剖
[19] **deductions:** 推理(から引き出される結論)
[22] **mortality tables:** 生命残存表，生命表，各年齢層の生存率・平均余命を列記した，生命保険用の統計表．
[23] **life span:** 寿命
[25] **growth rates:** 経済成長率の意味でよく使われるが，ここではもちろん，体の成長率のこと．

can examine teeth for cavities (signs of a high-carbohydrate diet) or enamel defects (signs of a poor diet in childhood), and can recognize scars that many diseases such as anemia, tuberculosis, leprosy, and osteoarthritis leave on bones.

One straightforward example of what paleopathologists have learned from skeletons concerns historical changes in height. Many modern cases illustrate how improved childhood nutrition leads to taller adults: for instance, we stoop to pass through doorways of medieval castles built for a shorter, malnourished population. Paleopathologists studying ancient skeletons from Greece and Turkey found a striking parallel. The average height of hunter-gatherers in that region toward the end of the Ice Age was a generous five feet ten inches for men, five feet six inches for women. With the adoption of agriculture, height crashed, reaching by 4000 B.C. a low value of only five feet three for men, five feet one for women. By classical times, heights were very slowly on the rise again, but modern Greeks and Turks have still not regained the heights of their healthy hunter-gatherer ancestors.

Another example is the study of thousands of American Indian skeletons excavated from burial mounds in the Illinois and Ohio river valleys. Corn, first domesticated in Central America thousands of years ago, became the basis of intensive farming in those valleys around A.D. 1000. Until then, Indian hunter-gatherers had skeletons "so healthy it is somewhat discouraging to work with them," as one paleopathologist complained. With the arrival of corn, Indian skeletons suddenly became interesting to study. The number of cavities in an average adult's mouth jumped from less than one to nearly seven, and tooth loss and abscesses became rampant. Enamel defects in children's milk teeth imply that pregnant and nursing mothers were severely undernourished. Anemia quadrupled in frequency; tuberculosis became established as an epidemic disease; half the population suffered from yaws or syphilis; and two-thirds suffered from osteoarthritis and other degenerative diseases. Mortality rates at every age increased, with the result that only 1 percent of the population survived past age fifty, as

AGRICULTURE'S MIXED BLESSING

[1] **for cavities:** 虫歯はないかと
a high-carbohydrate [kà:rbouháidreit] **diet:** 炭水化物の多い食生活
[2] **enamel:** 歯の表面のエナメル質のこと．
[3] **anemia** [əní:miə]**, tuberculosis** [tjubə̀:kjəlóusəs]**, leprosy** [léprəsi]**, and osteoarthritis** [àstiouɑ:rθráitəs]**:** 貧血症，結核，ライ病，骨関節症
[8] **stoop:** to bend the upper body forward and down; lean forward
[9] **malnourished:** poorly nourished; suffering from a poor diet. 32行目の undernourished も同義．
[12] **the end of the Ice Age:** 約200万年前にはじまった第四紀氷河時代は，約1万年前までつづいた．
[14] **crashed:** [a. went up / b. went down] dramatically
[16] **classical times:** 古代ギリシャ・ローマの時代．地中海にエーゲ文明が発生したのが紀元前20世紀ごろで，ローマ共和制が成立したのは紀元前6世紀末ごろ．
[21] **excavated:** found by digging
burial mounds: 埋葬塚
[22] **river valleys:** 川が流れる平地
Corn: イギリス英語では麦・トウモロコシ類の総称だが，北米やオーストラリアではトウモロコシを指す．筆者はアメリカ人．
domesticated: (野生植物を)農作物にした
[26] **work with them:** study them
[30] **abscess(es)** [ǽbses, -səs]**:** 膿瘍
rampant: [a. very rare / b. very widespread]
[31] **milk teeth:** 乳歯
[32] **quadrupled:** became four times greater
[33] **epidemic disease:** 伝染病
[34] **yaws or syphilis** [sífələs]**:** イチゴ腫(皮膚病の一種)や梅毒
[35] **degenerative:** 次第に悪化していく

compared to 5 percent in the golden days before corn. Almost one-fifth of the whole population died between the ages of one and four, probably because weaned toddlers succumbed to malnutrition and infectious diseases. Thus corn, usually considered among the New World's blessings, actually proved to be a public-health disaster. Similar conclusions about the transition from hunting to farming emerge from studies of skeletons elsewhere in the world.

There are at least three sets of reasons to explain these findings that agriculture was bad for health. First, hunter-gatherers enjoyed a varied diet with adequate amounts of protein, vitamins, and minerals, while farmers obtained most of their food from starchy crops. In effect, the farmers gained cheap calories at the cost of poor nutrition.

Second, because of that dependence on one or a few crops, farmers ran a greater risk of starvation if one food crop failed than did hunters. The Irish potato famine is merely one of many examples.

Finally, most of today's leading infectious diseases and parasites of mankind could not become established until after the transition to agriculture. These killers persist only in societies of crowded, malnourished, sedentary people constantly reinfected by each other and by their own sewage. The cholera bacterium, for example, does not survive for long outside the human body. It spreads from one victim to the next through contamination of drinking water with feces of cholera patients. Measles dies out in small populations once it has either killed or immunized most potential hosts; only in populations numbering at least a few hundred thousand people can it maintain itself indefinitely. Such crowd epidemics could not persist in small, scattered bands of hunters who often shifted camp. Tuberculosis, leprosy, and cholera had to await the rise of farming, while smallpox, bubonic plague, and measles appeared only in the past few thousand years with the rise of even denser populations in cities.

Besides malnutrition, starvation, and epidemic diseases,

AGRICULTURE'S MIXED BLESSING

[3]　**weaned toddlers:** 乳離れしたよちよち歩きの幼児．toddler は infant につづく年齢層で，ふつう1〜3歳の幼児を指す．
　　　succumbed to: yielded to; died from
[4]　**Thus corn ... actually proved to be a public-health disaster:** より厳密な言い方をすれば，Thus the way of life depending on corn ... proved to be responsible for a decline in public health.
[5]　**the New World:** 新たな富や資源への期待をこめて，アメリゴ・ヴェスプッチ (1454–1512) が新大陸を Mundus novus (the New World) と呼んで以来，この呼称が定着した．
[13]　**starchy:** 澱粉質の (having a high carbohydrate content)
　　　gained cheap calories at the cost of poor nutrition: i.e. [a. gained calories from easily available food / b. didn't gain enough calories], and/but [a. gained enough nutrition / b. didn't gain enough nutrition]
[17]　**The Irish potato famine:** アイルランドで1845年から49年にかけてジャガイモの疫病が原因で生じた大飢饉．アイルランドでは18世紀にもジャガイモの疫病が広まったが，当時はまだそれほどジャガイモに依存していなかったため，被害は比較的小さかった．だが1845年の段階では，住民の3分の1以上がほとんどジャガイモだけを主食としていて，飢饉による死者は数十万にのぼった．
[21]　**persist:** continue to exist; are difficult to get rid of
[22]　**sedentary:** 定住性の (この逆が p. 50, l. 9 の nomadic)
[23]　**reinfected by each other:** たがいに病気をうつしあう
　　　sewage [súːidʒ]: 下水
[26]　**contamination:** 汚染
　　　feces [fíːsiːz]: 糞便
[27]　**Measles:** はしか (単数扱い)
[28]　**immunize(d):** 免疫にする
　　　host(s): (寄生動植物の) 寄主，宿主
[30]　**indefinitely:** without a fixed end; for a long time
[31]　**shifted:** moved
[33]　**smallpox:** 天然痘
　　　bubonic plague: 腺ペスト

farming brought another curse to humanity: class divisions. Hunter-gatherers have little or no stored food, and no concentrated food sources like orchards or herds of cows. Instead, they live off the wild plants and animals that they obtain each day. Everybody except for infants, the sick, and the old joins in the search for food. Thus there can be no kings, no full-time professionals, no class of social parasites who grow fat on food seized from others.

Only in a farming population could contrasts between the disease-ridden masses and a healthy, nonproducing, elite develop. Skeletons from Greek tombs at Mycenae around 1500 B.C. suggest that royals enjoyed a better diet than commoners, since the royal skeletons were two or three inches taller and had better teeth (on the average, one instead of six cavities or missing teeth).

These signs of health differentials within local communities of farmers in the past appear on a global scale in the modern world. To most American and European readers, the argument that humanity could on the average be better off as hunter-gatherers than we are today sounds ridiculous, because most people in industrial societies today enjoy better health than most hunter-gatherers. However, Americans and Europeans are an elite in today's world, dependent on oil and other materials imported from countries with large peasant populations and much lower health standards. If you could choose between being a middle-class American, a Bushman hunter, and a peasant farmer in Ethiopia, the first would undoubtedly be the healthiest choice, but the third might be the least healthy.

While giving rise to class divisions for the first time, farming may also have exacerbated sexual inequality already in existence. With the advent of agriculture, women often became beasts of burden, were drained by more frequent pregnancies (see below), and thus suffered poorer health. For example, among the Chilean mummies from A.D. 1000, women exceeded men in osteoarthritis and in bone lesions from infectious disease.

AGRICULTURE'S MIXED BLESSING

- [4] **live off:** to get their food from
- [10] **disease-ridden:** -ridden は「〜に悩まされている，苛まれている」の意. *crime-ridden area*（犯罪の多発する地域）
- [11] **Mycenae** [maisíːniː]: ミュケーナイ．アガメムノン王の伝説やシュリーマンの発掘で有名な，古代ギリシャ文明黎明期（青銅時代）の中心都市．
- [12] **commoners:** 平民
- [16] **differentials:** 落差
- [26] **Bushman:** 南アフリカ，カラハリ砂漠付近にすむ採集狩猟民族．SESSION 6, p. 52 参照．
- [30] **exacerbate(d)** [iɡzǽsəbéit, iksǽs-]**:** to make worse
- [32] **beasts of burden:** 荷物運搬用の動物，役畜
  drained: deprived of strength; exhausted
- [35] **lesion(s)** [líːʒen]**:** 損傷

Instead of the progressivist party line that we chose agriculture because it was good for us, a cynic might ask how we got trapped by agriculture despite its being such a mixed blessing.

Perhaps the main reason we find it so hard to shake off the traditional view that farming was unequivocally good for us is that there's no doubt that it meant more tons of food per acre. Population densities of hunter-gatherers are typically one person or less per square mile, while densities of farmers average at least ten times higher. This is partly because nomadic hunter-gatherers have to keep their children spaced at four-year intervals by infanticide and other means, since a mother must carry her toddler until it's old enough to keep up with the adults. Because sedentary farmers don't have that problem, a woman can and does have a child every two years. We forget that farming also resulted in more mouths to feed, and that health and quality of life depend on the amount of food per mouth.

As population densities of hunter-gatherers slowly rose at the end of the Ice Age, bands had to "choose," whether consciously or unconsciously, between feeding more mouths by taking the first steps toward agriculture, or else finding ways to limit growth. Some bands adopted the former solution, unable to anticipate the evils of farming, and seduced by the transient abundance they enjoyed until population growth caught up with increased food production. Such bands outbred and then drove off or killed the bands that chose to remain hunter-gatherers, because ten malnourished farmers can still outfight one healthy hunter. It's not that hunter-gatherers abandoned their life-style, but that those sensible enough not to abandon it were forced out of all areas except ones that farmers didn't want. Modern hunter-gatherers persist mainly in scattered areas useless for agriculture, such as the Arctic and deserts.

AGRICULTURE'S MIXED BLESSING

- [1] **progressivist party line:** 進歩主義路線．人類の歴史を進歩と捉える見方を皮肉って言っている．
- [2] **cynic:** 醒めた，皮肉な見方をする人間
- [3] **mixed blessing:** 一見ありがたいようでいて，実はありがたくないもの
- [5] **unequivocally** [ʌ̀nikwívəkəli]: decidedly; absolutely
- [9] **nomadic:** 遊牧民の
- [11] **infanticide:** (慣行としての)「間引き」．cf. *suicide, genocide, etc.*
- [24] **transient abundance:** つかのまの豊かさ
- [26] **outbred** < outbreed: to produce more children than; outnumber in population

SESSION 6

Against Focused Attention

Mary Catherine Bateson

AMONG the San people such as the !Kung of the Kalahari (also known as Bushmen), the women are either pregnant or nursing (each child for three years or more) for most of their adult lives, but this does not prevent them from making a full contribution to subsistence tasks. The San used to be called a hunting people, when anthropologists focused almost exclusively on the male half of the societies they studied, but eventually they noticed that some two-thirds of the diet was actually provided by women's gathering and proposed that the San be called a hunting-gathering or a foraging people.

If you are a San hunter, a man, you go out with a small group of companions armed with poison-tipped arrows, hoping to track and wound a large grazing animal, an antelope or a giraffe. It would take the poison many hours to work on the animal, but unless you as hunter arrived quickly when it collapsed, other predators or scavengers would get to the meat before you. The San are extraordinarily skilled trackers, able to tell from tiny clues when the animal passed and how it was feeling, taking note of where it urinated, where it defecated, even of where it staggered and brushed against a bush. The veldt speaks to them in great detail, so rich in information that the difference from a city dweller's vision of the same landscape must be like the difference between black and white and color vision. They read the whole condition of the animal they

AGAINST FOCUSED ATTENTION

　フェミニズムという言葉が一般化してから30年経ったいま,「男性的」な思考や行動を中心に据え,「女性的」な思考や行動を周縁に据える発想から我々はどこまで自由になっただろう？　一見,性差など関係なさそうなところで,「男性的」なものに重きを置いてはいないだろうか——たとえば,「目標に向かってひた向きに進むのはよいことだ」と唱えるときに？

　著者メアリ・キャサリン・ベイトソンは人類学者マーガレット・ミードとグレゴリー・ベイトソンを両親として育ち,大学で教えるかたわら,現代人の生き方について考えさせるエッセーを精力的に発表している.

[Notes]
[1] **the San people:** サン族.アフリカ南部に住む,狩猟採集で暮らしていた民族.Sanはホッテントット語で「藪の人(ブッシュマン)」の意.
the !Kung: サン族の一部族.Kungの前に！がついているのは,Kの音がクリック音(舌打ちのようにして発音する「吸着音」)であることを示す.ホッテントットやブッシュマンの喋る「コイ＝サン系」の言語では,吸着音がきわめて多様に発達している.
[2] **the Kalahari:** カラハリ砂漠
Bushmen: San,特にその一部族である !Kungの旧称.最近は避けられる傾向にある.
[3] **nursing:** feeding infants with milk from their breasts
[5] **subsistence tasks:** work essential for survival
[7] **exclusively:** entirely
[10] **foraging** < forage: to wander about looking for food
[14] **track:** to follow
grazing: grass-eating
antelope: 羚羊(レイヨウ).ウシ科の動物のうち,スイギュウ,ヤギュウ,カモシカ,ヤギ,ヒツジの各類を除いた,シカに似た優美な形態をもつものの総称.
[17] **collapsed:** fell down
scavengers: animals that feed on dead animals
[20] **urinate(d) ... defecate(d):** 排尿する...排便する
[21] **stagger(ed):** よろめく,ふらつく
[22] **veldt** [velt]:(アフリカ南部の)草原.veltとも.

are pursuing from its spoor, as a modern physician might from an array of lab tests. The hunters, focused on the trail, knowing exactly what they are after, must move quickly because the quarry can cover a lot of country before it slows down. When the meat is eventually brought home, it will be shared with everyone in the band, providing a moment of celebration and excitement.

If you are a San woman, you also set off with a small group of companions, but not with the hope of getting one large piece of meat. For a day of gathering, you will probably head to an area where nuts rich in protein, say, or wild melons are known to be found, but in the course of the day you may find and bring home a dozen different foodstuffs: roots, nuts, gourds, melons, edible insects, eggs from a bird's nest, a tortoise, a whole variety of foods spotted along the way.

Because the women move more slowly, they can talk and gossip through the day, whereas the men tracking are moving faster and doing less talking. Several of the women will be carrying nursing infants, and there is probably another child or two along, who refused to be left in someone else's care back at the camp. Some of the children are more or less walking but need periods of rest and will probably ask to be picked up on the trip home, when everyone has the most to carry. In the meantime, the children on foot are zigzagging a little into the bush, so you are watching what each child is doing, looking up in the branches, scanning and checking along the ground for a burrow or a vine that betrays an edible root. Back in the camp women do a second shift, preparing food, looking after children and old people and the sick, carrying firewood and water — doing a variety of overlapping and enfolded tasks. If you imagine yourself as a San woman, you can get the sense of multiple focus that frees the men for the narrower focus of the hunt.

The food that the women bring home is shared without fanfare in the immediate family. Nobody has a party about it — no one gives it that much attention — so it is not surprising that anthropologists took so long to notice its importance. The

AGAINST FOCUSED ATTENTION

[1] **spoor:** 足あとや糞など，動物がそこを通ったことを知る手がかりとなるもの．臭跡，足跡 (track, trail)
[2] **array** [əréi]: collection; group
lab tests: 検査結果
[4] **quarry:** 獲物
a lot of country: a huge area
[11] **say:** for example
[13] **gourd(s)** [gɔːd, guəd]: ヒョウタン
[14] **edible:** good to eat; eatable
[17] **through the day:** all day
[19] **nursing infants:** infants that are still being fed with their mother's milk. cf. p. 52, l. 3
[26] **scanning and checking along the ground for . . . :** 〜はないかと道中地面に視線を走らせている
[27] **burrow:** a hole in the ground made by an animal, such as a rabbit hole
[28] **a second shift:** 二巡目の仕事．普通 a shift といえば，それだけで一日の十分な労働量．
[30] **overlapping and enfolded tasks:** 重なり合い，織り込まれあったさまざまな作業
[32] **frees the men for the narrower focus of the hunt:** i.e. allows the men to focus on hunting without having to worry about various other things
[35] **fanfare** [fǽnfɛə]: noticeable celebration
[36] **that much attention:** very much attention. *The new machine isn't that much different from the old one.*

response to the food gathered by the women is reminiscent of the old notion of a woman as "just a housewife": "not working," not contributing to the GNP, achieving nothing worthy of notice. Nobody celebrates the fruits of her effort. Hunting skills are reserved for men; men do sometimes gather food on the veldt, but they do so unenthusiastically, gathering less efficiently.

With contraception, alternative ways of feeding, and low infant mortality, we no longer need to let the division of labor be determined by reproduction. Men and women do a great variety of tasks, demonstrating a range of potential unexplored in the Kalahari, tasks that require myriad styles of attention. But the advantages that men have enjoyed and the extra value given to their contributions carry over in an extra value given to narrowly focused attention, to doing one thing at a time. The more our society moves toward specialization, the more women and men alike are forced to focus on single activities, living in narrow channels.

Increasingly in contemporary society, men and women do the same tasks, but there are still visible differences in the way they do them. Some tasks that traditionally were done by women were elaborated and turned into full-time professions by men. It used to be said that women cook and men become chefs. Women care for the sick and men become surgeons. Women sew and men become fashion designers. Today, of course, women are becoming chefs and surgeons and designers, and are able to compose their lives so that at appropriate times they can focus fully on these vocations instead of weaving them in with other activities. Still, one of the things that has been pointed out about the entry of women into the corporate world is that they often attend to process simultaneously with task — to how things are done as well as whether the goal is achieved. They notice whose feelings are being hurt and who is hesitating to voice an idea, even while working on improving the bottom line for the next quarterly report. A few corporations are beginning to value this skill, but all too often it is unrewarded.

AGAINST FOCUSED ATTENTION

- [1] **is reminiscent** [rèmənísnt] **of:** reminds you of; is like
- [2] **housewife:** 北米を中心に，次第に politically correct でなくなりつつある言葉．現在は homemaker (次頁 17 行目)と言う方が「正しく」聞こえる．
- [8] **With contraception . . . :** 避妊が可能な時代になって
  alternative ways of feeding: つまり，母乳以外の授乳法．
- [10] **reproduction:** 生殖機能
- [11] **potential:** possibilities
- [12] **myriad** [míriəd]**:** innumerable; a great variety of
- [14] **carry over in . . . :**（なくなってしまったわけではなく）～のなかに今日まで持ち越されている
- [22] **elaborated:** made complex; made sophisticated
- [28] **weaving them in with . . . :** doing them simultaneously (= at the same time) with . . . . **weave in:** 織り込む
- [30] **the corporate world:** 企業 (corporation) の世界
- [31] **process . . . task:** 2つの言葉の対照がダッシュに続いて説明されている．
- [34] **voice:** to express
- [35] **bottom line:** 決算表の最終行の数字．収益
  quarterly report: 四半期ごとに提出される報告書

SESSION 6

Life is complicated. It is simplifying but dangerous to have one overriding concern that makes others unimportant — rage or passion or the kind of religious exultation that seeks or inflicts martyrdom. The most striking cause of narrowed attention at the national level is warfare. In a complex world of conflicting priorities, going to war can be a tremendous relief. In peacetime, government has to balance off guns and butter, but when a nation goes to war, it goes to war to win, and everything else becomes unimportant. All of a sudden, the president no longer has to be concerned with the future of industry or education or human rights. Everyone can focus in on the supreme importance of victory. Warfare comes as a great relief to those who prefer thinking about one thing at a time. It is no coincidence that the language of warfare is so often used to focus on any urgent issue — poverty, or drugs, or the AIDS epidemic — yet the metaphor is ill chosen, for many of these wars cannot be won, any more than a homemaker can definitively win a war against mess. The world doesn't stop while a war is taking place, either, and the victories won on the battlefield leave other problems unsolved.

Even in warfare, there are issues of attention. Intelligence depends on the skillful use of peripheral vision. Strategy depends on recognizing change. Battles are often lost by attending too much to the lessons of previous conflicts, too little to the present. The United States went to Vietnam with fixed ideas of how to fight and was blindsided by the effectiveness of guerrilla warfare. From that debacle it drew the conclusion that wars should be fought only with narrowly drawn and highly specific goals, but such goals have the effect of narrowing attention in an unpredictable world. Focusing in 1991 on getting Iraq out of Kuwait, the generals ignored issues that we will be dealing with for years to come. The war not only left Saddam Hussein in power in Baghdad but also created a major environmental disaster in the gulf and a major human disaster for the Kurds, and it gave political legitimacy to Syria's Hafiz al-Assad, for in warfare it is easy to ignore the bad habits of allies. Wars almost always have unintended side effects, and

AGAINST FOCUSED ATTENTION

[2] **overriding:** dominant; urgent
[3] **exultation:** triumphant joy; ecstasy. ある種の religious exultation がいかに危険であるかを証明するような事件が，近年も後をたたない．
inflicts: forces an unpleasant experience on someone
[4] **martyrdom:** 殉教
[5] **a complex world of conflicting priorities:** 何を優先すべきか，利害が対立しあっている複雑な世界
[6] **tremendous:** huge; extreme
[7] **guns and butter:** "guns before butter" といえば「国民生活より軍事優先」
[13] **no coincidence:** cf. p. 4, l. 33; p. 22, l. 13
[16] **the metaphor is ill chosen:** it's not a good metaphor
many of these wars cannot be won:「受験戦争」「就職戦線」「企業戦士」といった日本語の例でも，同様の議論が成り立たないだろうか？
[21] **Intelligence:** 情報収集
[22] **peripheral vision:** 周辺視覚，周辺視野 (⇔ focused vision). この文章の出典である本の題名は *Peripheral Visions* (1995).
[26] **was blindsided:** 弱点をつかれた
[27] **debacle** [deibɑ́:kl, di-]: disaster; complete failure
[30] **in 1991 on getting Iraq out of Kuwait . . . :** いわゆる湾岸戦争 (the Gulf War) のこと．
[32] **The war not only left Saddam Hussein in power:** サダム・フセインが権力の座にとどまったということは，湾岸戦争の「勝利」は当初の目的すら十分には果たせなかったことになる．
[35] **the Kurds:** クルド人．イラン・イラク・トルコの国境地帯に居住する民族．湾岸戦争とその後の混乱のなかで，イラクに住む多数が難民化した．
legitimacy: lawful status
Hafiz al-Assad [hɑfíz ǽləsǽd]: (1930–2000) 1971 年からシリア大統領．ソ連崩壊後，西側接近を試み，91 年の湾岸戦争では西側に味方してサウジアラビアに出兵．

goals may need to change along the way. Winning is never as simple as it seems.

In warfare, domestic issues are left untended. Men have on the whole had the privilege of walking out the door and assuming that they could delegate many of life's concerns in order to concentrate elsewhere. Whether for the period of a workday or a military campaign, someone else would take care of the children, the laundry, the elderly, tonight's dinner, calling the plumber, getting on with the neighbors. Today women are meeting the demands of outside jobs, and some of these other concerns are beginning to be shared. It was interesting, in the criticism of the Bush administration that followed Operation Desert Storm, to notice that the electorate was increasingly feeling that it is unacceptable to ignore domestic issues during wartime, for often there are parallels between the household division of labor and the national priorities. This new insistence on the domestic may represent more than the familiar postwar spasm of isolationism.

Building peace, like women's work, is never done. A woman's work is never done because, although a particular task may be completed, she is always engaged in multiple tasks, long- and short-term, cycled and recycled, and there is never a moment when she can say that no task is waiting. The first proverb arguing against focused attention that comes to my mind is from the kitchen: A watched pot never boils. The reality is that the pot will boil, but the tea tray won't be ready. A homemaker cannot keep up with the full range of tasks by focusing on one thing at a time. In the same way, the health of a nation is always many-stranded.

[5] **delegate:** to leave (work, duty, etc) to somebody else
[12] **the Bush administration:** アメリカの「〜政権」はこの言い方が普通.
[13] **Operation Desert Storm:**「砂漠の嵐作戦」．1991年1月17日に開始された，米国を中心とする多国籍軍のクウェート奪回作戦．1か月以上にわたる空爆ののち2月24日から地上戦が開始され，27日にクウェートが解放されて終了．
      electorate: 有権者
[16] **national priorities:** 国外で戦うことと「家」を守ることのうち，どちらが「国家の優先事」かということ．
[18] **postwar spasm of isolationism:** 戦争が終わった直後，それまでの反動で孤立主義に固まる傾向．**spasm:** burst
[26] **tea tray:** お茶のセット
[29] **many-stranded:** made up of many elements

SESSION 7

The Flesh of Language

David Abram

EVERY attempt to definitively say *what language is* is subject to a curious limitation. For the only medium with which we can define language is language itself. It may be best, then, to leave language undefined, and to thus acknowledge its open-endedness, its mysteriousness. Nevertheless, by paying attention to this mystery we may develop a conscious familiarity with it, a sense of its texture, its habits, its source of sustenance.

Already in the *Phenomenology of Perception*, Merleau-Ponty had begun to work out a notion of human language as a profoundly carnal phenomenon, rooted in our sensorial experience of each other and of the world. In a famous chapter entitled "The Body as Expression, and Speech," he wrote at length of the gestural genesis of language, the way that communicative meaning is first incarnate in the gestures by which the body spontaneously expresses feelings and responds to changes in its affective environment. The gesture is spontaneous and immediate. It is not an arbitrary sign that we mentally attach to a particular emotion or feeling; rather, the gesture is the bodying-forth of that emotion into the world, it *is* that feeling of delight or of anguish in its tangible, visible aspect. When we encounter such a spontaneous gesture, we do not first see it as a blank behavior, which we then mentally associate with a particular content or significance; rather, the bodily gesture speaks directly to our own body, and is thereby understood

THE FLESH OF LANGUAGE

「ことばの生身」とは一体何だろう．Language といえば私たちはまず words を思い浮かべる．words とはなにか．それは「意味」のこもった「記号」である．そうした前提から言語についての思考はふつう始まる．だがそれだけでは足らないことも私たちは知っている．というのも言葉は怒りにふるえ，喜びにはずみ，悲しみにしずんだりもするからだ．そしてそれらの「ふるえ」「はずみ」「しずみ」自体が——その上に言葉が乗っていようといまいと——相手に伝わる．何か別の記号に置き換えられることなく，直接伝わる．ここでは，「ことば」にこもる抽象的な意味ではなく，伝達行動の身体的な深みを探っていこう．筆者デイヴィッド・エイブラムは生態学的な視点から人間の精神を考えようとする，いわば「環境哲学」または「生態心理学」の実践者．その立場は現代的であると同時に，西欧ロマン主義思潮の伝統をうけついでいる．

[Notes]

[2] **subject to a curious limitation:** never completely successful (for a special reason). **subject to:** likely to be affected by. *The time table is subject to alteration.*
For the only medium with which we can define language is language itself: Because we cannot define language without using language itself

[5] **its open-endedness:** 言語が open-ended であるということは，言語を言語でないものから画す(define する)ための境界がわからない，ということ．

[6] **develop a conscious familiarity with it:** become aware of the mystery

[7] **its texture:** 言葉の「手触り」(⇔ 抽象的な「意味」)
its habits, its source of sustenance: 本論では言葉を生き物として語るレトリックが多用される． **source of sustenance:** 滋養の源；生命を支えるもの

[9] **Merleau-Ponty:** モーリス・メルロー=ポンティ (1908–61) はフランスの哲学者．知覚と社会における身体の役割を探究して現象学に新たな地平を拓いた．主著 *Phénoménologie de la perception* (1945)，邦訳『知覚の現象学』(みすず書房)．

[10] **work out:** 案出する． *We never could work out what caused the accident.*

[11] **carnal:** bodily. 本論に登場する「身体」の関連語を 71 頁にまとめた．
sensorial experience: i.e. seeing, hearing, touching, etc.

[13] **at length:** in great detail

[14] **the gestural genesis of language:** ことばがジェスチャーに起源をもつこと．

[15] **incarnate** [inkáːnət, -nèit]: 抽象的な概念や特性が(目に見える形に)「具現化(受肉化)した」ということ． *She is a devil incarnate.*

[17] **affective:**「情動的な」．次の頁の本文 6 行目以下を参照. cf. *I was deeply affected* (= moved) *by the film.*

[18] **arbitrary:**「恣意的な」．記号の意味するもの(記号表現)と意味されるもの(記号内容)との間に，慣習的(conventional) に結びついているという以上の関係がないこと．犬という動物は "inu" "dog" "chien" などさまざまな音列で呼ばれるように，単語の大多数は arbitrary な性格をもつ．

[20] **bodying-forth:** いかにも身体全体を使って感情を表出するという感じの表現．

[21] **tangible, visible aspect:** that side of emotion we can see and touch

without any interior reflection. The gesture *does not make us think of anger*, it is anger itself.

Active, living speech is just such a gesture, a vocal gesticulation wherein the meaning is inseparable from the sound, the shape, and the rhythm of the words. Communicative meaning is always, in its depths, affective; it remains rooted in the sensual dimension of experience, born of the body's native capacity to resonate with other bodies and with the landscape as a whole. Linguistic meaning is not some ideal and bodiless essence that we arbitrarily assign to a physical sound or word and then toss out into the "external" world. Rather, meaning sprouts in the very depths of the sensory world, in the heat of meeting, encounter, participation.

We do not, as children, first enter into language by consciously studying the formalities of syntax and grammar or by memorizing the dictionary definitions of words, but rather by actively making sounds — by crying in pain and laughing in joy; by squealing and babbling and playfully mimicking the surrounding soundscape, gradually entering through such mimicry into the specific melodies of the local language, our resonant bodies slowly coming to echo it.

If that is the case, language cannot be genuinely studied or understood in isolation from the sensuous reverberation and resonance of active speech. James M. Edie attempts to summarize this aspect of Merleau-Ponty's thought in this manner:

> ... Merleau-Ponty's first point is that words, even when they finally achieve the ability to carry referential and, eventually, conceptual levels of meaning, never completely lose that primitive, strictly phonemic, level of 'affective' meaning which is not translatable into their conceptual definitions. There is, he argues, an affective tonality, a mode of conveying meaning beneath the level of thought, beneath the level of the words themselves ... which is much more like a melody — a 'singing of the world' — than fully translatable, conceptual thought.

Merleau-Ponty is not alone among philosophers of language

THE FLESH OF LANGUAGE

[1]   **interior reflection:** 内省
[3]   **vocal gesticulation:** 声による身ぶり；表現にみちた発声
[5]   **Communicative meaning:** 実際の会話でやり取りされる伝達内容
[7]   **born of ...:** 〜から生まれた
[8]   **resonate with ...:** 〜と共鳴(共振)する．cf. *resonant* (l. 20), *resonance* (l. 24)
[11]   **the "external" world:** 引用符がついているのは，発話者の「内なる」世界と「外的世界」が別者であるという考えが正しくないことを示そうとしているから．
[12]   **sprout(s):** 芽ぶく
[15]   **syntax and grammar:** syntax は「統語論」(単語を組み合わせて複合的な表現を構成する際に従わなければならない規則の体系)だが，ここでは grammar と併せて普通の意味での「文法」を指すと考えてよい．
[18]   **squealing and babbling:** キーキー，バブバブと言う
        surrounding soundscape: 自分をとりまく音の世界．cf. *landscape, techno-scape*
[20]   **the specific melodies of the local language:** (日本語なら日本語の)特有の節まわし
[23]   **reverberation:** echoing
[27]   **referential** [rèfərénʃəl]: 外界のものを指示 (refer to) する．言語表現と客観世界の事物が直接対応関係を結ぶという図式．次の行の **conceptual** はそうした指示的な意味がさらに抽象化し，(例えば "dog" は特定の犬ではなく犬の「概念」を表わすという具合に)抽象化した段階．いずれも身体性から遊離している点が重要．
[29]   **phonemic:** 本来は「音素の」だが，ここでは言語表現の音声と意味が表裏一体の段階を指している．
[31]   **affective tonality:**「情動の響き」．すぐ後で melody や singing of the world という言い方で比喩的に表現されている．
[33]   **much more like a melody:**「メロディ」が表わすのは「メロディ」そのものであって，「メロディ」とは別個に「メロディの表わす意味」があるわけではないことを考えてみよう．

in his sensitivity to this level of meaning. The expressive, gestural basis of language had already been emphasized in the first half of the eighteenth century by the Italian philosopher Giambattista Vico, who in his *New Science* wrote of language as arising from expressive gestures, and suggested that the earliest and most basic words had taken shape from expletives uttered in startled response to powerful natural events, or from the frightened, stuttering mimesis of such events — like the crack and rumble of thunder across the sky. Shortly thereafter, in France, Jean-Jacques Rousseau wrote of gestures and spontaneous expressions of feeling as the earliest forms of language, while in Germany, Johann Gottfried Herder argued that language originates in our sensuous receptivity to the sounds and shapes of the natural environment.

In his embodied philosophy of language, then, Merleau-Ponty is the heir of a long-standing, if somewhat heretical lineage. Linguistic meaning, for him, is rooted in the felt experience induced by specific sounds and sound-shapes as they echo and contrast with one another, each language a kind of song, a particular way of "singing the world."

The more prevalent view of language, at least since the scientific revolution, and still assumed in some manner by most linguists today, considers any language to be a set of arbitrary but conventionally agreed upon words, or "signs," linked by a purely formal system of syntactic and grammatical rules. Language, in this view, is rather like a *code*; it is a way of *representing* actual things and events in the perceived world, but it has no internal, nonarbitrary connections to that world, and hence is readily separable from it.

If Merleau-Ponty is right, however, then the denotative, conventional dimension of language can never be truly severed from the sensorial dimension of direct, affective meaning. If we are not, in truth, immaterial minds merely housed in earthly bodies, but, are from the first, material, corporeal beings, then it is the sensuous, gestural significance of spoken sounds — their direct bodily resonance — that makes verbal communication possible at all. It is this expressive potency —

THE FLESH OF LANGUAGE

[4] **Giambattista Vico:** ジャンバティスタ・ヴィーコ (1668–1744). 人間社会の円環的発展衰退理論を提唱. 『新しい学』 *New Science* は, 西洋思潮史の指標のひとつと言われ, ゲーテ, マルクス, ニーチェ, ジョイスらにも強い影響を与えた.

[6] **take(n) shape from ...:** 〜にもとづいた形をしている
expletive(s) [iksplítiv]: (「アー」「ウー」のように慣習化された意味をもたない) 間投詞的な表現

[8] **stuttering mimesis** [məmí:səs]: 思わず口をついて出る模倣的な声

[10] **Jean-Jacques Rousseau:** 『社会契約論』や教育論『エミール』で知られるフランスの思想家ジャン=ジャック・ルソー (1712–78) は「言語の起源についての試論——メロディと音楽的模倣」という論文を書いている.

[12] **Johann Gottfried [von] Herder:** ヨハン・ゴットフリート・フォン・ヘルダー (1744–1803) は疾風怒濤運動を率いたロマン主義の思想家で, やはり「言語の起源についての試論」という論文を残した. 邦訳『言語起源論』(大修館書店).

[13] **receptivity to:** sensitivity to

[15] **embodied philosophy of language:** 言語を身体化した (embodied) ものとして捉える考え方

[16] **heir** [ɛə]: 後継者
of ... lineage: 〜の系譜に属する
heretical [hərétikəl]: contrary to what is generally accepted. (< heresy: 異端)

[21] **prevalent:** widely accepted

[22] **the scientific revolution:** 「科学革命」. 17 世紀にデカルトやニュートンらによってなしとげられた知の変革. これにより客観的な対象を要素に分解して分析する方法が確立された. 言語を単語や音素に分解し, それらの要素間の客観的な結びつきの規則を扱う言語学も, 同じ方法論を受け継いでいると言えるが, 最近の言語理論にはこうした還元主義的な考え方からの離脱の試みも目立つ.

[26] ***code***: 符号の体系. 「意味」を「符号」化することを encoding, 「符号」を解読することを decoding という.
representing: イタリックスでの強調により「(本来の姿とは直接関係のない音や文字記号の姿で) 表わし直す」という意味が押し出されている.

[30] ***denotative***: (< denote) 前頁 27 行目の referential とほぼ同義.

[32] **severed from:** cut off from

[33] **immaterial minds merely housed in earthly bodies:** 「(本来神に由来する) 霊的な精神が (もともと土くれから造られた) 肉体に宿る」というのは, ユダヤ=キリスト教文化の伝統的な人間観. このような心身二元論の克服が 20 世紀哲学の大きなテーマのひとつとなった.

[34] **from the first:** from the beginning

[36] **direct bodily resonance:** cf. "the sensuous reverberation and resonance of active speech" (p. 64, l. 23)

[37] **potency** [póutənsi]: power; ability

the soundful influence of spoken words upon the sensing body — that supports all the more abstract and conventional meanings that we assign to those words. Although we may be oblivious to the gestural, somatic dimension of language, having repressed it in favor of strict dictionary definitions and the abstract precision of specialized terminologies, this dimension remains subtly operative in all our speaking and writing — if, that is, our words have any significance whatsoever. For meaning, as we have said, remains rooted in the sensory life of the body — it cannot be completely cut off from the soil of direct, perceptual experience without withering and dying.

Yet to affirm that linguistic meaning is primarily expressive, gestural, and poetic, and that conventional and denotative meanings are inherently secondary and derivative, is to renounce the claim that "language" is an exclusively human property. If language is always, in its depths, physically and sensorially resonant, then it can never be definitively separated from the evident expressiveness of bird-song, or the evocative howl of a wolf late at night. The chorus of frogs gurgling in unison at the edge of a pond, the snarl of a wildcat as it springs upon its prey, or the distant honking of Canadian geese veeing south for the winter, all reverberate with affective, gestural significance, the same significance that vibrates through our own conversations and soliloquies, moving us at times to tears, or to anger, or to intellectual insights we could never have anticipated. Language as a bodily phenomenon accrues to *all* expressive bodies, not just to the human. Our own speaking, then, does not set us outside of the animate landscape but — whether or not we are aware of it — inscribes us more fully in its chattering, whispering, soundful depths.

If, for instance, one comes upon two human friends unexpectedly meeting for the first time in many months, and one chances to hear their initial words of surprise, greeting, and pleasure, one may readily notice, if one pays close enough attention, a tonal, melodic layer of communication beneath the explicit denotative meaning of the words — a rippling rise and fall of the voices in a sort of musical duet, rather like two birds

THE FLESH OF LANGUAGE

[1]   **sensing body:** body that feels the meaning. cf. *I could sense her growing irritation.*
[3]   **oblivious to:** not aware of
[4]   **somatic:** bodily; physical; corporeal. cf. *psychosomatic*: 心身(症)の
[5]   **repressed it in favor of . . . :** それ (gestural, somatic dimension of language) を抑圧して〜を優先する. *They rejected my suggestion in favor of hers.*
[7]   **subtly operative:** at work almost unnoticeably
[11]   **without withering and dying:** "rooted in" や "soil" という表現にこもる「意味＝生き物」の比喩を膨らませ，次の段落の議論へつなげていくための表現. **wither:** (植物等が)枯れる
[15]   **renounce:** [a. to abandon / b. to support]
        an exclusively human property: unique to human beings
[18]   **evocative:** producing an emotional response
[19]   **in unison:** 一斉に，声を合わせて. *The drunken men sang — not quite in unison.*
[21]   **veeing south:** Ｖの字をなして南へ渡る
[24]   **soliloquies** < soliloquy [səlíləkwi]: ひとりごと
        at times: sometimes
[26]   **accrues to *all* expressive bodies:** 身体的表現を行なう生き物すべてに付いている. **accrue to:** to be added to
[28]   **does not set us outside of the animate landscape:** does not separate us from the world of the affective communication shared by animals
[29]   **inscribes us more fully in its chattering, whispering, soundful depths:** i.e. makes us participate more fully in the depths of tonal communication
[35]   **layer** [léiə]: 層
[36]   **a rippling rise and fall of the voices:** 声が盛り上がったり静まったり，細やかに変化すること. **ripple:** さざなみ(が立つ)
[37]   **rather like:** somewhat like

singing to each other. Each voice, each side of the duet, mimes a bit of the other's melody while adding its own inflection and style, and then is echoed by the other in turn — the two singing bodies thus tuning and attuning to one another, rediscovering a common register, *remembering* each other. It requires only a slight shift in focus to realize that this melodic singing is carrying the bulk of communication in this encounter, and that the explicit meanings of the actual words ride on the surface of this depth like waves on the surface of the sea.

It is by a complementary shift of attention that one may suddenly come to hear the familiar song of a blackbird or a thrush in a surprisingly new manner, not just as a pleasant melody repeated mechanically, as on a tape player in the background, but as active, meaningful speech. Suddenly, subtle variations in the tone and rhythm of that whistling phrase seem laden with expressive intention, and the two birds singing to each other across the field appear for the first time as attentive, conscious beings, earnestly engaged in the same world that we ourselves engage, yet from an astonishingly different angle and perspective.

Ultimately, then, it is not the human body alone but rather the whole of the sensuous world that provides the deep structure of language. As we ourselves dwell and move within language, so, ultimately, do the other animals and animate things of the world; if we do not notice them there, it is only because language has forgotten its expressive depths. It is no more true that we speak than that the things, and the animate world itself, *speak within us.*

THE FLESH OF LANGUAGE

[1] **mime(s):** to imitate; echo
[2] **inflection:** 抑揚
[4] **attuning:** 音を合わせる (= tuning)
[5] **common register:** 共通の声域, 音域
[7] **carrying the bulk of communication:** taking the main role of communication. **bulk:** a very large volume
[10] **a complementary shift of attention:** i.e. shifting attention to [a. explicit meanings / b. the "song" of language]. **complementary:** 足りないところを補う
[12] **thrush:** ツグミ
[16] **laden with:** loaded with; full of
[23] **dwell:** to inhabit; live
[25] **notice them there:** i.e. notice other animals and animate things in the same language within which we all live
[26] **It is no more true that . . . *speak within us*:** If it is correct to say that we speak, it is just as correct to say that the things . . . speak within us.

ことばの身体を表わすことば

flesh of language

the *body* as expression (62: 13) / language as a *bodily* phenomenon (68: 26) / the *bodying-forth* of emotion (62: 20) / his *embodied* philosophy of language (66: 15)

a *carnal* phenomenon (62: 11) / meaning *incarnate* in the gestures (62: 15) / *corporeal* beings (66: 34)

the *somatic* dimension of language (68: 4)

a spontaneous *gesture* (62: 22) / the *gestural* significance (66: 35) / vocal *gesticulation* (64: 3)

to *resonate* (64: 8) / our *resonant* bodies (64: 20) / their direct bodily *resonance* (66: 36)

the *sensing* body (68: 1) / the *sensual* dimension of experience (64: 7) / our *sensuous* receptivity (66: 13) / our *sensorial* experience (62: 11); physically and *sensorially* resonant (68: 16)

its *tangible*, *visible* aspect (62: 21)

affective tonality (64: 31); direct, *affective* meaning (66: 32)

SESSION 8
The Fabrication of Race

Matthew Frye Jacobson

WE tend to think of race as being indisputable, *real*. We see it plainly on one another's faces. It seems a product not of the social imagination but of biology. However, scholars in several disciplines have recently shaken faith in this biological certainty. The conventions by which "race mixing" is understood, they point out, is one site where the unreality of race comes into view. Why is it that in the United States a white woman can have black children but a black woman cannot have white children? Doesn't this bespeak a degree of arbitrariness in this business of affixing racial labels?

The history of racial classification over time is a second such site: entire races have disappeared from view, from public discussion, and from modern memory, though their flesh-and-blood members still walk the earth. What has become of the nineteenth century's Celts and Slavs, for instance? Its Hebrews, Iberics, Mediterraneans, Teutons, and Anglo-Saxons?

In Philip Roth's *Counterlife* (1988) a Gentile woman chances to comment that she seldom repays the attention of Jewish men "because there are enough politics in sex without racial politics coming into it." "We're not a race," objects her Jewish listener. The ensuing exchange cuts to the very heart of "difference" and the epistemology of race.

"It *is* a racial matter," she insisted.
"No, we're the same race. You're thinking of Eskimos."

アメリカでは，黒人と白人のあいだに生まれた子は社会的には黒人とみなされる．では，そのふたりの子どもと白人のあいだに生まれた子はどうだろう．さらに，その子と白人のあいだに生まれた子は白人だろうか，黒人だろうか．一般的にアメリカでは，とにかく黒人の血が入っていれば「黒人」と考えられてきたが，他の社会では同様のひとが「白人」とみなされもする．人種とは一見したところ，人間を分類する自然な枠組みに思えるが，実はそれは歴史的に特定の社会環境のなかで生成された概念である．他者の特徴を分類しようとする「目」は，その視点を持つ者が属する文化環境によって規定されている．人種を区別するその「目」の背景に潜む文化の構造を探ることによって，人種という概念がいかに歴史的に構築されてきたかを意識できるのではないか．著者のジェイコブソンは新進気鋭のアメリカ史研究者で，人種概念，とりわけ「白人」という範疇がいかに形成されてきたかについての分析で知られている．

[Notes]

[1] **indisputable:** beyond dispute or doubt; undeniable. *indisputable evidence*

[4] **discipline(s):** field of academic study

[8] **a white woman can have black children . . . :** In the United States, a girl born to a white mother and a black father is "black" by social convention. But if that girl marries a white man, her baby is still "black."

[9] **bespeak a degree of arbitrariness in this business of affixing racial labels:** show that decisions about race are to some extent unreasonable. **arbitrary:** cf. p. 22, l. 21, p. 62, l. 18. **affix:** to attach

[13] **flesh-and-blood members:** direct descendants of the races that have disappeared from today's view and public discussion

[14] **What has become of the nineteenth century's Celts . . . ?:** Today, Celts (the Irish, the Scots and others), Slavs (Russians, Poles, Czechs, etc.), Iberics (Spaniards and Portuguese), Mediterraneans (Italians, Greeks, etc.), Teutons (Germans and Scandinavians) and Anglo-Saxons are rarely seen as racially unique groups.

[17] **Phillip Roth's *Counterlife*:** See Box on page 81.

Gentile: non-Jewish

[19] **"because there are enough politics in sex without racial politics coming into it":** She thinks that *sexism* among men and women of the same race is complicated enough, and doesn't want to complicate the matter further by arguments concerning *racism*. And that's why she "seldom repays the attention" of (i.e. tends not to get involved with) men of other "racial" descents.

[21] **ensuing:** following

cuts to the very heart of: captures the essence of

[22] **epistemology of race:** the whole question of how we know one race from another. **epistemology:** (from Greek *epistēmē* : knowledge) the study of the nature of knowing

"We are *not* the same race. Not according to anthropologists, or whoever measures these things. There's Caucasian, Semitic — there are about five different groups. Don't look at me like that."

"I can't help it. Some nasty superstitions always tend to crop up when people talk about a Jewish 'race.'"

". . . All I can tell you is that you *are* a different race. We're supposed to be closer to Indians than to Jews, actually; — I'm talking about Caucasians."

"But I am Caucasian, kiddo. In the U.S. census I am, for good or bad, counted as Caucasian."

"*Are* you? *Am* I wrong?"

This passage beautifully conveys the seemingly natural but finally unstable logic of race. The debate over Jews' racial identity begins merely as a matter of conflicting classification: at the outset stable, meaningful categories are assumed, and the question is simply where a particular group belongs — which pigeonhole do Jews fit into, Caucasian or Semite? But the question itself points to a more profound epistemological crisis: if he is certain that he is a Caucasian, and she is certain that he is not, then what does it mean to call a person a Caucasian in the first place? And where does all this certainty come from?

Once the two characters recognize the slippage in what they had each thought an uncompromising natural fact, both scramble to appeal to some higher authority in order to uphold their initial views. She invokes science ("according to anthropologists . . ."); he invokes the state ("in the U.S. census . . ."). They thus identify what, historically, have been two key actors in the creation and enforcement of these public fictions called races. (Not incidentally, the narratives and images of popular culture, like Roth's best-seller itself, represent another.) Caucasians are not born, these combatants now seem to understand; they are somehow made. It's just a question of who does the making.

The racially inflected caricatures of the Irish in the middle of

THE FABRICATION OF RACE

[1] **Not according to . . . :** We are not the same race according to . . .
[2] **Caucasian** [kɔːkéiʒən]: "the White race"
[3] **Semitic:** One scientific way to group peoples of the world is to compare their languages. The Hebrew language of the Jewish people belongs, along with the Arabic language, to a group called "Semitic languages," which also include ancient tongues such as the Assyro-Babylonian language.
   "Don't look at me like that": "Why are you looking so doubtful? Did I say something strange?"
[6] **crop up:** come up, appear
[8] **closer to Indians than Jews:** The ancestors of the founders of the Hindu religion in India were light-skinned "Aryans," who came down from the northwest to conquer an earlier civilization.
[10] **kiddo:** a term of familiar address (not recommended because in many situations if you say "kiddo" or "kid" it would give the impression that you think you are talking to somebody inferior).
[18] **pigeonhole:** category (particularly, a meaningless or oversimplified one)
[23] **recognize the slippage:** i.e. come to understand that there isn't any hard reality underlying the concept of race
[24] **uncompromising:** [a. definite / b. dubious]
[25] **scramble:** to move quickly or desperately
[26] **invoke(s):** to resort to; appeal to
[30] **Not incidentally . . . popular culture . . . represent another:** Imagine how Hollywood movies used to present the Chinese and the Japanese.
[32] **Caucasians are not born:** cf. *He is a born musician.*
[35] **racially inflected caricatures of the Irish:** distorted images of the Irish as an inferior race. *See Figure 1.*

SESSION 8

Fig. 1. Racially charged portraits of the two leading threats to the Republic, the Negro and the Celt. *Harper's Weekly,* 1876

the nineteenth century are well known, as when *Harper's* depicted the "Celt" and the "Negro" weighing in identically on the scales of civic merit, but in the 1890s even the Irish novelist John Brennan could write that the Irishness of the emigrants' children showed in their "physiognomy, or the color of their countenances." When in 1891 a *Detroit News* reporter asked a black whitewasher whether or not he worked with any white men, the laborer answered (in a dialect provided by the journalist), "No, dere's no wite men. Dere's some Polacks, but dey ain't wite men, you know. Ha! ha! ha!" In his 1908 study *Race or Mongrel?* Alfred Schultz lamented in unambiguously biological language:

> The opinion is advanced that the public schools change the children of all races into Americans. Put a Scandinavian, a German, and a Magyar boy in at one end, and they will come out Americans at the other end. Which is like saying, let a pointer, a setter, and a pug enter one end of a tunnel and they will come out three greyhounds at the other end.

THE FABRICATION OF RACE

[1] *Harper's*: a long-lasting magazine in the United States, founded in 1850
[2] **weighing in identically:** equally balanced. See Figure 1.
[3] **civic merit:** usefulness to society; qualification as a civilized people
even the Irish novelist John Brennan could write that . . . : i.e. even an educated Irishman was led to believe that . . .
[5] **physiognomy:** facial characteristics
the color of their countenances: See how black the Irish faces were in the caricatures.
[7] **whitewasher:** wall painter
[9] **dere's no wite men:** there are no white men
Polacks: To call a person from Poland "a Polack" is not permissible, just as calling a Jew "a Kike" or calling a Japanese "a Jap" is now almost unthinkable.
[11] *Mongrel*: a cross between different breeds (of dogs and other domestic animals)
lamented: expressed his dissatisfaction
[13] **advance(d):** to put forward; suggest (an opinion, etc.)

77

SESSION 8

Fig. 2. White yet Other — Other yet White. Rudolph
Valentino menaces Agnes Ayres in *The Sheik*, 1921.

    In her 1910 study of Homestead, Pennsylvania, the sociologist Margaret Byington broke the community down along the "racial" lines of "Slav, English-speaking European, native white, and colored." H. L. Mencken later casually alluded to the volume of literature crossing his desk by "Negro and other non-Nordic writers," by which, evidently, he meant people like John Fante and Louis Adamic. In *The Sheik* (1921), Rudolph Valentino traded on his physiognomical ability to be both the exotic, racial Other and the acceptable, chivalric European — first, as a "savage" Arab, kidnapping Agnes Ayers, and later (safely revealed to be of English and Spanish descent), rescuing her from an even darker African foe. When *Porgy and Bess* appeared (1935), critics broadly attributed George Gershwin's talent for "American-Negroid music" to the "common Oriental ancestry in both Negro and Jew."

    So this history of whiteness and its fluidity is very much a history of power and its disposition. But there is a further point: race is not just a conception; it is also a perception. The problem is not merely how races are comprehended, but how they are seen. In her 1943 obituary of Franz Boas, Ruth Benedict recounted how Boas the physicist, having gone to the Arctic to study the properties of water, became Boas the anthropologist upon discovering that his observations did not at all match those of the Eskimos he encountered. Remarked Benedict, "He

THE FABRICATION OF RACE

[3] **native white:** people born in the United States and categorized as "white"

[4] **colored:** Usually, African Americans; here, all the non-European races including native Americans and "Orientals"

H. L. Mencken: (1880–1956) one of the most influential critics in America during the 1920s and 1930s

[7] **John Fante:** (1909–83) a second-generation Italian American writer

Louis Adamic: (1899–1951) a native of what is now Slovenia, who emigrated to America as a young man, and became a well-regarded writer

Rudolph Valentino: (1895–1926) Italian-born American actor, with dark, intense eyes that charmed millions of women

[8] **traded on his physiognomical ability:** made use of his racially ambiguous looks

[9] **racial Other:** The "white" audiences of the film would never identify themselves with a Sheik (an Arab leader), who, to them, remained a threatening outsider.

chivalric European: a European knightly figure. **chivalry:** 騎士道

[13] **attributed George Gershwin's talent for "American-Negroid music" to the "common Oriental ancestry in both Negro and Jew":** thought that Gershwin was able to incorporate elements of black music persuasively in his operatic work because Jews and "Negroes" both came originally from the same area (centered on the Nile). **George Gershwin:** (1898–1937) a famous Jewish American composer. His masterpiece, *Porgy and Bess* (1935), has been praised by some as the opera that captured in music the soul of the black people.

[16] **this history of whiteness and its fluidity is very much a history of power and its disposition:** i.e. the idea of who belonged to the white race shifted as power relations changed. **fluidity:** changeability. **disposition:** distribution

[21] **obituary:** an account of a person's life and work published to mark the person's death

Franz Boas: (1858–1942) a founder of modern anthropology. One of his most important conclusions was that no truly pure race exists, and that no race is innately superior to any other.

Ruth Benedict: (1887–1948) best known in Japan for her probing analysis of Japanese culture in *The Chrysanthemum and the Sword* (『菊と刀』).

[22] **Boas the physicist ... became Boas the anthropologist:** i.e. Boas found that even descriptions of something as basic as water were influenced by culture and education, and as a result became interested in studying human culture and society rather than non-human matter.

returned with an abiding conviction that if we are ever to understand human behavior we must know as much about the eye that sees as about the object seen. And he had understood once and for all that the eye that sees is not a mere physical organ but a means of perception conditioned by the tradition in which its possessor has been reared."

If this passage sums up Boas's understanding of the power of culture, it also nicely sums up the properties of race itself. In racial matters above all else, the eye that sees is "a means of perception conditioned by the tradition in which its possessor has been reared." The American eye sees a certain person as black, for instance, whom Haitian or Brazilian eyes might see as white. Similarly, an earlier generation of Americans *saw* Celtic, Hebrew, Anglo-Saxon, or Mediterranean physiognomies where today we see only subtly varying shades of a mostly undifferentiated whiteness. (If pressed, we might come to a consensus on the physiognomical properties of Irishness, Slavicness, or Jewishness, but at a glance these certainly do not strike most Americans with anything like the perceptible force that they did a century ago, or that live racial distinctions do today.)

Thus, it is essential for us to see not only the history of various conceptions of racial "difference," but also the ways in which those conceptions of difference successfully masquerade as nature. The awesome power of race as an ideology resides precisely in its ability to pass as a feature of the natural landscape. Perhaps our most far-reaching ambition should be, then, to help loosen the grip of race by laying bare the moribund, and now quite peculiar, circuitry of an earlier era's racial conceptions and perceptions.

[1] **abiding:** long-lasting
[4] **once and for all:** decisively; forever
[12] **Haitian** [héiʃən, -tiən]: < Haiti [héiti]
[15] **subtly varying shades:** varying degrees of very small color differences
[18] **do not strike . . . with anything like the perceptible force that they did:** are no longer powerful enough to be perceived as racially distinct features
[20] **live racial distinctions:** By using the word "live" [laiv], the author implies that even (some of) the racial distinctions made today between Caucasians, Asian Americans, and African Americans could disappear in the future.
[24] (those conceptions of difference) **masquerade as nature:** lead us to believe that they are natural, unalterable facts, not something we ourselves have created in our heads. **masquerade:** to be in disguise. cf. p. 20, l. 31
[28] **the grip of race:** the [a. natural / b. ideological] power of race
   laying bare: showing clearly; revealing
   moribund: dying or disappearing
[29] **circuitry of . . . racial conceptions and perceptions:** the whole system of racial beliefs and perceptions which people used to accept

---

Philip Roth, *Counterlife* について
 ある男が性的不能を治すために大手術を受け，死ぬ．
 これが Philip Roth の *Counterlife* 第1章の結末である．
 ところが第2章では，同じ男が同じ手術を受け，手術は成功するが，なぜか人間がすっかり変わってしまい，男はエリート歯科医の地位も捨て，家族も愛人も捨て，イスラエルに移住して熱烈なユダヤ民族主義者になる．
 音楽でいう counterpoint (対位法) のように，二つの人生が対位的に並置されている．ゆえに，"Counterlife."
 Counterlife に限らず，Roth の近年の小説は，Roth 自身の姿に限りなく近い，作家 Nathan Zuckerman を主人公にしたものが多い (*Counterlife* で手術を受ける男は Nathan の弟)．といっても，単に実生活を申し訳程度に脚色した自伝的小説というのではない．むしろ，小説を書くということ自体，自分について書くということ自体がそこでは主題になっている．言ってみれば小説自体が，Roth の作家人生に対する Counterlife という感じなのだ．
 などというと，理屈が先走りした観念的小説と思えるかもしれないが，さにあらず．Roth の場合，枠組としては観念的でも，〈ユダヤ人〉〈セックス〉という二大テーマがほとんどどの作品でも濃密に描き込まれることによって，ひどく生ぐさい小説になっている．この二大テーマが一番明らかな形で現われるのが，この章にも出てくるユダヤ人と非ユダヤ人との性的関係というわけ． (柴田元幸)

SESSION 9
Multiple Personality

Ian Hacking

THERE has always been a popular face to the idea of multiple personality. The romantic fiction and poetry of the nineteenth century positively reeks of duality. *Dr. Jekyll and Mr. Hyde* is the best known, Dostoyevsky's Mr. Golyadkin of *The Double* is the greatest artistic creation, and James Hogg's *The Private Memoirs and Confessions of a Justified Sinner* is the one that scares me the most. The modern movement has thrived not on fiction but on a new genre, the multobiography. This is the book-length story of a multiple, usually packaged as an "as-told-to," and often turned into a movie or TV special.

The book that introduced the movement was *Sybil*. Published in 1973, it is a fictionalized story of Cornelia Wilbur and her multiple patient Sybil. Wilbur's professional accounts of the case were routinely rejected by scholarly and medical journals, apparently on the grounds that no one could take multiple personality seriously. One crushing insult followed upon a paper she read at the annual meeting of the American Academy of Psychoanalysis. Wilbur believed that the academy published all the papers that were read, but she was telephoned and told there were "space problems." Since Sybil's story would not be received by the experts, it had to be told for the public. It was written up by a journalist, Flora Rheta Schreiber. Schreiber insisted that Sybil be cured before she began work. A book without a happy ending would not sell. When Sybil was cured,

客観的な現実とみえて多分に歴史的・文化的産物であるものは,「人種」以外にもいろいろあるだろう．たとえば「病い」——とくに心の．

1970年代末から北米をはじめとして児童虐待が大きく問題視されるようになり，これまで考えられていたよりはるかに多くの虐待が行なわれてきたことが明らかになってきた．それとともに浮上してきたのが，子供のころ受けた心的苦痛が原因とされる「多重人格」．80年代に入って，multiplesと呼ばれる人々がつぎつぎと「発見」され，それをマスメディアが派手に取り上げたこともあって，この「障害」をめぐる議論はかなりスキャンダラスな様相を呈している．はたして，どこまでが真実なのか．カナダの著名な哲学者が，この問題を第三者の目で冷静に整理してみせる．

[Notes]

[1] **a popular face:** 大衆受けする側面

[3] **positively reeks of duality:** 露骨に分身の匂いがする＝分身が至るところに見られる．**reek:** to make a strong smell

[4] ***Dr. Jekyll*** [dʒékəl] ***and Mr. Hyde***: 『ジキル博士とハイド氏』(1886). Robert Louis Stevenson (1850–94) による有名な分身物語．Jekyll という名はフランス語の je (私は)と英語の kill に通じ，科学者の破壊的な側面を示唆する．一方 Hyde は hide (「隠す」「獣の皮」)に通じ，人間の隠れた獣性を示唆する．

Dostoyevsky's Mr. Golyadkin of *The Double*: ドストエフスキーの『二重人格』(1864)では，さえない下級官吏ゴリャートキン氏の前に，外見は彼そっくりの世渡り名人(実は彼が秘かになりたいと思っているような人物)が現われる．

[6] **James Hogg's *The Private Memoirs and Confessions of a Justified Sinner*:** スコットランドの文人 James Hogg (1770–1835) が 1824 年に発表した作品．邪悪な分身に唆された男が恐ろしい罪を重ねる話．邦題『悪の誘惑』(国書刊行会)．

[7] **The modern movement has thrived ... on a new genre, the multobiography:** ジャンルだけでなく，「主人公」の性別も大きな違い．19世紀の分身物語の主人公はほとんど男性だが，今日の multobiography はほとんど女性の物語である．

[9] **a multiple:** このように multiple という語が「多重人格者」の意味で名詞として使われるようになったのは，近年の「ブーム」が訪れてから．

[10] **an "as-told-to":** 語り手(本人)と書き手(プロのライター)の共作になる，聞き書に基づく自叙伝．

[15] **routinely:** regularly; repeatedly

[16] **on the grounds that no one could take multiple personality seriously:** 北米以外では，たとえば 1987 年にイギリスで刊行された事典でも，"Dissociation of the personality [i.e. multiple personality] is not only bizarre but also extremely rare — so rare, indeed, that one has to take seriously the possibility that it may be a social and psychiatric artefact." と依然懐疑的な見解が述べられている (*The Oxford Companion to the Mind*).

[20] **all the papers that were read:** 学会で発表することを "read a paper" という．

[23] **written up:** prepared for publication

SESSION 9

Schreiber came to live in what had virtually become the Wilbur-Sybil ménage, and wrote the book.

Wilbur's work broke new ground because she actively sought out childhood traumas. She traced Sybil's multiplicity to perverse, vindictive, and usually sexually oriented assaults by Sybil's mother. Wilbur was no orthodox Freudian. She worked on Sybil's memories with both hypnosis (anathema to Freud) and Amytal. She did not believe in the ritualized distancing between patient and analyst demanded by American psychoanalysis. The two women became friends, went for long rides in the country, and lived for a while in the same house. Sybil's treatment involved 2,534 office hours. It took so long, Wilbur was to tell people, only because in the 1960s there was simply no knowledge about multiple personality.

A doctrinaire Freudian would work with Sybil's memories of abuse in order to help the patient understand what they meant to her in the present. It would be of little moment whether these were true memories or fantasies. Wilbur went on to confirm, as best she could, that the events Sybil painfully came to remember really had happened. She went to the family home and saw at least the instruments of torture, the enema bag, the tool for lacing boots that had been stuck into Sybil's orifices. The passive father did not contradict the stories. Of course the existence of the objects of torture — which were also, in those days, common household furnishings — did not prove that they had been perverted for sadistic uses. But Wilbur believed Sybil, and by the time of the book and above all the film, no one could doubt the reality.

Sybil became a prototype for what was to count as a multiple. She was an intelligent young woman, with a promising career, who experienced substantial periods of lost time. She had fugue episodes; she would recover herself in a strange place with no idea how she got there. But other features are more important. Patients in the past had tended to have two or three or even four alters. Sybil had sixteen. There were child alters. There were two alters of the opposite sex. Some alters knew about others. They argued, fought, tried to help or destroy each

MULTIPLE PERSONALITY

[2] **ménage** [meinɑ́:ʒ]: household
[3] **broke new ground:** [a. opened / b. destroyed] a new field
[4] **trauma(s)** [trɔ́:mə]: トラウマ．その影響があとあとまで残るような大きな精神的打撃を指す．
       perverse, vindictive: abnormal, extremely cruel
[7] **hypnosis (anathema to Freud):** フロイトは初期には師ブロイアーの影響でhypnosis（催眠術）を使った治療を行なったが，やがてこれを否定し，自由連想法を開発して精神分析の新しい世界を切り拓いた．**anathema** [ənǽθəmə]: something one strongly dislikes and disapproves of
[8] **Amytal:** 鎮静剤 amobarbital（アモバルビタール）の商品名．多重人格状態を引き出しやすくすると言われている．
       ritualized distancing: 分析医が患者をあくまで治療の対象として捉え，密な関係を結ばない慣行
[15]   **doctrinaire:** 教義にしばられた，融通の利かない
[17]   **of little moment:** of little importance
[21]   **enema:** 浣腸
[22]   **orifices:** 人体その他について広く「開口部」を指す言葉．
[25]   **household furnishings:** 一家の備品，生活用具
[26]   **perverted:** used for bad purposes
[27]   **the film:** *Sybil* は1976年にテレビ映画として放映され，16の人格を演じわけた主演サリー・フィールドはエミー賞を獲得．
[28]   **doubt the reality:** doubt that Sybil's story was real
[29]   **prototype:** 原型；モデル
[31]   **substantial periods:** periods long enough (to be significant)
[32]   **fugue episodes:** fugue は音楽では「フーガ」（遁走曲）だが，精神医学では，衝動的に出奔し，あとで記憶に残らないようなケースをいう．episodes は医学で「症状の発現」の意味．
[35]   **alter(s)** [ɔ́:ltə]: alter ego（分身）という表現は以前からあったが，alter 一語で多重人格者の個々の「人格」を表わすようになったのは最近．

other. This idea of dynamic relationships between different personalities had been glimpsed before, but it was the reports of Sybil that made them prominent. Above all, the etiology of her disorder was writ large. She really had been abused as a child. "Sybil," the main presenting personality, had no memory of those sorry events. But her alters did remember. Indeed they had been created in order to cope with horror. They would be dissociated from the main personality, so that Sybil, herself, did not need to be conscious of those scars. She did not need to hate her mother, who had done those things to her. She could even love her mother, while some of the alters were full of hate. Other alters lived out a life that Sybil would like to have lived, had she not been so assaulted when she was growing up.

During the 1970s the public conception of child abuse and neglect was shifted to sexual abuse and incest. The theory of multiple personality followed in train. By 1986 a questionnaire survey of clinicians treating multiple personality produced a sample of one hundred patients, ninety-seven of whom reported experiencing significant trauma in childhood, most often sexual in nature.

There is now no difficulty in summarizing the 1980s prototype for multiple personality: a middle-class white woman with the values and expectations of her social group. She is in her thirties, and she has quite a large number of distinct alters — sixteen, say. She spent a large part of her life denying the very existence of these alters. The alters include children, persecutors, and helpers, and at least one male alter. She was sexually abused on many occasions by a trusted man in her family when she was very young. She has previously been through parts of the mental health system and has been diagnosed with many complaints, but her treatments have not helped her in the long run until she came to a clinician sensitive to multiple personality. She has amnesia for parts of her past. She has the experience of "coming to" in a strange situation with no idea of how she got there. She is severely depressed and has quite often thought about suicide.

In 1972, multiple personality had seemed to be a mere curi-

- [3] **etiology:** 病因
- [4] **writ large:** clearly visible. write の過去分詞は現在では written が普通だが，この慣用句に限り writ large と言う。
- [6] **sorry:** sad; pitiful
- [8] **dissociated from the main personality:** 主たる人格から切り離されて
- [16] **followed in train:** あとにつづいた；風潮になびいた
  questionnaire survey: アンケート調査
- [23] **the values and expectations of her social group:** 中流の女性としての標準的な価値観と人生への期待
- [26] **persecutors:** alters who treat her cruelly, who cause pain
- [30] **has been diagnosed with many complaints:** さまざまな病気 (complaints) を患っていると診断されてきた．complaints は「不満，不平」ではない．
- [32] **a clinician sensitive to . . . :** a doctor or a therapist who quickly recognizes the sign of . . .
- [33] **amnesia** [æmníːʒə, -ziə]: 記憶喪失
- [34] **"coming to":** regaining consciousness
- [35] **severely depressed:** 鬱病 (depression) 的傾向が強い
- [37] **In 1972, multiple personality had seemed to be a mere curiosity:** 1957 年に *The Three Faces of Eve* という三重人格の女性を描いた映画が話題になったが，それもただ「奇怪な話」という受けとめ方が一般的だった．

osity. In 1992, there were hundreds of multiples in treatment in every sizable town in North America. What has happened? Is a new form of madness, hitherto almost unknown, stalking the continent? Or have multiples always been around, unrecognized? Were they classified, when they needed help, as suffering from something else? Perhaps clinicians have only recently learned to make correct diagnoses. Or, as a majority of psychiatrists still contend, is there simply no such thing as multiple personality disorder? Is the epidemic the work of a small but committed band of therapists, unwittingly aided and abetted by sensational stories in the tabloids and afternoon TV talk shows?

We hear moral conviction on all sides. Psychiatrists who reject multiple personality are accused of complacently dismissing the victims, the abused, the women and children. Is that true? There are doctors who see themselves as scientists, dedicated to objective fact, not social movements. They resent the media hype that surrounds multiple personality. They are dubious about the sheer scope of the epidemic. How can a mental disorder be so at the whim of place and time? How can it disappear and reappear? How can it be everywhere in North America and nonexistent in the rest of the world until it is carried there by missionaries, by clinicians who seem determined to establish beachheads of multiple personality in Europe and Australasia? The only place that multiples flourish overseas is in the Netherlands, and that florescence, say skeptics, was nourished by intensive visiting by the leading American members of the movement.

Is multiple personality a real disorder as opposed to a product of social circumstances, a culturally permissible way to express distress or unhappiness? That question makes a presupposition that we should reject. It implies that there is an important contrast between being a real disorder and being a product of social circumstances. The fact that a certain type of mental illness appears only in specific historical or geographical contexts does not imply that it is manufactured, artificial, or in any other way not real.

MULTIPLE PERSONALITY

[2]　**sizable:** fairly large
[3]　**hitherto:** up to now
　　　stalking the continent: (北米)大陸を(獲物を求めて)歩き回る
[5]　**Were they classified ... as suffering from something else?:** 多重人格を信じる人のあいだでは、かつて分裂病患者と診断された人々の相当数は実は多重人格だったのではないか、などとも言われる．
[8]　**psychiatrist(s)** [saikáiətrist]:「精神医学者」．clinician (l. 6) に比べ、患者の診療より理論的研究に取りくんでいるというニュアンスが強い．
[10]　**committed:** firmly believing
　　　unwittingly: without knowing it
[11]　**abetted:** そそのかされて
　　　tabloid(s):『日刊ゲンダイ』サイズの大衆紙で、ゴシップその他センセーショナルな記事を売り物にする．イギリスでは *The Sun*、アメリカでは *The National Enquirer* が業界トップ．
　　　afternoon TV talk shows: 現代のアメリカでは、"Oprah Winfrey" など主婦層向けトークショーだけでなく、"Inside Edition" などのニュースショーでも、「家庭内暴力の犠牲者による涙の訴え」的な企画が絶えない．
[13]　**We hear moral conviction on all sides:** 信じる側も信じない側も、自分の正しさに対して感情的な思い込みを抱くのが、多重人格をめぐる議論の特徴．
[14]　**complacently:** in a self-satisfied manner; ignoring a genuine problem
[18]　**media hype:** メディアによる扇情的な誇張報道
[19]　**dubious about the sheer scope of the epidemic:** 多重人格を流行病のように考え、そのあまりの広がりようをうさん臭く思っている、ということ．
[20]　**at the whim of ... :** 〜に左右されて
[23]　**missionaries:** multiples の存在を明らかにすることを mission と考えている「布教活動家」
[24]　**beachheads:** 上陸拠点
[25]　**Australasia** [ɔ̀:strəléiʒə, -ʃə]: オーストラリア・ニュージーランドとその近海諸島
[26]　**florescence:** 開花；繁栄
[29]　**as opposed to:** "A as opposed to B" は、A の意味を明確にするために対立概念 B を提示する言い方．*I'm looking for a biological, as opposed to psychological, explanation for her strange conduct.*
[31]　**presupposition:**（しばしば無根拠な）前提

89

SESSION 9

In a 1992 talk Frank Putnam, author of *Diagnosis and Treatment of Multiple Personality Disorder* (1989), candidly stated that "very little is known about the alter personalities and what they represent." His increasing reservations about alter personalities are shared by an influential group of psychiatrists within the multiple movement who have long held that the emphasis on personalities is wrongheaded. In 1993 David Spiegel, chair of the dissociative disorders committee for the 1994 edition of the *Diagnostic and Statistical Manual of Mental Disorders*, wrote that "there is a widespread misunderstanding of the essential psychopathology in this dissociative disorder, which is failure of integration of various aspects of identity, memory, and consciousness. The problem is not having more than one personality; it is having less than one personality." One is reminded of Alice (in Wonderland), "for this curious child was very fond of pretending to be two people. 'But it's no use now,' thought poor Alice, 'to pretend to be two people! Why, there is hardly enough of me left to make one respectable person!'"

We shall find over and over again that multiple personality is a moving target. Yet two things are constantly in view, memory and psychic pain. Whether the illness involves more than one personality or less than one, the disorder is supposed to be a response to childhood trauma. Memories of the early cruelties are hidden and must be recalled to effect a true integration and cure. Multiple personality and its treatment are grounded upon the supposition that the troubled mind can be understood through increased knowledge about the very nature of memory.

[4]　**reservations:** 慎重な姿勢
[7]　**wrongheaded:** mistaken
[8]　**dissociative disorders:** multiple personality という，センセーショナルな響きがこびりついてしまった名称を避けて，Dissociative Identity Disorder（解離性人格障害）という呼称を使う関係者もいる．
[10]　**misunderstanding of the essential psychopathology:** 根本的にいかなる精神の病いであるかという点についての誤解
[12]　**integration of various aspects of . . . :** 〜のさまざまな側面をうまく統合すること
[17]　**Why, there is hardly enough of me left to make one respectable person!:** *Alice's Adventures in Wonderland* (1865) 第1章の終わり近くで，DRINK ME と書かれた瓶の中身を飲んで 30 センチくらいに縮んでしまったアリスの言葉．このあと彼女は，EAT ME と書かれたケーキを食べて，何メートルもの大きさになってしまう．なお，respectable は「尊敬すべき」ではなく「まともな」．
[20]　**a moving target:** something which is constantly being re-defined
[26]　**grounded upon the supposition that . . . :** 〜という考えを基盤にしている

SESSION 10

The Pleasure of Music

Robert Jourdain

ONE way of regarding pleasure of any kind is to see it [1] as inherent in the satisfaction of anticipations. This generalization seems also to apply to the pleasure of music. As music's promises (anticipations) are fulfilled, we experience pleasure; as they are betrayed, we feel anxiety or [5] worse. When skillful composition arouses strong, far-reaching anticipations, intense pleasure accompanies their fulfillment; by comparison, the weak anticipations generated by poor composition hardly touch us.

Yet the deepest pleasure in music comes with deviation from [10] the expected: dissonances, syncopations, kinks in melodic contour, sudden booms and silences. Isn't this contradictory? Not if the deviations serve to set up an even stronger resolution. Banal music raises common anticipations then immediately satisfies them with obvious resolutions. There's pleasure to be [15] had, but it is the pleasure of the bread roll, not of caviar. Well-written music takes its good time satisfying anticipations. It teases, repeatedly instigating an anticipation and hinting at its satisfaction, sometimes swooping toward a resolution only to hold back with a false cadence. When it finally delivers, all [20] resources of harmony and rhythm, timbre and dynamics, are brought to bear at once. The art in writing such music lies less in devising resolutions than in heightening anticipations to preternatural levels. If this process sounds as much like the recipe for good love-making as for good music-making, it's [25]

THE PLEASURE OF MUSIC

音楽は感じるもの．音楽は楽しむもの．それはたしかにそうだけれども，なぜ音楽は楽しいのか，その理由を科学するのも心弾むことである．というわけで，*Music, the Brain & Ecstasy* (1997) という話題の書物をひもといてみよう．ここに引いたのはその最終章「エクスタシーへ」の一節．著者ジャーデインは認知科学に詳しい作曲家兼ピアニスト．だが，心配無用，分析に使っているのは「ピンク・パンサー」のテーマ1曲だけだ．あのメロディは，私たちの感情に，どのように作用するといえるのか？

[Notes]

[1] **see it as inherent in the satisfaction of anticipations:** さまざまな期待の充足こそが快感なのだと見る．**anticipation:** その後の進行についての前もって与えられる感覚

[3] **generalization:** 一般則

[9] **hardly touch us:** so weak that we are hardly aware of them

[10] **deviation:** departure（逸脱）

[11] **dissonance(s):** 不協和音（⇔ consonance）
syncopation(s): 規則的なビートをはずして正規の強拍の位置をずらすこと
kinks in melodic contour: メロディラインの異様な動き．**melodic contour** [kóntuə]: メロディの上下するさまを大まかになぞった輪郭線

[13] **resolution:** 解決．緊張がとけて落ち着き感が得られること．宇多田ヒカルの「Automatic」でいえば，"I just can't help" で作られた緊張が "it's au-to-" でさらに押し上げられ，"ma-tic" で一瞬「解決」を見る．演劇論でもドラマが盛り上がって climax に至った後の落ち着きを resolution という．

[14] **Banal** [bənáːl, -ǽl]: commonplace; predictable; uninteresting

[17] **takes its good time satisfying . . . :** takes ample time before satisfying. . . .
cf. *She never lets anything hurry her; she always takes her own good time.*

[18] **instigating** < instigate: to stir up; arouse

[19] **swooping toward a resolution only to hold back with a false cadence:** 解決に一挙に近づいていきながら，最後のところで落ちつくはずのところにいかない．**swoop:** to move in a sudden sweep. *The hawk swooped down on a running rabbit.* **hold back:** おあずけにする．**cadence** [kéidns]: 音楽では，終止（休止）に向けてのコード展開．$G_7 \to C$, $E_7 \to Am$ などのパターン．

[20] **delivers:** i.e. reaches its resolution

[21] **timbre** [tǽmbə, tím-]: 音色．pitch（音の高さ），volume（強さ）とともに音の3要素の1つ．
dynamics: 楽音の強弱の変化．クラシック系音楽では「デュナーミク」と言う．

[22] **brought to bear:** exerted; applied

[23] **in devising resolutions:** working out interesting resolutions

[24] **preternatural:** beyond what is natural or normal; extraordinary

because the nervous system functions the same way in all its reaches. The same basic mechanism applies to all pleasures, artistic and otherwise, for the simple reason that this mechanism *is* pleasure.

Consider harmony. Once we've mastered the harmonic system of our culture and know how to follow tonal centers and anticipate harmonic resolutions, we bring a flood of anticipations to all our listening. Particular chords lead in particular harmonic directions, and so long as harmony travels in that direction we register immediate pleasure. Conversely, an inappropriate change of key can be quite jarring, even painful. However, carefully controlled dissonances are frequently employed to postpone the resolution of harmonic anticipations, and thus to make them larger, sometimes integrating many smaller anticipations into a towering hierarchy. Most such dissonances are related to the underlying harmony so that they will not be too jarring. They do not so much violate anticipations as reshape them.

Melodic pleasure arises in similar fashion, but through the anticipation of melodic contour. When contour rises and falls "naturally" — that is, in ways that we anticipate — we register pleasure; when contour wavers recklessly, we register distress as our brains struggle to make sense of the patterns before them.

The role of anticipation in rhythmic pleasure is equally clear. We enjoy meter by anticipating a train of pulses. Any sudden deviation in tempo, or in the number of beats per measure, sends our nervous systems reeling. But carefully controlled syncopations can set us up for a pleasurable reaccentuation of the underlying beat.

The rhythm of phrase is more elaborately constructed, relying on a panoply of cues that make us strongly anticipate phrase boundaries. Composers meticulously construct sequences of evolving phrases, each suggesting the next, but sometimes deviating toward the unexpected, then moving to reaffirm the overall form.

This way of thinking about pleasure may explain the surge we feel in the climax of a Beethoven symphony, but what of the

THE PLEASURE OF MUSIC

[1] **in all its reaches:** それが支配している全領域で
[5] **the harmonic system of our culture:** 西洋音楽の和音体系．ひらたく言えば，ハ長調ではC（I度：ドミソ），F（IV度：ファラド），G（V度：ソシレ）を基本に進行する．
[6] **tonal centers:** （和音進行の）中心になる音
[8] **Particular chords lead in particular harmonic directions:** ある特定のコードが現われたことで，その後のコード展開が（およそのところ）決まってくるということ．たとえばハ長調の曲がC→Fのコード展開をしたとすると，その後はG→CまたはC→G→Cの展開が常識的には予測される．
[10] **register:** to feel; show
[11] **jarring:** harsh; shocking; disturbing
[12] **carefully controlled dissonances:** きちんと制御された不協和音
[15] **a towering hierarchy:** 「積み上がった期待感のヒエラルキー」．次の和音への期待感（直接的なレベル），8小節単位の進行パターン等，レベルの違った期待感を階層構造に組織したもの．
[22] **contour wavers recklessly:** メロディラインがいい加減に上下する
[23] **the patterns before them:** （脳が）直面するパターン
[25] **meter:** 拍子
   a train of pulses: 拍動の連続
[26] **the number of beats per measure:** 1小節中の拍数．measure = bar
   sends our nervous systems reeling: i.e. confuses and upsets the brain
[28] **set us up for:** make us ready for
   a pleasurable reaccentuation of the underlying beat: ビートの基本進行の上に生じる快い拍動の変化．たとえばチャック・ベリーのロック曲「ジョニー・B・グッド」の冒頭（いきなりリードギターが始まるところ）では，ビートが4拍子の基本パターンを裏切って次のようにシンコペートする．

[30] **phrase:** 楽句（ふつう4小節または8小節からなる）．the rhythm of phraseとは各楽句の連続がつくり出す，[A, A', B, A']というような，より高次の進行形式のこと．
[31] **a panoply of cues:** 楽曲全体を見渡す高みにおいて得られる手がかり
[32] **meticulously:** very carefully
[35] **reaffirm the overall form:** 楽曲全体の統一感を再び押し出すこと
[36] **surge:** （波や感情の）盛り上がり
[37] **what of ... ?:** what about ... ?

"simple" pleasure we find in the individual sounds of instruments? Because the experience of music arises as our brains model hierarchies of relations among sounds — hierarchies that are "invisible" in the sense that they can't be readily shared with others, or even described to oneself — it's impossible to sort out the degree to which the pleasure we find "purely" in instrumental sound actually arises from surrounding musical relations. Any three notes on a viola can sound uninteresting when heard as the violist tunes up, yet might ravish us when they appear at the climax of a piece. Although pleasure appears to be embodied in the "sound" of the notes, it mostly resides in high-level relations that we keenly experience, but to which we bring little self-awareness.

Still, just a lone note from a viola can bring bliss to a keen ear. How is this possible? In truth, no one has a clue. But it's likely that, at the microscale of music cognition where the auditory cortex assembles individual sounds, somehow anticipations are suggested and fulfilled, but too quickly to be consciously observed. Significantly, we find no pleasure in a pure-frequency tone generated by a computer. Lacking variation of any kind, such sounds have no basis for generating anticipations. Musical sounds are complex, constantly changing entities of many undulating components. The architecture of such sounds varies with the skill of the musician. We celebrate a violist who "has good tone." Somehow, through years of practice, such a violist learns to tease sounds of a particular structure out of the strings. He does this without understanding how, just as we tie shoelaces without having to think about it. Conversely, a novice violist can torture a sensitive ear by producing sounds that are "grating" — that is, sounds broken into disconnected segments, where one moment does not lead to the next, where every nascent anticipation is foiled.

Music's large structures can as readily result in wincing pain. When a well-trained but overambitious composer generates strong anticipations and then fails to deliver on them, we're soon in agony. Most such music quickly disappears from the concert repertory. But new music often inflicts pain upon its

THE PLEASURE OF MUSIC

[1] **the individual sounds of instruments:**「楽器を弾いたり弾いたりしたときの単一の音」．14〜15行目で同じ問いかけを行なっているが，その前に「単一の音そのもの」について考えることが適切かどうか考察される．

[3] **model hierarchies of relations among sounds:** 音と音との関係を階層的に組織する．

[6] **sort out the degree to which the pleasure . . . actually arises from . . . relations:** i.e. (it's impossible) to tell how much of the pleasure comes directly from the individual sounds of instruments, and how much of it arises from the relations between many musical sounds.

the pleasure we find "purely" in instrumental sound:「楽器の音"それ自体"に見いだされる快感」．引用符がついているのは，他の楽音と関係づけられない純粋な楽音というものの存在が疑われているため．

[9] **tune(s) up:** 調弦する

ravish us: overwhelm us with [a. pleasure / b. pain]

[11] **"sound" of the notes:**「音」に引用符がついているのは，脳が情報処理しているのは音そのものではないという認識がはたらいているため．

[12] **high-level relations:**「高次の諸関係」．単にいくつかの楽音がつくる関係ではなく，メロディ，コード，リズム全体にわたる推移プロセス全体をつくる要素間の複雑な関係．

to which we bring little self-awareness: of which we are hardly conscious

[14] **lone note:** single, separate, musical sound

bliss: delight; ecstacy

[16] **the microscale of music cognition:**「音楽認知の極小レベル」とは，マクロな関係レベルを一応無視して一つの楽音の認知のみを考えるレベル．

the auditory cortex: the part of the brain which processes data about sounds

[19] **a pure-frequency tone:** 純音(音叉の音やラジオの時報のように最も基本的で単純な振動だけによる音)

[22] **entities of many undulating components:**「多くの波動的に変化する構成音からなる存在」．楽器の音は，どの音も，あるピッチ(高さ)の音を中心に，それと整数比の周波数比をもつさまざまな「倍音」が割合を変化させながら聞こえている．

[23] **architecture:** 構成 (structure)

[24] **varies with:** depends on

[26] **tease . . . out of the strings:** 弦をうまく操って引き出す

[30] **grating:** ギーギーきしる

[32] **every nascent anticipation is foiled:** 期待が生じかけたとたんにすぐしぼむ

nascent: emerging. **foiled:** prevented from reaching its goal

[33] **as readily:** as easily (as a lone note)

wincing pain: 辟易するほどの苦痛感

[35] **deliver on them:** satisfy those anticipations. cf. p. 92, l. 20

Fig. 1. Emotion in "The Pink Panther"

audiences until they learn how to anticipate it properly — or until they realize that the fault is not theirs and that the composer has failed to achieve his aims.

For a specific example of how music creates emotion and pleasure, let's take a look at Henry Mancini's "The Pink Panther" (Fig. 1). Mancini directs melody, harmony, and rhythm toward a point of high tension at the start of the third bar as the tune plateaus on a long, accentuated dissonance. This note violates several kinds of anticipation. Melody suddenly stops accelerating and freezes. Melodic contour ends its overall rise. Harmony veers from the prevailing tonal center. Meter pounces on a strong accentuation. And phrasing that is formed largely by melodic contour ends its accelerating pattern of stealthy footsteps, first in twos and then in fours. For a moment the music becomes motionless, much as a stalking cat might.

What is the emotional content of this music? And wherein lies its pleasure? Clearly, this theme is not constructed from the regular, predictable patterns that characterize "intellectual" music. This fragment is filled with violated anticipation and so emotional tension, tension that peaks on the long dissonance in the third bar. Yet it's hard to characterize the nature of the emotion other than as a rising sense of apprehension. None of the usual monikers from our inventory of emotions — joy, grief, triumph, whatever — make a good match for what we feel when we listen to this passage.

Nonetheless, it makes perfect sense to call the experience of stealth "emotional" even though we don't normally think of it that way. We're quite accustomed to feeling the emotional content of stealth when we have occasion to sneak around. We make motions that alternate between jarring restraint and

THE PLEASURE OF MUSIC

[2] **the fault is not theirs . . . :** i.e. the music is painful because [a. the audience is unaccustomed to it / b. it is simply bad].

[5] **Henry Mancini's "The Pink Panther":** 今のテレビの番組でも探偵の登場する場面によく BGM として使われる．もともとはピーター・セラーズ演じるフランス人警部 ジャック・クルーゾ の珍活躍を描く英国の喜劇映画 (1964)．その後テレビのアニメ・シリーズとしてもヒットした．映画音楽の巨匠ヘンリー・マンシーニ (1924–94) はイタリア系アメリカ人．『ティファニーで朝食を』(1961) の挿入曲「ムーン・リバー」でアカデミー賞主題歌賞に輝き，「シャレード」(1963)，「ロミオとジュリエットのテーマ」(1969) など多くのスタンダード曲を残した．

[7] **the third bar:** 第 3 小節

[8] **plateau(s)** [plətóu]: 一定の高さを長く保つ

[11] **veers from the prevailing tonal center:**「支配的な中心音から逸脱する」．ちなみにこの長く伸びた音は，ホ短調の階名で読むと「ミ♭」．ブルースやジャズなど黒人起源の音楽ジャンルではよく使われる．
Meter pounces on a strong accentuation: 拍が強いアクセントによって前方に跳びあがる動きをとる．cf. *A cat pounced on a mouse.*

[12] **phrasing:** 楽句の区切り方，まとめ方 (cf. p. 95, note [30])．この 4 小節分のまとまりを指している

[13] **stealthy** < stealth [stelθ]: こそこそ歩き．cf. *He stole up behind her.*

[14] **in twos:** 2 歩ずつ

[16] **wherein lies its pleasure?:** in what does its pleasure lie?

[18] **"intellectual" music:** （情動に訴えるというよりは）頭で聴くタイプの音楽

[19] **fragment:** ひと切れ．いま検討している 2 小節のこと．

[21] **it's hard to characterize the nature of the emotion other than as . . . :** i.e. the only way to describe the nature of the emotion is to see it as (a rising sense of apprehension)

[22] **apprehension:** 不安，危惧

[23] **monikers from our inventory of emotions:**「我々が感情と呼んでいるものの目録に並んだラベル」．この音楽から得られる感情は「喜び」「悲しみ」というラベルでは表わせないということ．

[24] **make a good match for:** fit well with; can describe well

[28] **the emotional content of stealth:** 忍び歩きに含まれる感情；コソコソした動きに伴う情動

[29] **when we have occasion to sneak around:** 実際忍び歩きをする（機会がある）ときには

[30] **make motions that alternate between jarring restraint and sudden over-reaching:** ぎこちない抑止の動きと突然グイと前に進む動きを繰り返す．**jarring:** cf. p. 94, l. 11

sudden overreaching, all the while violating the normal pacing of physical movement. And so we experience little bouts of the pain of constriction and the pleasure of leaping. Notice that we *feel* stealth by moving in certain ways with certain timings; when music follows similar patterns, it *sounds* stealthy, just as the pink panther's slinking around *looks* stealthy.

But "The Pink Panther" sounds not just stealthy, but also *funny*, and we would find levity in this theme even without its visual associations. There's something going on here, some sort of contrast of opposites that's found in all humor. The timings of the panther's creeping are modified in ways that are contradictory, making our hero seem both courageous and cowardly at the same time, and thus ridiculous.

It would seem, then, that what this theme generates is not a statement produced by a "language" of emotions, but rather by a "language" of physical movement, a language that sounds "emotional" when anticipations are consistently violated, and merely "intellectual" when they are not. It is a language in which sonic objects move together in time, much as body parts move together as we navigate the world. No wonder music makes us want to dance.

THE PLEASURE OF MUSIC

[2] **little bouts of the pain of constriction and the pleasure of leaping:** cf. a bout of depression/flu/nausea = an attack or period of ...

[6] **the pink panther's slinking around:** ピンク・パンサー独特のくねくね (?) 歩き

[8] **levity:** 軽み (⇔ gravity)

even without its visual associations: このテーマから(ピンクパンサーの)視覚イメージを想起しなくても

[10] **contrast of opposites that's found in all humor:** ここで筆者は人が笑う理由について，ハチソン寄りの見解を示している (See SESSION 1, Box on p. 11).

[15] **a "language" of emotions:** 音楽は「感情の言語」だと昔から言われてきた．その考えを筆者はどのように否定しているのだろう．

[16] **a language that sounds "emotional" when anticipations are consistently violated, and merely "intellectual" when they are not:** The author asserts that good music should give us [a. emotional / b. intellectual] experiences by keeping anticipations and resolutions constantly [a. in harmony / b. at war].

[19] **sonic objects move together in time:** さまざまな音響物が一体になって(身体のように)時間の中を動いてゆく

SESSION 11
None Was for a Party; All Were for the State

Frank Muir

THE only bit of Spanish I remember after wrestling with it for a term at school is an ancient proverb which went: 'Whoever Spitteth at Heaven Shall Have it Fall Back in his Eye.' A good thought; cautionary, ballistically sound. And it seems to me that we should have a similar proverb in English to warn the impulsive of the dangers of doing the opposite; not spitting at Heaven but trying to get a bit nearer to it. I propose the following: 'Whoever Foolishly Attempteth to Bring About a Social Reform Very Likely will Find that it Falleth Upon Cloth Ears and Lo the Ground Will be Stony and Before He Knoweth Where He is He Will be Back Where He Started having Achieved Sweet Fanny Adams and Made to Feel an Utter Nana.'

That's only a first draft, of course. It will need honing before it goes into *The Oxford Dictionary of English Proverbs*.

The need for such a proverb was brought home to me recently when I attempted to set on its way a small but, it seemed to me, vital social reform.

The Classless Society is the dearest wish of all of us but spreading the word that beans-on-toast are chic and Rolls-Royces are heavy on brake-linings is only nibbling at the problem. There is one real bastion of class-consciousness which must be removed.

Until recently the main Class giveaways were speech and dress. If somebody spoke a little too loudly, with a pre-war BBC

NONE WAS FOR A PARTY; ALL WERE FOR THE STATE

Frank Muir is a well-known British humorous writer, who has appeared in several radio and television game series featuring word play and verbal humour. In this passage he talks about Britain's complicated class system, and its influence on English.

This passage comes from a series of radio programs in which participants competed to tell the funniest story. One rule of the competition was that their story had to end with a sentence resembling a well-known phrase or saying, which they were given at the start. The phrase given to Muir at the beginning of his story was 'None was for a party: all were for the state', a quotation from *The Lays of Ancient Rome* (1842) by Thomas Babington Macaulay (See Box on p. 109).

[Notes]

[2] **term:** The school year in Britain is divided into three terms (not two semesters).

[3] **Spitteth:** verb + eth is an old form of verb + s. A tongue-twister which uses this old form is: *The Leith police dismisseth us and sympathiseth with us.*

[4] **cautionary, ballistically sound:**「戒告的であるし，弾道学的にも問題はない」. In this case 'ballistically sound' only means that if you spit upwards, it will fall back down. By seeming to present something very obvious as if it was a serious reason for liking the proverb, the author suddenly makes himself look foolish. In lines 8–13, Muir again makes fun of himself by proposing a proverb which is simply too long. For all its length it only means: 'it's no use trying to change society'.

[10] **Cloth Ears:** ears which do not hear well. 'Have you got cloth ears?' is an idiom meaning 'Are you deaf?' **Lo:** an old form of 'Look!' **the Ground Will be Stony:** the idea will not be well received (a phrase from the Bible).

[12] **Sweet Fanny Adams:** nothing at all. **an Utter Nana:** a complete idiot

[14] **honing** < hone: to sharpen. (Of course, the suggested proverb would need much more than 'honing' before it could be accepted.)

[16] **brought home to me:** made very clear to me

[17] **set on its way:** to start; put into motion

[19] **The Classless Society:** Class divisions, once strongly marked in Britain, have become weaker during the twentieth century, but, according to the writer, everyone wants them to disappear completely.

[20] **beans-on-toast:** a snack associated with the lower class

[21] **heavy on brake-linings:** ブレーキのライニング(内張り)の持ちが悪い **nibbling at the problem:** tackling the problem in a small-scale or unserious way. **nibble:** to take small delicate bites

[22] **bastion of class-consciousness:** a place where class feelings are strong. **bastion** [bǽstʃən]: 砦

[24] **giveaway(s):** sign; clue; indicator

announcer's accent, keeping the vowels well open, then he or she was an Upper. If all this was attempted and it just failed, then he or she was a Middle. Mumbling mangled vowels, and local colour in the accent indicated Lower. But nowadays, thanks to telly, pop-music, and the media generally, our youth and our trendier middle-aged now talk what might be termed Standard Received Disc-Jockey. If you meet a lad in Windsor High Street it is now no longer possible to tell from his speech whether he is Eton or Slough Comprehensive. Clothes have also ceased to be reliable indicators of Class. If you spot a little riot of colour ambling along the King's Road it could well be the rhythm guitarist of The Who. It could also be The Right Hon. Leo Abse M. P. on his way to the opening of Parliament.

But there is still one infallible way of separating the sheep from the lambs, the ewes from the non-ewes, and that is what we call the place where we all, from time to time, are compelled to go. Roughly speaking, Uppers go to the Lavatory, Middles to the Loo and Lowers go to the Toilet.

This is oversimplifying the picture to an enormous extent; in fact, the situation is in a state of flux. Loo is holding its own fairly well but there is a strong, perhaps 14%, swing to Toilet and most of these gains are at the expense of Lavatory.

These terms are totally non-interchangeable in society. Uppers and Middles recoil from the vulgarity of the word Toilet. Uppers and Lowers both regard 'Loo' as being a hopelessly twee euphemism. And Lowers and Middles join in finding the aristocratic use of the word 'Lavatory' utterly disgusting.

Now it wouldn't be too bad if we had just those three words — the U.S.A. manages happily with two, the John and the Can — but unfortunately we have a great many more words for the Unmentionable Thing. Consequently when strangers meet in an English house, and nature calls, our society breaks into a *mille-feuille* of social strata, the guest trying frantically to sort out in his mind which euphemism his host is most likely to embrace and the host similarly trying to fit euphemism to guest.

NONE WAS FOR A PARTY; ALL WERE FOR THE STATE

[3] **Mumbling mangled vowels:** speaking unclearly, with unpleasant vowel sounds
[5] **telly:** television
[7] **Standard Received Disc-Jockey:** Received pronunciation (RP) is a name for the English upper-class accent, now rarely heard. It is certainly not used by disc-jockeys. Muir's point is that the disc-jockey's classless way of speaking has become widely accepted.
Windsor High Street: the most important or central street in Windsor, a historically important city situated on the Thames just west of London
[9] **Comprehensive:** a kind of secondary school which accepts all the pupils who live nearby, irrespective of academic ability. This kind of school was introduced in Britain in the early seventies in an attempt to make educational opportunity more equal. **Eton,** by contrast, is an expensive, and famously upper-class, private school. **Slough** [slau]: an ordinary town near Windsor
[11] **riot:** literally, a crowd of people behaving violently; here, someone wearing clothes of many bright colours
ambling < amble: to walk in a relaxed, easy way
[12] **The Who:** a British rock band once famous for their violent stage act
The Right Hon. . . . M.P.: In Parliament, politicians are required to politely describe each other as 'My *right honourable* friend'. **M.P.:** Member of Parliament
[14] **infallible:** unmistakable, certain
separating the sheep from the lambs: separating good people from bad. The author changes 'goats' to 'lambs' because 'lamb' means not only a young sheep, but a gentle or kindly person (and so, perhaps, a person of the upper class).
[15] **ewe(s)** [juː]: a female sheep. A pun on 'U', a term which means upper class.
[20] **Loo is holding its own:** the word 'loo' is not losing popularity. **hold one's own:** not to weaken or retreat. In this sentence, Muir is imitating the style of commentators on the night of a general election.
[26] **twee:** so correct or charming as to be pretentious; too polite
euphemism [júːfəmizm]: a polite or pleasant-sounding way of referring to something unpleasant. Some euphemisms in English for 'to die' are 'to pass away', 'to go before', 'to pass on', 'to depart this vale of tears', 'to go to meet one's Maker', 'to join the choir celestial', 'to be gathered up', 'to be received into the bosom of one's ancestors', etc. Many of these euphemisms are limited to religious contexts and would rarely be used in ordinary speech except for humour.
[30] **the U.S.A. manages happily with two, the John and the Can:** Muir oversimplifies American usage for the sake of contrast. American women would rarely say 'the John' or 'the Can'. The commonest, all-purpose euphemisms in America are 'the bathroom' (in someone's home), and 'the restroom' (in a public place).
[34] *mille-feuille* [milfœːj] **of social strata:** 3つの階級どころか無数の層に分かれる

SESSION 11

Many older hosts and hostesses, who grew up in a protected, non-permissive society, can't bear to apply any word at all to It. They say, "Would you like to . . . (faint upward wave of right hand) . . .?" Or simply, "Are you . . . all right?"

Schoolchildren are brought up to avoid a confrontation by being taught to use such evasions as "Please, Miss, may I be excused?" "Please, Sir, may I leave the room?" The confusion which this produces in the delicate, growing mind is illustrated by the small boy who suddenly put his hand up and said "Please Miss, Johnny's left the room on the floor".

Keen euphemismaticians often study a stranger's house for clues before taking the plunge. Framed prints of vintage cars on the walls, pewter tankards, and 'Match of the Day' on the telly indicate an approach along the lines of:

"Where's the geography, old son?" Or:

"Excuse me, but I must go and see whether my horse has kicked off its blanket".

(*Note:* These phrases are rarely necessary as this host invariably greets his guests with a cheerful, "By the way, the bog's on the landing".)

Colour Supplements lying about, Hi-Fi, and Spanish Claret indicate a slightly more roguish approach from the host:

"Ah — if anyone needs the House of Lords it's at the end past the au-pair's room". Or:

"Comforts anyone?"

And in between these phrases there are a hundred others, each one clung to by a section of the population as being the one socially acceptable phrase which will protect them from hideous embarrassment.

Obviously something must be done to straighten this situation out, and the answer to the problem is to find a word for the Thing which is acceptable to all ranks. But which word? 'Lavatory' is useless; it is the word plumbers use for a washbasin. 'Toilet' is a horrid euphemism, imported from the U.S.A., which really means a lady's dressing-table. 'Loo' doesn't mean anything at all, being a hangover from eighteenth-century Edinburgh when folks were wont to empty their cham-

- [5] **confrontation:** a difficult situation. それを口にしなくてはならない状況
- [6] **evasions:** それを言わずにすます言い方
- [11] **euphemismaticians:** a word invented by Muir for those who enjoy or study euphemisms
- [12] **taking the plunge:** literally, diving into water; figuratively, making an important decision, in this case, about which expression to use

    Framed prints of vintage cars: pictures of cars made many years ago. Muir takes it that the person who puts this kind of picture on their walls does not have the educational level to appreciate real art.
- [13] **pewter tankards:** metal mugs for drinking beer. The more upper-class **Spanish Claret** wine is mentioned in l. 21.

    'Match of the Day': a television program showing the best football match played that day (taken by Muir to indicate lower or middle class)
- [14] **indicate an approach along the lines of . . . :** suggest that one should use euphemisms such as . . .
- [15] **the geography:** 家の間取りのこと．トイレの婉曲語として使われる．

    old son: an affectionate term of address from male to male (associated particularly with lower or middle-class London speech)
- [18] **invariably:** always
- [19] **bog:** literally, soft, wet ground. トイレの言い換えとしてはきわめて直接的．
- [20] **the landing:** (階段の)踊り場
- [21] **Colour Supplement(s):** a kind of magazine often included in Sunday newspapers read by middle- or upper-class people
- [22] **roguish:** humorously pretending to be bad or unreliable; mischievous
- [23] **the House of Lords:** the upper house of the British (and Canadian) parliament (⇔ the House of Commons)
- [24] **au-pair:** usually a female student from abroad who lives (perhaps for a year or so) in a family's house, in exchange for occasional baby-sitting
- [25] **"Comforts anyone?":** 'Would anyone like comforts?' cf. *'Tea anyone?'*
- [27] **each one clung to . . . as being the one socially acceptable phrase:** 多数に分化した層のそれぞれが自分たちの婉曲表現に固執しているということ．
- [29] **hideous** [hídiəs]: horrible; horrid (l. 34)
- [35] **dressing-table:** 化粧台．フランス語で化粧台を意味する toilette が 19 世紀末のアメリカで「浴室兼用化粧室」の意味で使われだし，そこから婉曲表現としての toilet が生まれたのだが，現代のアメリカ人にこの言葉は日本語の「トイレ」よりもっと直接的に響く．
- [37] **Edinburgh:** [édinbərə]

    were wont to empty: used to empty; would often empty

    chamber pot(s): a receptacle used in the past as a portable toilet

ber pots out of the top stories of tenement buildings with a cheerful warning cry of, "Guardy-loo!"

The problem was solved for me one evening when a small, round, innocent face looked up into mine and said, simply, "I want potty". It wasn't a child who spoke, in fact, it was a shortish Rural Dean who had come round about a subscription and had stayed to bash the sherry. But the simple, child's word 'Potty' was the word I had been searching for. An old, honourable, easily remembered word, and the only word of the whole bunch which described the Thing itself.

My mind went immediately into overdrive (unhappily, I recall, forgetting the Rural Dean and his pressing problem) and it seemed to me that I should form a society to promote the use of the word 'Pot'. Perhaps calling the society Pointers of Truth (thus making clever use of the initial letters), with myself as (paid) President. Perhaps I would write the society a brief, expensive manifesto . . .

I saw the Rural Dean out of the front door and into the bushes and immediately sat down and wrote out a questionnaire, to send to a hundred people to test whether I had judged the people's mood correctly. I asked them to state clearly whether they would be in favour of everybody settling to call the Thing something like 'Potty' rather than messing about pretending that they were nipping outside to check whether the trusty steed had kicked off its saddle.

It was when the results of my referendum were all in that I realised a sad truth. A truth encapsulated in the proverb 'Whoever Foolishly Attempteth to Bring About a Social Reform Very Likely Will Find that it Falleth Upon Cloth Ears . . . (etc.)' The figures were conclusive: None was for a Potty; all were for the Steed.

NONE WAS FOR A PARTY; ALL WERE FOR THE STATE

[2] **Guardy-loo:** (from pseudo-French *'Gare de l'eau!'*) 'Look out for the water!'
[5] **potty:**「おまる」. a more childish version of 'chamber pot'
[6] **Rural Dean:** the minister of a country church
  subscription: money given regularly, as a contribution (or to pay for a magazine, club membership, etc.)
[7] **to bash the sherry:** to drink some sherry. cf. *to hit the bottle* (to drink too much alcohol)
[14] **'Pot'... Pointers of Truth:** A word formed from the initial letters of other words is called an ACRONYM. e.g. 'radar' from Radio Detecting and Ranging; 'laser' from Light Amplification by Stimulated Emission of Radiation.
[17] **manifesto:** a statement of beliefs or program of action. It will be "expensive" because he is intending to charge a lot of money for writing it.
[18] **saw the Rual Dean out:** escorted him out of the house
  into the bushes: The writer has hurried the Dean out so quickly that he (the Dean) has been unable to go to the toilet in the writer's house and has to relieve himself in the garden.
[24] **nipping outside:** going outside quickly or briefly
  trusty steed: faithful horse (see p. 106, l. 16)
[26] **when the results... were all in:** when the replies to the questionnaire were all collected or analysed
  referendum:「国民投票」. questionnaire を大げさに言った言葉
[27] **encapsulated:** summed up, contained
[30] **conclusive:** leaving no room for further argument; decisive

---

The Lays of Ancient Rome (excerpt)
by Thomas Babington Macaulay　　　　　　　　（山本史郎 訳）

Then none was for a party;	そのかみ人に私なく,
Then all were for the state;	なべて国を思い, 公に尽くせり.
Then the great man helped the poor,	そのかみ貴きは賤きを扶け,
And the poor man loved the great;	賤きは貴きに親しめり.
Then lands were fairly portioned;	そのかみ地を頒くるに偏りなく
Then spoils were fairly sold:	商ひにも, たへて偽はることなし.
The Romans were like brothers	おお, 輝ける古代のローマ人
In the brave days of old.	みな同胞のごとく昵めり.

Part II

SESSION 12

The Imam and the Indian

Amitav Ghosh

WHEN I first came to that quiet corner of the Nile Delta I had expected to find on that most ancient and most settled of soils a settled and restful people. I couldn't have been more wrong.

The men of the village had all the busy restlessness of airline passengers in a transit lounge. Many of them had worked and travelled in the sheikhdoms of the Persian Gulf, others had been in Libya and Jordan and Syria, some had been to the Yemen as soldiers, others to Saudi Arabia as pilgrims, a few had visited Europe: some of them had passports so thick they opened out like ink-blackened concertinas. And none of this was new: their grandparents and ancestors and relatives had travelled and migrated too, in much the same way as mine had, in the Indian subcontinent — because of wars, or for money and jobs, or perhaps simply because they got tired of living always in one place. You could read the history of this restlessness in the villagers' surnames: they had names which derived from cities in the Levant, from Turkey, from faraway towns in Nubia; it was as though people had drifted here from every corner of the Middle East. The wanderlust of its founders had been ploughed into the soil of the village: it seemed to me sometimes that every man in it was a traveller. Everyone, that is, except Khamees the Rat, and even his surname, as I discovered later, meant 'of Sudan'.

'Well, never mind *ya doktor*,' Khamees said to me now, 'since

THE IMAM AND THE INDIAN

Amitav Ghosh was born in Calcutta in 1956. He grew up in Bangladesh (then East Pakistan), Sri Lanka, Iran and India. After graduating from the University of Delhi, he went to Oxford to study Social Anthropology and received a Master of Philosophy, and a Ph. D. in 1982. In 1980, he went to Egypt to do field work in the village of Lataifa. The work he did there resulted in *In an Antique Land* (1993), which is, according to the book's cover, "history in the guise of a traveller's tale." Novels by Ghosh include *The Circle of Reason* (1986), and *The Shadow Lines* (1988). He now lives in New York and teaches at Columbia University.

[Notes]
[1] **Nile Delta:** ナイル川はカイロの北で2つの支流に分かれ，広大なデルタを形成して地中海に注ぐ．
[3] **soils:** regions (literally, fertile land for farming)
I couldn't have been more wrong: I was completely wrong. *I couldn't have picked a worse time.* (= I picked the worst possible time.)
[5] **had all the ... restlessness:** cf. *She has all the courage of a lion.*
[7] **sheikhdoms of the Persian Gulf:** The United Arab Emirates, or U.A.E. (アラブ首長国連邦) is a federation of seven sheikhdoms. **Sheikh:** the leader of an Arab village or tribe. *Sheik* (p. 78, l. 7) is the American spelling.
[8] **to the Yemen as soldiers:** イエメンではそれぞれ異なった歴史的背景をもつ南北地域間の紛争がたえない．1989年の統一達成のあとも緊張は続き，1994年に勃発した9週間の内戦は，北軍が旧共産勢力の率いる南を制圧する形で決着した．
[9] **to Saudi Arabia as pilgrims:** Making a pilgrimage to the holy cities of Mecca and Medina is the lifetime dream of many Muslims.
[11] **concertina(s):** 蛇腹のついた小型のアコーディオンのような楽器．左右の6角形のボードのボタンを押して演奏する．
[13] **the Indian subcontinent:** 国土の広さを強調する「インド亜大陸」という言葉はかつて日本でもよく聞かれた．
[18] **the Levant** [ləvǽnt]: 地中海東岸の地方
Nubia: ヌビア(エジプト南部からスーダン北部の砂漠地方)
[20] **wanderlust:** strong impulse to travel
[23] **Khamees:** [kəmíːz]

you're not going to make it back to your country by sundown anyway, why don't you come and sit with us for a while?'

He smiled and moved up to make room for me.

I liked him at once. He was about my age, in the early twenties, scrawny, with a thin, mobile face deeply scorched by the sun. He had that brightness of eye and the quick, slightly sardonic turn to his mouth that I associated with faces in the coffee-houses of universities in Delhi and Calcutta; he seemed to belong to a world of late-night rehearsals and black coffee and lecture rooms, even though, in fact, unlike most people in the village, he was completely illiterate. Later I learned that he was called the Rat — Khamees the Rat — because he was said to gnaw away at things with his tongue, like a rat did with its teeth. He laughed at everything, people said — at his father, the village's patron saint, the village elders, the Imam, everything.

That day he decided to laugh at me.

'All right *ya doktor*,' he said to me as soon as I had seated myself. 'Tell me, is it true what they say, that in your country you burn your dead?'

No sooner had he said it than the women of the group clasped their hands to their hearts and muttered in breathless horror: *'Haram! Haram!'*

My heart sank. This was a conversation I usually went through at least once a day and I was desperately tired of it. 'Yes,' I said, 'it's true; some people in my country burn their dead.'

'You mean,' said Khamees in mock horror, 'that you put them on heaps of wood and just light them up?'

'Yes,' I said, hoping that he would tire of this sport if I humoured him.

'Why?' he said. 'Is there a shortage of kindling in your country?'

'No,' I said helplessly, 'you don't understand.' Somewhere in the limitless riches of the Arabic language a word such as 'cremate' must exist, but if it does, I never succeeded in finding it. Instead, for lack of any other, I had to use the word 'burn'.

[1] **make it back:** be able to go back
[5] **scrawny:** unattractively thin; skinny; bony
       mobile: able to move expressively
       scorched: burnt
[7] **sardonic:** cynical; mocking
[13]   **gnaw away at things with his tongue:** i.e. keep talking until he makes his point.
       gnaw: to bite or eat, using the front teeth like a rat
[15]   **patron saint:** 守護聖人
       Imam [imá:m]: a recognized leader or a religious teacher. See Box on page 119.
[23]   *Haram!*: (*Arabic*) God forbid!
[28]   **in mock horror:** pretending to feel horror himself
[30]   **sport:** mockery; play
       if I humoured him: if I complied with his mood; if I let him have his way
[32]   **a shortage of kindling:** This reference, of course, comes from Khamees' own phrasing "you put them on heaps of wood and just light them up?"

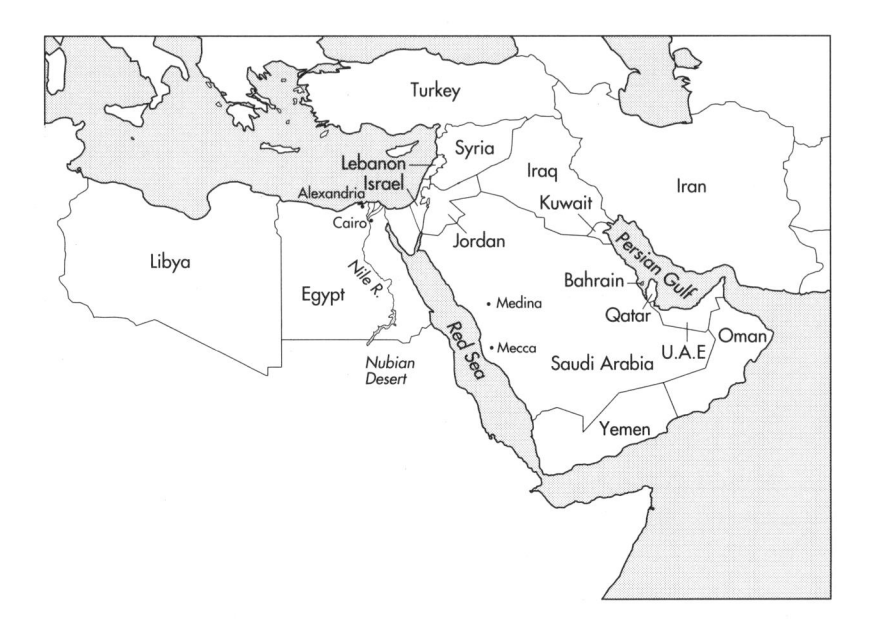

SESSION 12

That was unfortunate, for 'burn' was the word for what happened to wood and straw and the eternally damned.

Khamees the Rat turned to his spellbound listeners. 'I'll tell you why they do it,' he said. 'They do it so that their bodies can't be punished after the Day of Judgement.'

Everybody burst into wonderstruck laughter. 'Why, how clever,' cried one of the younger girls. 'What a good idea! We ought to start doing it ourselves. That way we can do exactly what we like and when we die and the Day of Judgement comes, there'll be nothing there to judge.'

Khamees had got his laugh. Now he gestured to them to be quiet again.

'All right then *ya doktor*,' he said. 'Tell me something else: is it true that you are a Magian? That in your country everybody worships cows? Is it true that the other day when you were walking through the fields you saw a man beating a cow and you were so upset that you burst into tears and ran back to your room?'

'No, it's not true,' I said, but without much hope: I had heard this story before and knew that there was nothing I could say which would effectively give it the lie. 'You're wrong. In my country people beat their cows all the time; I promise you.'

I could see that no one believed me.

'Everything's upside-down in their country,' said a dark, aquiline young woman who, I was told later, was Khamees's wife. 'Tell us *ya doktor*, in your country, do you have crops and fields and canals like we do?'

'Yes,' I said, 'we have crops and fields, but we don't always have canals. In some parts of my country they aren't needed because it rains all the year around.'

'*Ya salám*,' she cried, striking her forehead with the heel of her palm. 'Do you hear that, oh you people? Oh, the Protector, oh, the Lord! It rains all the year round in his country.'

She had gone pale with amazement. 'So tell us then,' she demanded, 'do you have night and day like we do?'

'Shut up woman,' said Khamees. 'Of course they don't. It's day all the time over there, didn't you know? They arranged it

[2] **the eternally damned:** those condemned by God to suffer forever
[6] **wonderstruck:** cf. *thunderstruck; awestruck*
[11] **had got his laugh:** had got people laughing
[14] **Magian** [méidʒiən]: a believer in Zoroastrianism
[21] **give it the lie:** prove it to be false
[25] **aquiline** [ǽkwəlain]: eagle-like (particularly in the profile of the face). cf. canine (dog-like), feline (cat-like)
[31] *Ya salám*: literally 'Oh, peace!' cf. *'For Heaven's sake!' 'Good Heavens!'* (*Salám* is a respectful ceremonial greeting in Islamic countries.)

Why Hindus Regard the Cow as Sacred

Hinduism is truly a way of life and certain traditions such as treating cows as sacred are symbolic. In Hindu families the parents and grandparents are givers and children are the takers, and this relationship is seen as something sacred. During the Vedic period, the cow was an integral part of a Hindu family, so it is no wonder that cows, the greatest sacrificers of their possessions for the benefit of the family, became sacred.

According to the Rigveda, a collection of ancient hymns, the cow symbolically represents the maternal aspect of the Earth. Hindus believe that God resides everywhere and in everything, so that the whole of Nature is a divine gift, which we receive. In Hindu scriptures there are references to Kamadhenu, the mythical and miraculous 'wish-cow', and Karpakavirucha, the incredible-tree. Kamadhenu, the cow that gives everything that anyone wishes, became the symbolic representation of all other creatures to the Hindu. Trees and plants accept the garbage that is discarded by all living creatures and in return give everything that they possess. It is no wonder that Hindus treated flowers, fruits and milk as sacred. All materials such as the flowers, fruits, milk, honey and other natural products used in Hindu Temples represent the symbolic presence of God everywhere.

Lord Krishna in the Bhagavadgita ('song of God') advises Hindus to perform their duties spontaneously without expecting rewards. Trees, flowers, plants and selfless animals like cows remind good Hindus to follow their generous example.

(Ram Chandran, adapted)

like that so that they wouldn't have to spend any money on lamps.'

We all laughed, and then someone pointed to a baby lying in the shade of a tree swaddled in a sheet of cloth. 'That's Khamees's baby,' I was told. 'He was born last month.'

'That's wonderful,' I said. 'Khamees must be very happy.'

Khamees gave a cry of delight. 'That Indian knows I'm happy because I've had a son,' he said to the others. 'He understands that people are happy when they have children: he's not as upside-down as we thought.'

He slapped me on the knee and lit up the hookah and from that moment we were friends.

One evening, perhaps a month or so after I first met Khamees, he and his brothers and I were walking back to the village from the fields when he spotted the old Imam sitting on the steps that led to the mosque.

'Listen,' he said to me, 'you know the old Imam, don't you? I saw you talking to him once.'

'Yes,' I said. 'I talked to him once.'

'My wife's ill,' Khamees said. 'I want the Imam to come to my house to give her an injection. He won't come if I ask him, he doesn't like me. You go and ask.'

'He doesn't like me either,' I said.

'Never mind,' Khamees insisted. 'He'll come if you ask him — he knows you're a foreigner. He'll listen to you.'

While Khamees waited on the edge of the square with his brothers I went across to the Imam. I could tell that he had seen me — and Khamees — from a long way off, that he knew I was crossing the square to talk to him. But he would not look in my direction. Instead, he pretended to be deep in conversation with a man who was sitting beside him, an elderly and pious shopkeeper whom I knew slightly.

When I reached them I said 'Good evening' very pointedly to the Imam. He could not ignore me any longer then, but his response was short and curt, and he turned back at once to resume his conversation.

[4] **swaddle(d):** In this part of the world, babies wear swaddling clothes, a long sheet of cloth wrapped around the body like bandages.
[11] **hookah** [húkə]: a tobacco pipe which uses water to cool the smoke; a water pipe
[27] **I could tell:** I was certain; I was positive; I knew
[35] **curt:** rudely brief

Imam

The literal meaning of the word 'imam' is 'exemplar, model', and in this sense, the imam is the man who leads prayers in the mosque. He might not be a trained priest or minister, but simply someone recognised in his community as being of good character. Larger mosques might have a salaried imam who would organise festivals, the religious education of the young and so on, but an imam in a small village might equally well be a shopkeeper or craftsman.

The second meaning of the word applies particularly to Shi'ite Islam (and so not to a Sunni Muslim country like Egypt). In Shi'ite Islam, an imam is a charismatic religious leader, believed to be morally perfect and authoritative in interpreting the Koran. Sunni Muslims, by contrast, tend to follow tradition and the consensus of the community in matters of interpretation. Shi'ite Muslims (such as the people of Iran and Iraq) expect the appearance of a new imam, who will establish justice and peace on earth.

The word 'imam' can also simply mean 'leader', in which meaning it can apply to a secular ruler without any specifically religious role.

SESSION 12

The old shopkeeper was embarrassed now, for he was a courteous, gracious man in the way that seemed to come so naturally to the elders of the village. 'Please sit down,' he said to me. 'Do sit. Shall we get you a chair?'

Then he turned to the Imam and said, slightly puzzled: 'You know the Indian *doktor*, don't you? He's come all the way from India to be a student at the University of Alexandria.'

'I know him,' said the Imam. 'He came around to ask me questions. But as for this student business, I don't know. What's *he* going to study? He doesn't even write in Arabic.'

'Well,' said the shopkeeper judiciously, 'that's true; but after all he writes his own languages and he knows English.'

'Oh those,' said the Imam. 'What's the use of *those* languages? They're the easiest languages in the world. Anyone can write those.'

He turned to face me for the first time. His eyes were very bright and his mouth was twitching with anger. 'Tell me,' he said, 'why do you worship cows?'

I was so taken aback that I began to stammer. The Imam ignored me. He turned to the old shopkeeper and said: 'That's what they do in his country — did you know? — they worship cows.'

He shot me a glance from the corner of his eyes. 'And shall I tell you what else they do?' he said to the shopkeeper.

He let the question hang for a moment. And then, very loudly, he hissed: 'They burn their dead.'

The shopkeeper recoiled as though he had been slapped. His hands flew to his mouth. 'Oh God!' he muttered. '*Ya Allah.*'

'That's what they do,' said the Imam. 'They burn their dead.'

Then suddenly he turned to me and said, very rapidly: 'Why do you allow it? Can't you see that it's a primitive and backward custom? Are you savages that you permit something like that? Look at you: you've had some kind of education; you should know better. How will your country ever progress if you carry on doing these things? You've even been to the West; you've seen how advanced they are. Now tell me: have you ever seen them burning their dead?'

120

[2] **in the way that seemed to come so naturally to the elders of the village:** 村の老人たちはそうした物腰を自然に身につけていた. *New ideas seem to come naturally to her — she's a born designer.*
[9] **as for this student business, I don't know:** I'm dubious about what he's doing being a student
[11] **judiciously:** trying to arrive at a good or balanced judgment
[17] **twitch(ing):** to move suddenly and involuntarily
[19] **taken aback:** stunned; left speechless
[26] **hissed:** i.e. said in a sharp, contemptuous tone
[33] **Look at you:** an expression usually followed by a strong criticism. *Look at you — a disgrace to your family and friends.*

SESSION 12

The Imam was shouting now and a circle of young men and boys had gathered around us. Under the pressure of their interested eyes my tongue began to trip, even on syllables I thought I had mastered. I found myself growing angry — as much with my own incompetence as the Imam.

'Yes, they do burn their dead in the West,' I managed to say somehow. I raised my voice too now. 'They have special electric furnaces meant just for that.'

The Imam could see that he had stung me. He turned away and laughed. 'He's lying,' he said to the crowd. 'They don't burn their dead in the West. They're not an ignorant people. They're advanced, they're educated, they have science, they have guns and tanks and bombs.'

'We have them too!' I shouted back at him. I was as confused now as I was angry. 'In my country we have all those things too,' I said to the crowd. 'We have guns and tanks and bombs. And they're better than anything you have — we're way ahead of you.'

The Imam could no longer disguise his anger. 'I tell you, he's lying,' he said. 'Our guns and bombs are much better than theirs. Ours are second only to the West's.'

'It's you who's lying,' I said. 'You know nothing about this. Ours are much better. Why, in my country we've even had a nuclear explosion. You won't be able to match that in a hundred years.'

So there we were, the Imam and I, delegates from two superseded civilizations vying with each other to lay claim to the violence of the West.

At that moment, despite the vast gap that lay between us, we understood each other perfectly. We were both travelling, he and I: we were travelling in the West. The only difference was that I had actually been there, in person: I could have told him about the ancient English university I had won a scholarship to, about punk dons with safety pins in their mortar-boards, about superhighways and sex shops and Picasso. But none of it would have mattered. We would have known, both of us, that all that was mere fluff: at the bottom, for him as for me and

[3] **trip:** [a. to move smoothly / b. to stumble]. cf. *slip of the tongue*
[5] **incompetence:** inability; inefficiency; impotence
[9] **stung** < sting: to pierce or attack like a bee; cause sharp pain
[17] **way ahead of you:** cf. *way before, way behind, way beyond* (Humpty Dumpty's lecture, Box on p. 17)
[24] **nuclear explosion:** On May 11, 1998, India announced that it had conducted three underground nuclear tests.
[26] **two superseded civilizations:** The author is not only talking about the ancient civilizations of Egypt and India. In their heyday, India's Gupta Dynasty (グプタ朝 *c.* 320–*c.* 540) and the Islamic Empire, especially the Abbasid Caliphate (アッバース朝 749–1258), were each of them far more prosperous in arts and sciences than any kingdom in Medieval Europe. **supersede:** to displace as inferior
[27] **vying . . . to lay claim to the violence of the West:** competing for the right to be thought [a. as violent as / b. victims of the violence of] the West. **vying** < vie: to strive to be superior; compete
[31] **travelling in the West:** よそ者としてヨーロッパ文明に生きていることのたとえ．
[34] **punk dons with safety pins in their mortar-boards:** 「(大学で式典の時にかぶる)角帽に安全ピンを通したパンクな教師」．2つの衣服文化の衝突がおかしい表現．元来スペイン語の敬称である don は日本語では政治家等に使われるが，イギリスの大学では(やや古風ながら)教師に対して使われる．時には頬にも通したという安全ピンは，過激なパンク・ファッションを代表する小道具．
[37] **fluff:** something trivial or superficial

SESSION 12

millions and millions of people on the landmasses around us, the West meant only this — science and tanks and guns and bombs.

And we recognized too the inescapability of these things, their strength, their power — evident in nothing so much as this: that even for him, a man of God, and for me, a student of the 'humane' sciences, they had usurped the place of all other languages of argument. He knew, just as I did, that he could no longer say to me, as Ibn Battuta might have when he travelled to India in the fourteenth century: 'You should do this or that because it is right or good or because God wills it so.' He could not have said it because that language is dead: those things are no longer sayable; they sound absurd. Instead he had had, of necessity, to use that other language, so universal that it extended equally to him, an old-fashioned village Imam, and great leaders at SALT conferences: he had had to say to me: 'You ought not to do this because otherwise you will not have guns and tanks and bombs.'

Since he was a man of God his was the greater defeat.

For a moment then I was desperately envious. The Imam would not have said any of those things to me had I been a Westerner. He would not have dared. Whether I wanted it or not, I would have had around me the protective aura of an inherited expertise in the technology of violence. That aura would have surrounded me, I thought, with a sheet of clear glass, like a bullet-proof screen; or perhaps it would have worked as a talisman, like a press card, armed with which I could have gone off to what were said to be the most terrible places in the world that month, to gaze and wonder. And then perhaps I too would one day have had enough material for a book which would have had for its epigraph the line, *The horror! The horror!* — for the virtue of a sheet of glass is that it does not require one to look within.

But that still leaves Khamees the Rat waiting on the edge of the square.

In the end it was he and his brothers who led me away from the Imam. They took me home with them. And there, while

[1] **the landmasses:** the vast expanses of land
[7] **'humane' science:** 人文科学は humanities または humane studies (sciences) と呼ばれる．'humane' [hju:méin] は文字どおりには kind, compassionate の意．
had usurped the place of all other languages of argument: それ以外の論じ方を不可能にしてしまった．
[9] **Ibn Battuta:** イブン・バトゥータ (1304?–1377?) は 'the traveller of Islam' と呼ばれて，インドからスペインまで総計約 12 万キロを旅し，各地の 60 人以上の支配者と出会い，膨大な日誌を残して当時の各国の様子を詳細に記録した．
[16] **SALT:** Strategic Arms Limitation Talks（戦略[核]兵器制限交渉）
[19] **his was the greater defeat:** i.e. his acceptance of the language of violence was more damaging to his (religious) beliefs
[20] **I was desperately envious:** i.e. envious of [a. the Imam / b. a Westerner]
[23] **the protective aura of an inherited expertise in the technology of violence:** 過去から受け継がれた，武力のテクノロジーに秀でた者としての護身のオーラ
[26] **would have worked as a talisman:** would have given me supernatural powers of protection
[27] **press card:** 報道関係者の身分証明証
[31] **epigraph:** 本の巻頭につける気の利いた科白または引用句
The horror! The horror!: 出典はポーランド出身の英国作家コンラッド (Joseph Conrad, 1857–1924) の中編小説『闇の奥』(*Heart of Darkness*, 1902). コンゴの奥地で原住民の権力者として君臨する白人商人クルツ (Kurtz) が臨終の際に叫んだ言葉．具体的に何を意味するかは明確でないが，劣等と見なしてきた異文化との遭遇によって西洋文明が 19 世紀末に経験したリアリティーの喪失感を広く表わしていると考えられる．もっとも，このテクストの文脈では，非西洋との遭遇を単に恐怖の経験としか見ない心性を象徴する一句ととるのが適当だろう．なお『闇の奥』は，ベトナム戦争の恐怖を描いたアメリカ映画『地獄の黙示録』('Apocalypse Now' 1979) の原作でもある．
[32] **the virtue of a sheet of glass is that it does not require one to look within:** 最初 'protective aura' として描かれ，羨望の対象だった透明ガラスが，ここでは安全な覗き窓として批判的に捉え直されていることに注意．批判のターゲットは自省的な意識をもたずに政情不安定な「危険地帯」のルポを売り物にする作家やジャーナリストであろう．
[34] **But that still leaves ... waiting on the edge of the square:**「そうしたところで，カミーズが広場の片隅で待たされていることにかわりはない」．第三世界をめぐる報道の中で一般庶民が見過ごされていることをにおわせる書き方．

SESSION 12

Khamees's wife cooked dinner for us — she was not so ill after all — Khamees said to me: 'Do not be upset, *ya doktor*. Forget about all those guns and things. I'll tell you what: I'll come to visit you in your country, even though I've never been anywhere. I'll come all the way.'

He slipped a finger under his skull-cap and scratched his head, thinking hard.

Then he added: 'But if I die, you must bury me.'

[3] **and things:** だの何だの；とか　cf. *Oh, was that why? I thought she hated me or something.*
I'll tell you what:「そうだ，こうしよう」．何かを提案するときの表現．*I'll tell you what. Why don't you go in and finish your shopping while I make a phone call.*
[6] **skull-cap:** つばのない，お椀を伏せた形の帽子
[8] **you must bury me:** [a. I want *you* to bury me. / b. Don't *burn* me.]

SESSION 13

Sarajevo: Survival Guide 1993

FAMA

C **LIMATE** Sarajevo's climate is very continental, with [1] a short hot summer, when nights are still cold due to the constant breeze coming from the surrounding mountains. Winters are rich with snow, from November until April. Snow has been recorded in August and in June — a fact [5] which can be found in old Sarajevo chronicles. War so far hasn't changed the climate. The moon is still shining, the sun rises, rains fall, and it snows, too.

Accommodation Those who were lucky still live in their apartments. Refugees and those whose apartments have been [10] burned or destroyed by grenades are inhabiting the apartments of those who left Sarajevo before or during the war. Temporary leases and bills of sale are being issued. Some entered flats by breaking the doors and changed locks. You can change apartments if one of your friends manages to leave town. Some [15] people have two or three apartments. Depending on what each of them can offer — electricity, gas, water, or minimal security — people move from one apartment to another. Some are living in communes. Old families have disintegrated — new ones are being formed. [20]

Windows are gone, destroyed by perpetual detonations. It was kind of pleasant during the summer — plastic came only with the first rains. People fixed it to the window-frames with the wide tape used in factories for packing, but the glue gave

SARAJEVO: SURVIVAL GUIDE 1993

　第一次世界大戦のはじまりを 20 世紀の「真の」はじまりと見る人は多いが，その未曾有の大戦争のきっかけとなったのは，サラエヴォで起きたオーストリア=ハンガリー帝国の帝位継承者暗殺事件であった．それから 4 分の 3 世紀後の 1992 年，ボスニア内乱が激化するなかで，サラエヴォはふたたび世界の注目を浴びることになる．260 台の戦車，120 台の迫撃砲，その他無数の対空機関砲や狙撃用ライフルに街が包囲され，ここでその一部を読む *Sarajevo: Survival Guide* の表現を借りれば，街全体が巨大な dart game と化したのである．

　Sarajevo: Survival Guide は，そうした悪夢のような状況のさなかから世界に向けて発信されたメッセージである．ミシュランの旅行ガイドそっくりの装丁と，文章を貫くしたたかなユーモアで，多くの読者に感銘を与えた．出版元の FAMA は「噂，伝説」を意味するセルビア・クロアチア語で，1952 年生まれの Suada Kapić（スアダ・カピッチ）を中心とするサラエヴォの芸術家グループ．

[Notes]

[1] **Sarajevo's climate is very continental:** continental climate（大陸性気候）とは oceanic climate（海洋性気候）と対比して用いられる言葉．昼夜の温度差，季節間の温度差が大きい．
[3] **the surrounding mountains:** 92 年 4 月に包囲がはじまると，街を囲むそれらの山々に戦車の迫撃砲が出現した．
[6] **War so far hasn't changed the climate:** このガイドブックには，苦みの効いたこの手のユーモアが随所に見られる．次の The moon is still shining...の一文からは，静かな悲しみも感じられる．
[9] **Accommodation:** ガイドブックとなれば宿泊施設の情報は欠かせないが，ここで述べられるのは……？
[11] **grenades:** 手榴弾
[12] **who left Sarajevo before or during the war:** と，ここではあっさり書いてあるが，包囲がはじまってからサラエヴォを抜け出すのは容易でなかった．このガイドの "Going Out of Town" というセクションには，"Officially, there is no such thing as 'going out of town'. Since April of 1992, the City has been forced to turn in on itself [孤立を強いられている]" とある．
[13] **bills of sale:** 売渡証
　　　flats: apartments
[19] **disintegrated:** fallen apart; gone to pieces
[21] **detonations:** explosions
[22] **plastic:** 日本語でいう「プラスチック」だけでなく「ビニール」も含む．英語で vinyl [váinəl] というと，今日ではアナログ・レコードを指すことが多い．

up under the rain and winds. Then they used nails. Whoever had no plastic — a more than precious item on the black market — would cover the windows with cardboard boxes left behind from humanitarian aid. However, the best for the purpose proved to be those smaller sacks for the rice provided by UNPROFOR.

Water Water shortages may last for days, or weeks. The reasons are always the same — no electricity, or an act of terror. Then the search starts. First, one checks a basement. Then you may go to Konak (which serves only the privileged), then to Sedam Brace on Bistrik, where long lines form, then in the neighborhood of Pionirska Dolina, where one waits under the snipers. Those who carry water, depending on their strength and the number of canisters, do so several times a day, traveling several kilometers, waiting in each line for at least three hours. The lucky ones are those with bicycles, which are pushed rather than ridden. The same with the owners of baby-carriages or former supermarket carts. Anything that rolls will do, for anything is easier than carrying the water by hand.

People stand in lines, in the rain, waiting with buckets for their portion of rainwater. Day or night — it doesn't really matter. People drink it and use it for doing laundry. It is very good for your hair, which becomes silky and shiny.

The washing machine is a household appliance from some long-gone time. It has no function. The women of Sarajevo are again first-class laundresses. The only thing lacking is a battledore, lye soap and a clean river to wash what they have.

Sarajevo by Night Sarajevo life is dependent on the cycle of the sun. Without civilization based on inventions of two Americans — Tesla, who was born in the neighborhood and who we are proud of, and Edison, who they are proud of — you have to learn to go to sleep early and wake up early. So many evenings are spent in envy of those who have electricity.

Sleeping Sleeping is entirely conditioned by the arrival of

SARAJEVO: SURVIVAL GUIDE 1993

[6] **UNPROFOR:** United Nations Protection Force; 国連保護軍. 旧ユーゴスラヴィア紛争を食い止めるため 1992 年 3 月から活動を開始, 95 年 12 月に任務を終了. 94 年 4 月には, PKO (国連平和維持活動) としては最大級の 45000 人の規模があった.
[8] **an act of terror:** テロ行為
[10] **Konak:** 元来「宿舎」の意だが, 長年にわたってユーゴスラヴィアの指導者だったチトー (1892–1980, 首相 1945–53, 大統領 1953–80) の邸宅を指す.
[11] **Sedam Brace on Bistrik:** ビストリク(地区名)のセダム・ブラーチェ(「七人兄弟」を意味する, 墓地の名)
[12] **Pionirska Dolina:** ピオニール渓谷
[13] **snipers:** 狙撃兵. 同じく FAMA が制作した "Sarajevo Survival Map" という一見楽しげなイラストマップに付した説明によれば, "According to the data gathered in 1995, the snipers, shooting from small holes made in the walls of the buildings or from the bushes, had wounded 1,030 and killed 225 persons, 60 of whom were children."（口絵参照）
[14] **canisters:** 缶. ガイドに収められた写真で見るかぎりポリタンクが多いようだ.
[17] **The same with:** It's the same with; The same can be said about
[24] **household appliance:** 家庭電器製品
[26] **battledore:**（洗濯板を叩く）へら
[27] **lye:** 灰汁(あく). 古くから洗剤として使われてきた.
[28] **Sarajevo by Night:** 普通のガイドブックだったら, ナイトクラブやデートスポットなどが紹介されるところ.
[30] **Tesla, who was born in the neighborhood:** エディソンの直流電気に対して交流電気の技術を開発し, いわゆる「交直論争」に勝利を収めたニコラ・テスラ (Nicola Tesla, 1857–1943) は, クロアチアのスミリャン生まれのセルビア人で, 1884 年アメリカに渡った. ベオグラードには彼を記念するテスラ博物館がある.
[34] **Sleeping is entirely conditioned by the arrival of water and electricity:** When we can sleep depends entirely on when water or electricity arrives

from *Sarajevo: Survival Guide* © FAMA

water and electricity. If they appear at the same time, the shock is complete. The race against time starts — in order to use both in the best possible way. It doesn't matter that it is two or five o'clock in the morning. We cook, we wash, we clean, we take baths. Sometimes even a loaf of bread can be baked, the most wonderful gift.

Heating   The major problem is fuel. You cannot buy wood or coal.

During the first summer, all dry benches, trees and wooden material were collected. This autumn, in parks, alleys, courtyards and cemeteries trees started to fall — birches, poplars, ash-trees, plane-trees, plum-trees, apple-trees, cherry-trees, pear-trees, all the way down to brushwood. The wooden backs of benches in parks were taken away, doors and doorframes of ruined apartments, handrails from the hallways, shelves from abandoned stores and kiosks, wooden stools and bars from restaurants, even the crosses and pyramids from the cemeteries. All bombed houses and barracks were dismantled with dismaying speed. But fuel is still scarce. Those who were wise took scrap wood from their garages early in the summer. Then they used paper. Now, new kinds of fuel are being manufactured. Plastic bags from US lunch packages — a leftover from the Persian Gulf War — can heat five liters of water.

UNHCR supplied the city with numerous but not sufficient thermal foils for windows. On every window, from the outside, one can read their name: UNHCR — they are the owners of our lives.

November temperatures were very nice last year. Meteorologists have informed us they were very high, in comparison with times no one remembers any more: about 9 degrees Centigrade in the apartment. It was warmer to take a walk than to sit inside. Fortunately, everyone can get warm while searching for water and wood.

Eating   The main dishes of 1992 were macaroni and rice. You wouldn't believe how many different ways they can be

[11] **birches, poplars, ash-trees, plane-trees, plum-trees ...:** カバノキ，ポプラ，トネリコ，スズカケノキ，スモモノキ……
[13] **brushwood:** small branches broken off from trees or bushes
[15] **handrails from the hallways:** 建物内の玄関ホールや通路などからとってきた手すり
[16] **kiosks:** 広場や駅の売店．日本語の「キヨスク」のように駅の売店とは限らない．
[18] **dismantled with dismaying speed:** taken apart with depressing speed
[23] **the Persian Gulf War:** 1990年8月にイラクがクウェートに侵攻したことに端を発し，91年1月17日にアメリカ主導の多国籍軍がイラク空爆を開始，2月26日にクウェートを解放し，28日戦闘は終わった．
[24] **UNHCR:** (the office of the) United Nations High Commissioner for Refugees; 国連難民高等弁務官（事務所）．これまで2500万人以上の難民に対する救済活動を行なってきた．
[25] **thermal foils:** 保温用金属箔
[28] **Meteorologists:** 気象学者

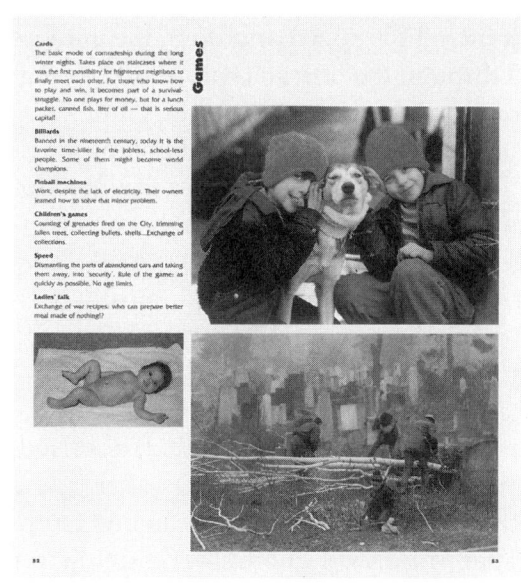

prepared! They couldn't be bought except on the black market. That was the case during the first months of the siege. Now, everyone is saving them, jealously, if they still have any. With additions and a lot of imagination, one US lunch package can feed five people. Rice, macaroni and bread are often eaten together — otherwise it is difficult to survive. For each resident of Sarajevo, during the first seven months of war, you couldn't count more than six packages of humanitarian aid. One had to invent ways to preserve and make last for as long as possible what is normally envisioned for one person, one meal, one use. In spring, summer and fall, all kinds of leaves it is possible to find were used as ingredients — from parks, gardens, fields and hills which were not dangerous to visit. Combined with rice, and well seasoned, everything becomes edible. Each person in Sarajevo is very close to an ideal macrobiotician, a real role model for the health-conscious, diet-troubled West. People are healthy, in spite of everything, for no one eats animal fat anymore, nor meat, nor cheese — meals are made without eggs, without milk, onions, vegetables. We eat a precious mix of wild imagination.

Rumors Rumors are the most important source of information. They spread with incredible speed and often mean more than news transmitted through the official channels. They regularly — "this time for sure" — report on military intervention, on the siege of the city being lifted, on establishing corridors and safe havens. And they are regularly, each time "for sure," wrong. Rumors are spread by all: housewives, university professors, teenagers, doctors. No one is immune. Rumors travel the city quicker than you can, and they are mostly optimistic. Only later you might hear opinions that they were too optimistic.

Shopping Stores have been broken into, shelled, deserted. This situation lasted for months and then, in October, a few brave owners reopened some of them. There you can find toothpaste, soap, toilet paper (rarely), light bulbs and foil for

SARAJEVO: SURVIVAL GUIDE 1993

- [2] **siege:** 包囲，封鎖状態．サラエヴォ封鎖は 1992 年 5 月 2 日から 96 年 2 月 26 日まで 1395 日間つづいた．その間に殺された人数は 10615 人と言われる．
- [3] **jealously:** なくならないよう用心して
- [9] **make last ...:** ～をもたせる．last は動詞．
- [10] **envisioned:** conceived; seen
- [14] **well seasoned:** きちんと味つけすれば
  edible: suitable to eat
- [15] **macrobiotician:** macrobiotics は日本でもマクロバイオティック，マクロビオティックの名で実践されている，自然との調和を重視して主に穀類と豆に頼る食事法．
  role model: （見習うべき）お手本
- [17] **animal fat:** 動物性脂肪
- [22] **mean more:** i.e. are more reliable
- [23] **transmitted:** communicated; sent
  the official channels: 政府の公式見解などを流す新聞，テレビ等．
- [24] **"this time for sure":**「今度こそは確かだ」という触れ込みで
  military intervention: 軍事介入
- [25] **lifted:** removed; brought to an end
  corridors and safe havens: 通行ルートや安全避難所
- [28] **immune:** able to ignore rumors. 本来の意味は「免疫のある」．噂を病原菌にたとえた言い方．
- [32] **shelled:** bombed

© FAMA

preserving food — remnants from the pre-war rich Sarajevo. Supermarkets are gone. Some, completely ravaged, since December have been selling just the one and only kind of bread. People got food stamps sometime in June, but they never served their purpose — you could never buy anything with them. Only one card works, the one that appeared in December, for bread. If you manage to wait in a line, you can get 233 grams per person daily. Single men and women are forming trios, so that each of them gets a whole loaf every third day. Business hours are from 8 a.m. to 3 p.m., but most places close at noon.

Recreation
Walking: Six kilometers a day — that is the average for those who don't need to go far. Some believe it helps you to keep in good shape.
Running: This is the favorite sport, practiced by everyone in Sarajevo. All crossroads are run through as are all the dangerous neighborhoods. Running with stolen wood, you run to the line where others are standing. Something is on sale, and you will know what it is only when you join the line.
Rock-climbing: Urban rock-climbing is a compulsory sports discipline. Instead of adequate ropes, one uses sheets. Climbers calculate the distances between balconies, from higher ones to the lower ones which have not yet been reached by fire.

Transportation Imagine driving through streets with no street lights (they have been torn down or are not working), without any traffic signs (they are gone), without any attention paid to pedestrians, at maximum speed across the crossroads and other dangerous spots. People are driving recklessly in all directions. No one pays any attention to crashes. Broken cars are abandoned easily and damages are negotiated in quick conversations. This is the war with the biggest ever civilian motor pool. The war is being waged in Audis, in BMWs, in Mercedes and VW Golfs, as well as in expensive yuppie jeeps.

General Tips When you come to Sarajevo, be prepared and

[1] **the pre-war rich Sarajevo:** 封鎖がはじまるわずか8年前のサラエヴォ冬季オリンピック大会は，サラエヴォが豊かで美しい街であることを世界中に印象づけた．
[2] **ravaged:** ruined and destroyed
[4] **food stamps:** 政府支給の食料引換券
[9] **Business hours are . . . :** これも「ガイド」をもじった表現．
[13] **keep in good shape:** 元気を保つ（「体型を」ではない）
[20] **compulsory sports discipline:** 必修の体育教科
[31] **civilian motor pool:** 集められた民間車．その前の ever は the biggest を強調する．
[32] **Audis . . . BMWs . . . Mercedes** [mə:sí:di:z, mɔ́:si] . . . : いずれも日本でもおなじみのドイツ車．
[33] **yuppie jeeps:** ヤッピーが乗るような，ファッショナブルなジープ
[34] **Tips:** helpful pieces of advice

© FAMA

SESSION 13

be mature. It might prove to be the most important decision [1] you have made in your life. Bring: good shoes which allow you to walk long and run fast, pants with many pockets, pills for water, Deutsche Marks (small denominations), batteries, matches, jars of vitamins, canned food, drinks and cigarettes. [5] Everything you bring will be consumed or exchanged for useful information. You should know when to skip a meal, how to turn trouble into a joke and be relaxed in impossible moments. Learn not to show emotions and don't be fussy about anything. Be ready to sleep in basements, be eager to walk and [10] work surrounded by danger. Give up all your former habits. Use the telephone when it works, laugh when it doesn't. You'll laugh a lot. Laugh, don't hate.

[3] **pills for water:** 水を飲めるようにする浄水剤
[4] **small denominations:** 少額の貨幣・紙幣
[9] **fussy:** too concerned about small things

SESSION 14

The Birth of Fractal Geometry

James Gleick

A PICTURE of reality built up over the years in Benoit Mandelbrot's mind. In 1960, it was a ghost of an idea, a faint, unfocused image. But Mandelbrot recognized it when he saw it, and there it was on the blackboard in Hendrik Houthakker's office.

Mandelbrot was a mathematical jack-of-all-trades who had been adopted and sheltered by the pure research wing of the International Business Machines Corporation. He had been dabbling in economics, studying the distribution of large and small incomes in an economy. Houthakker, a Harvard economics professor, had invited Mandelbrot to give a talk, and when the young mathematician arrived at Littauer Center, the stately economics building just north of Harvard Yard, he was startled to see his findings already charted on the economist's blackboard. Mandelbrot made a querulous joke — *how should my diagram have materialized ahead of my lecture?* — but Houthakker didn't know what Mandelbrot was talking about. The diagram had nothing to do with income distribution; it represented eight years of cotton prices.

From Houthakker's point of view, too, there was something strange about this chart. Economists generally assumed that the price of a commodity like cotton danced to two different beats, one orderly and one random. Over the long term, prices would be driven steadily by real forces in the economy — the rise and fall of the New England textile industry, or the open-

140

THE BIRTH OF FRACTAL GEOMETRY

　自然のカタチの背後に不思議な整合性を見せてくれるフラクタル図形は，今では癒し系のビデオなどにも使われているが，それが一人の天才の直感のなかで育まれていったエピソードは，カオス理論の登場にまつわる 20 世紀後半の知の変革の物語のなかでも，ひときわ興味をひく．ブノワ・マンデルブロは 1924 年ワルシャワ生まれのユダヤ系リトアニア人．ナチスから解放されたばかりのパリで，英才校エコール・ノルマルに入学したが，純粋数学の厳密な論法になじめず，パリ大学で博士号を取得してからも，数学界ではまったく浮いた存在だった．ジェイムズ・グリックの名著 *Chaos: Making a New Science* (1987) からとったこの一節は，1960 年，まだ彼の直感的世界像がはっきりと形をなしていなかったころの物語である．

[Notes]

[1]　**built up:** developed by degrees; accumulated
[2]　**a ghost of an idea:** a ghost-like idea.　cf. *She is an angel of a baby.*
[5]　**Houthakker** [háuthækə]: 1924 年オランダ生まれ．ハーヴァード大教授 (1960–94). 現在同大学名誉教授．
[6]　**jack-of-all-trades:**「何でも屋」．マンデルブロは IBM 就職後もハーヴァード大学で経済学の，イェール大学で工学の，アインシュタイン医科大学で生理学の客員教授をつとめている．
[7]　**wing:** メイン・ビルディングとつながった別棟の建物
[8]　**International Business Machines Corporation:** 1911 年創立のキャッシュ・レジスター販売会社が，1920 年代にこう改名．30〜40 年代の電動タイプライターのビジネスを通して，また 50 年代に始まったコンピュータの生産販売を通して，IBM は 20 世紀情報産業を代表する企業になった．60 年代と 70 年代のコンピュータ業界シェア率は約 80%．
[9]　**dabbling in economics:** 経済学に手を出す．**dabble in:** to engage in (a secondary activity, usually without serious intent)
[10]　**an economy:** 経済的にひとまとまりをなす地域
[12]　**Littauer** [litáuə] **Center:** ハーヴァード大学経済学部が本拠とする建物
　　　stately: impressive; majestic
[13]　**Harvard Yard:** 縦・横・斜めに歩道が走る，芝生と木々が美しいハーヴァード大学のシンボル．映像で見たい向きは，www.news.harvard.edu/tour/ へ．
[15]　**querulous:** complaining
[16]　*materialize*(*d*): to become real or present; emerge
[22]　**danced to two different beats:** i.e. changed according to two different factors
[25]　**rise and fall:** 盛衰

ing of international trade routes. Over the short term, prices would bounce around more or less randomly. Unfortunately, Houthakker's data failed to match his expectations. No matter how he plotted them, Houthakker could not make the changes in cotton prices fit the bell-shaped model.

But they made a picture whose silhouette Mandelbrot was beginning to see in surprisingly disparate places. Unlike most mathematicians, he confronted problems by depending on his intuition about patterns and shapes. He mistrusted analysis, but he trusted his mental pictures. And he already had the idea that other laws, with different behavior, could govern random, stochastic phenomena. When he went back to the giant IBM research center in Yorktown Heights, New York, in the hills of northern Westchester County, he carried Houthakker's cotton data in a box of computer cards. Then he sent to the Department of Agriculture in Washington for more, dating back to 1900.

Like scientists in other fields, economists were crossing the threshold into the computer era, slowly realizing that they would have the power to collect and organize and manipulate information on a scale that had been unimaginable before. Not all kinds of information were available, but at least the economists' environment produced a constant supply of numbers. From Mandelbrot's point of view, cotton prices made an ideal data source. The records were complete and they were old, dating back continuously a century or more. Cotton was a piece of the buying-and-selling universe with a centralized market — and therefore centralized record-keeping — because at the turn of the century all the South's cotton flowed through the New York exchange en route to New England, and Liverpool's prices were linked to New York's as well.

Economists in those days shared certain articles of faith about how price changes worked. One was a conviction that small, transient changes had nothing in common with large, long-term changes. Fast fluctuations come randomly. The small-scale ups and downs during a day's transactions are just noise, unpredictable and uninteresting. Long-term changes, however, are a

THE BIRTH OF FRACTAL GEOMETRY

[4] **plot(ted):** to represent graphically on a chart
[5] **the bell-shaped model:**「正規分布曲線」をさす．下図参照．
[6] **silhouette:** outline image.　cf. "a faint, unfocused image" (p. 140, l. 3)
[7] **disparate places:** entirely different fields
[12] **stochastic phenomena:** occurrences that involve randomness, chance or probability. Examples: throwing of dice, some card games, natural selection.
[13] **Yorktown Heights, New York:** ニューヨーク州ヨークタウン・ハイツは，マンハッタンから真北に60マイルほど行ったあたり．
[15] **computer cards:** 旧型のコンピュータにデータを入力するためのパンチカード
sent to . . . for more: より多くのデータを取りよせた
[19] **threshold** [θréʃ(h)òuld]: a doorway; the point at which something begins
[26] **continuously:** i.e. with no missing period
[28] **the turn of the century:** 世紀の変わり目（の境の数年間）．cf. *the turn of the millenium*
[29] **the South:** アメリカ南部
[30] **exchange:** 取引所
en route [ā:(n) rú:t] **to:** on the way to.　"on route to"とも．
Liverpool: 英国最大の港湾都市として大英帝国の繁栄を支えた．背後にManchesterを中心とする工業地帯が控える．
[32] **articles of faith:** 確信している事がら．cf. He gave me *two pieces of advice*.
[34] **transient** [trǽnʃ(i)ənt/-ziənt]: passing or disappearing in a short while
[35] **fluctuations:** 波動；変動
[36] **transactions:** 取引
noise: irrelevant or meaningless data (⇔ signal/information)

THE
STANDARD
MODEL FOR PLOT-
TING VARIATION IS THE
BELL-SHAPED CURVE ◇ IN THE
MIDDLE, WHERE THE HUMP OF THE
BELL RISES, MOST DATA CLUSTER AROUND THE
AVERAGE ◇ ON THE SIDES, THE LOW AND HIGH EXTREMES FALL OFF RAPIDLY.

Fig. 1　The Bell-Shaped Curve

different species entirely. The broad swings of prices over months or years or decades are determined by deep macroeconomic forces, the trends of war or recession, forces that should in theory give way to understanding. On the one hand the buzz of short-term fluctuation; on the other, the signal of long-term change.

As it happened, that dichotomy had no place in the picture of reality that Mandelbrot was developing. Instead of separating tiny changes from grand ones, his picture bound them together. He was looking for patterns not at one scale or another, but *across* every scale — a symmetry not of right and left or top and bottom, but rather a symmetry of large scales and small.

Indeed, when Mandelbrot sifted the cotton-price data through IBM's computers, he found the astonishing results he was seeking. Each particular price change was random and unpredictable. But the sequence of changes was independent of scale: curves for daily price changes and monthly price changes matched perfectly. Incredibly, analyzed Mandelbrot's way, the degree of variation had remained constant over a tumultuous sixty-year period that saw two World Wars and a depression.

Soon after his study of commodity prices, he came upon a practical problem of intense concern to his corporate patron. Engineers were perplexed by the problem of noise in telephone lines used to transmit information from computer to computer. Electric current carries the information in discrete packets, and engineers knew that the stronger they made the current the better it would be at drowning out noise. But they found that some spontaneous noise could never be eliminated. Once in a while it would wipe out a piece of signal, creating an error.

Although by its nature the transmission noise was random, it was well known to come in clusters. Periods of errorless communication would be followed by periods of errors. And the more closely the engineers looked at the clusters, the more complicated the patterns of errors seemed. An hour might pass with no errors at all. Then an hour might contain errors. Then

THE BIRTH OF FRACTAL GEOMETRY

[2]   **deep macroeconomic forces:**「マクロな経済を根本から動かす力」．個々のマーケットや消費者の動向に焦点を合わせる「ミクロ経済学」に対し，インフレ，デフレ，景気循環のような経済全体についての学を「マクロ経済学」という．

[3]   **the trends of war or recession:**「戦争や不景気の動向」．ある一定期間にそれらが起こる頻度や深刻さのこと．

that should . . . give way to understanding: that are . . . probably not impossible for us to understand

[4]   **in theory:** ⇔ in practice; in actual reality

On the one hand the buzz: On the one hand, there is the noise.   **buzz:** the sound made by bees or a power saw; here, meaningless data.   cf. "just noise" (p. 142, l. 36)

[7]   **dichotomy:**「二分法」．対立する二項に分けて考える思考法．

had no place in: was not part of

[10]   **patterns . . . *across* every scale:** すべての(時間的)スケールに通底するパターン

[12]   **a symmetry of large scales and small:** In technical terms, such symmetry is called "self-similarity." See Figure 3 on p. 148.

[14]   **sifted the cotton-price data through IBM's computers:** i.e. entered the information and let the computers plot it.   sift の原意は「ふるい(にかける)」．

[17]   **the sequence of changes was independent of scale:** the ways the price changed over time [a. varied widely / b. did not vary] from one scale of time to another.

[19]   **analyzed Mandelbrot's way:** マンデルブロの方法では(次の)分析結果が出た

[20]   **tumultuous** [t(j)umʌltʃuəs]: noisy and disorderly. (< tumult: [tjúːmʌlt])

[21]   **depression:** a period of drastic decline. 具体的には1930年代の世界不況をさす．

[23]   **problem of intense concern to . . . :** a problem that greatly worried . . .

his corporate patron: IBM was his *patron* because it provided him with research facilities and paid him for his unique studies.

[24]   **perplexed by:** confused by; troubled by

[26]   **in discrete packets:**「それぞれ離散した固まりにして」．つまり，たとえば強弱2つの電流値を設けて，「強強強弱弱強強」という1パケットが，アルファベットのどれか1文字を表わす——という形で情報を伝える．(*The Universe of English II*, SESSION 8, p. 78 下段のパラグラフ参照)

[28]   **drowning out noise:** 多量の電流でノイズを消し去るというイメージ．

[29]   **spontaneous:** self-generated; having no external cause

[32]   **in clusters:** 集団をなして

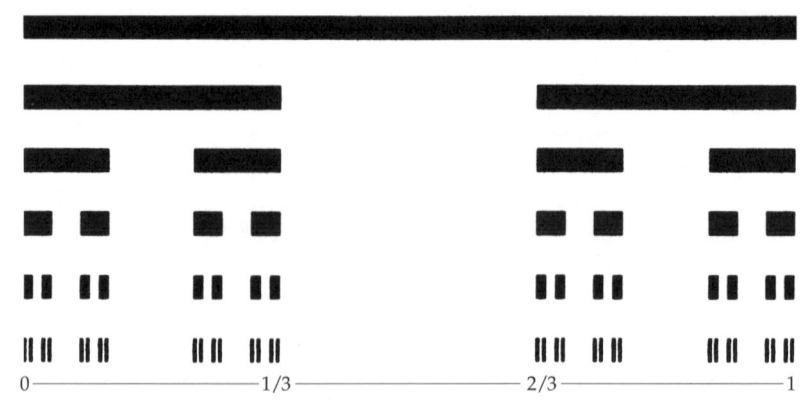

Fig. 2 The Cantor Dust
Begin with a line; remove the middle third; then remove the middle third of the remaining segments; and so on. The Cantor set is the dust of points that remains. They are infinitely many, but their total length is 0.

an hour might pass with no errors. But suppose you then divided the hour with errors into smaller periods of twenty minutes. You would find that here, too, some periods would be completely clean, while some would contain a burst of errors.

Mandelbrot argued — contrary to intuition — that you could never find a time during which errors were scattered continuously. Within any burst of errors, no matter how short, there would always be periods of completely error-free transmission. Furthermore, he discovered a consistent geometric relationship between the bursts of errors and the spaces of clean transmission. On scales of an hour or a second, the proportion of error-free periods to error-ridden periods remained constant.

Engineers had no framework for understanding Mandelbrot's description, but mathematicians did. In effect, Mandelbrot was duplicating an abstract construction known as the Cantor set, after the nineteenth-century mathematician Georg Cantor. To make a Cantor set, you start with the interval of numbers from zero to one, represented by a line segment. Then you remove the middle third. That leaves two segments, and you remove the middle third of each (from one-ninth to two-ninths and from seven-ninths to eight-ninths). That leaves four segments, and you remove the middle third of each — and so

[6]   **a time:** a period of time
[11] **the proportion of error-free periods to error-ridden periods:** エラーのない時間帯とエラーが続く時間帯との長さの比
[13] **framework for understanding:** 理解の枠組み (a basic structure of ideas)
[14] **In effect, Mandelbrot was duplicating:** Mandelbrot was making virtually the same pattern as
[16] **Georg Cantor:** ゲオルグ・カントール (1845–1918). 集合論の創始者として知られるドイツの数学者.
[17] **start with the interval of numbers from zero to one:** まず最初に 0 から 1 に至る数値の区間をとる
[18] **line segment:** 線分. 単に segment とも.
[21] **four segments:** i.e. from zero to one ninth, from two ninths to one third, from two thirds to seven ninths and from eight ninths to one

SESSION 14

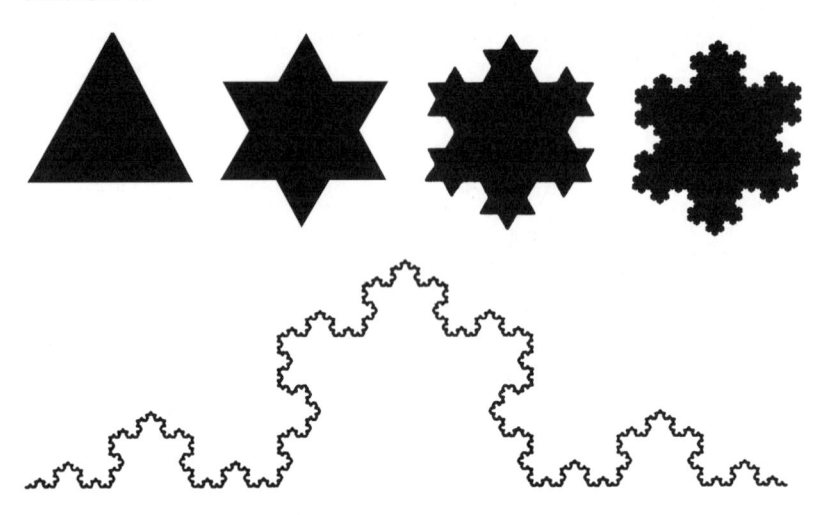

Fig. 3 The Koch Snowflake
Begin with a triangle with sides of length 1. At the middle of each side, add a new triangle one-third the size; and so on. The length of the boundary is 3 × 4/3 × 4/3 × 4/3 . . . — infinity. Yet the area remains less than the area of a circle drawn around the original triangle. Thus an infinitely long line surrounds a finite area.

on to infinity. What remains? A strange "dust" of points, [1] arranged in clusters, infinitely many yet infinitely sparse. Mandelbrot was thinking of transmission errors as a Cantor set arranged in time.

Discontinuity, bursts of noise, Cantor dusts — phenomena [5] like these had no place in the geometries of the past two thousand years. The shapes of classical geometry are lines and planes, circles and spheres, triangles and cones. They represent a powerful abstraction of reality, and they inspired a powerful philosophy of Platonic harmony. Euclid made of them [10] a geometry that lasted two millennia, the only geometry still that most people ever learn. Artists found an ideal beauty in them, Ptolemaic astronomers built a theory of the universe out of them. But for understanding complexity, they turn out to be the wrong kind of abstraction. [15]

Clouds are not spheres, Mandelbrot is fond of saying. Mountains are not cones. Lightning does not travel in a straight line. The new geometry mirrors a universe that is rough, not

THE BIRTH OF FRACTAL GEOMETRY

[2] **infinitely many yet infinitely sparse:**「無限数ありながら無限にまばら」．"dust" の数は n 回の操作後には，2^n になるので無限回後には無限になる．しかしその間のスペースも無限に 1 に近づいていく．つまり，無限個の "dust" を合わせても総計の長さはゼロにしかならない．

[6] **the geometries of the past two thousand years:** ユークリッドが『原論』(Elements) で 5 つの公準をもとに幾何学の体系化に着手したのは紀元前 300 年ごろのこと．

[9] **inspire(d):** 生み出す力となる

[10] **powerful philosophy of Platonic harmony:** プラトン (Plato [pléitou], 427?–347 B.C.) のイデア論は，後に延々と展開されるヨーロッパの形而上学と美学に決定的な影響を与えた．この世にある皿はどれも完全な円ではなく，その円さは「イデア的」(ideal) なものである．しかし世界は円を装い，円に収斂し，円を希求する多くのものから成っている．そうしたイデア的構成要素こそが真に実在する——という真理観と美意識は，ユークリッド幾何学のそれと強い整合性をもつ．

[13] **Ptolemaic** [tàləméiik] **astronomers:** プトレマイオス (Ptolemy, A.D. 2 世紀) 派の天文学者．天動説の立場から天体の統一美にあふれる運行を説明した．

[14] **understanding complexity:**「複雑性を理解する」ことは，1960 年代以降の科学の動きの一大スローガンと言える．流体の運動や気候の変動などを扱う「カオス理論」以外でも，現象を一義的に切るのではなく，矛盾や無限性を内包するものとしてみるアプローチが，理系・文系の諸学に広がっている．

rounded, scabrous, not smooth. It is a geometry of the pitted, [1] pocked, and broken up, the twisted, tangled, and intertwined. The understanding of nature's complexity awaited a suspicion that the complexity was not just random, not just accident. It required a faith that the interesting feature of a lightning bolt's [5] path, for example, was not its direction, but rather the distribution of zigs and zags. Mandelbrot's work made a claim about the world, and the claim was that such odd shapes carry meaning. The pits and tangles are more than blemishes distorting the classic shapes of Euclidean geometry. They are often the [10] keys to the essence of a thing.

THE BIRTH OF FRACTAL GEOMETRY

[1] **scabrous:** ざらざら(がさがさ，でこぼこ)した
the pitted, pocked, and broken up: ぼこぼこで，ぶつぶつして，きれぎれになったもの
[2] **the twisted, tangled, and intertwined:** ねじれ，もつれ，からまりあったもの
[3] **The understanding of nature's complexity awaited a suspicion . . . :** Before we could understand nature's complexity, someone had to suspect . . . .
[4] **the complexity was not just random, not just accident:** たとえばマンデルブロは，海岸線の複雑な形が「単にでたらめに」できているのではないことを，単純なモデルによって示した．Figure 3 および巻頭のカラー図版参照． **accident:** 偶然の(出来事)．*I ran into him by accident.*
[6] **distribution of zigs and zags:** ある方向への動きと別な方向への動きが全体としてどのような分布を見せているかということ
[9] **blemishes:** 美観をそこねるもの；キズ

On the Word "Fractal"

While he was preparing his first major book, Mandelbrot came across the adjective *fractus* (from the verb *frangere* — to break) in a Latin dictionary. The same Latin root gives the words 'fracture' and 'fraction' in modern English. A fracture is a break, for example in a bone: a fraction is a 'broken part' of a whole number — 1/2, 2/3, etc.

Mandelbrot was inspired to create the new word 'fractal' to describe his new geometry.

The Fractal Geometry of Nature came out in 1977, and was hailed as one of the few revolutionary books of mathematics that could be appreciated by general readers.

SESSION 15
The Return of Depression Economics

Paul Krugman

A COUNTRY that does not need to defend its exchange rate can fight recessions easily simply by cutting interest rates as low as necessary, even all the way to zero. But what if a zero interest is not low enough? What if, even at a zero rate, businesses do not want to invest as much as consumers want to save? This is the dreaded "liquidity trap," in which monetary policy finds itself "pushing on a string." Attempts to expand the economy by easing credit fail because banks and consumers alike prefer holding safe, liquid cash to investing in risky, less-liquid bonds and stocks.

On the face of it, the U.S. and British economies seemed to approach a liquidity trap during the 1930s. The average interest rate on U.S. Treasury bills during 1939 was only 0.023 percent. But in the postwar years some economists, notably Milton Friedman and Anna Schwartz, argued that monetary policy could nonetheless have been effective in the 1930s if only the Fed had tried harder. Others questioned whether a true liquidity trap is even possible in principle. In any case, the topic seemed to become one of purely historical interest. By 1990 the general view was that a liquidity trap did not happen and will not happen.

Then came Japan. After its "bubble economy" burst in 1991, Japanese authorities were at first reluctant to cut interest rates for fear of reinflating the bubble. Since 1996, however, short-term rates have been well under one percent and have slipped

THE RETURN OF DEPRESSION ECONOMICS

　1991年のバブル崩壊以降，日本経済は停滞システムのなかにとらわれた．その問題を国際的・歴史的視野から眺める論考を読んでみよう．著者 ポール・クルーグマン (1953－)はマサチューセッツ工科大学教授で，自由経済の健全な発展のために慎重な規制の必要を説くケインズ派寄りの経済学者．共和党などの保守派勢力(市場の力を信じる自由経済礼賛者)に対し，政府の果たすべき機能の重要性を訴える論を展開している．1999年の *Foreign Affairs* 誌に載ったこの記事では，日本を含むアジアの経済危機が，社会の立ち後れと未熟な資本主義精神によるものだという考え方に異議を唱え，矛盾を受け入れつつ経済を統制していくべきだと提唱している．

[Notes]

[1] **defend its exchange rate:**「為替レートを防衛する」．Lowering interest rates usually causes inflation and brings down the value (= exchange rate) of the nation's currency.

[4] **What if, even at a zero rate . . . :** Normally, zero interest rates will [a. boost / b. freeze] the economy because businesses will be [a. willing / b. unwilling] to borrow money for investments, and consumers will choose to [a. spend / b. save] money.

[5] **businesses:** any commercial organizations (e.g. companies, corporations, etc.)

[6] **"liquidity trap":**「流動性の罠」．a state in which reducing interest rates fails to boost the economy.

[7] **"pushing on a string":** i.e. ineffective　cf. *pull strings:*（陰で)糸を引く

[8] **easing credit:** making it easier to borrow money

[9] **holding safe, liquid cash:** 流動性の高い(すぐに使える)現金の方が安全なので，それをキープしておくということ．**liquid:** easy to move from place to place

[10] **bonds and stocks:** 債券や株

[11] **On the face of it:** On the surface; at first sight

[13] **Treasury bills:**（米国)財務省短期証券

[15] **Milton Friedman:** ミルトン・フリードマン(1912－)．アメリカの経済学者．ケインズの理論を批判し，政府の統制に批判的な勢力の中心的スポークスマンとなった．主著『資本主義と自由』．1976年ノーベル経済学賞受賞．
Anna Schwartz: アンナ・シュワーツ(1915－)．フリードマンと共に『米国貨幣史 1867–1960』を著した貨幣経済の専門家で，自由市場の擁護者．

[16] **nonetheless:** despite the difficulties
if only the Fed had tried harder: if only the federal government had pursued monetary policy more strongly. 1929年の株価大暴落のあとでも，金融当局が破産の危機に瀕していた銀行に資産を投入して，倒産パニックを未然に防いでいたら大恐慌にまではいたらなかったという見方は現在でも根強い．

[19] **one of purely historical interest:** a topic that is no longer relevant to us

[24] **reinflating:** ふたたび膨らませる．inflation/deflation は，もともと(風船などが)膨らむ／しぼむ，というイメージ．

to a quarter of one percent. Yet these extremely low rates were unable to prevent a slide into recession, let alone reverse the stagnation that has plagued the Japanese economy since 1992. Since few economists believe that shaving the last few decimal points off interest rates would make any significant difference, Japan really is caught in a classic trap, where zero is not low enough.

Japan's experience shows not only that advanced modern economies can get into a liquidity trap, but that the easy assumption that fiscal policy can get an economy out of that trap is far too optimistic. We may castigate Japan's leaders for their failure to act decisively; but similar mistakes could easily be made in the United States or Europe.

If it is true that the ghosts of the 1930s are once again stalking the earth, the obvious question is why now, after all these years? The standard answer is that some nations are paying for their failure to obey the necessary dictates of free markets. Asian economies, in particular, are being punished for the sins of crony capitalism. And every country that has gotten into trouble does turn out, once the crisis puts its policies in the spotlight, to have made major mistakes. It allowed banks to take unsupervised risks yet retain implicit government backing, encouraged corporations to take on excessive debt, and so on. Yet the idea that economies are being punished for their weaknesses is ultimately unconvincing on at least two grounds. For one, the scale of the punishment seems wholly disproportionate to the crime. Why should bad investment decisions lead not merely to a slowdown in growth but to a massive collapse in output and employment? Furthermore, if the fault lies with the countries, why have so many of them gotten into trouble at the same time?

A parable may be useful here. Imagine that some stretch of road has recently been the scene of an unusual number of accidents. Those who get into accidents naturally become the subject of special attention, and it becomes clear that in just about every case the victims of accidents were themselves partly to blame: they had had too much to drink, their tires were bald,

[2] **recession:** 景気後退 (< recede: to move back). クルーグマンは1990年代のアジアの長引く不況を，30年代の the Great Depression に対して the Great Recession と呼んでいる．
let alone . . . : not to mention . . . ; much less . . .
[3] **stagnation:** 景気低迷 (< stagnant: not moving)
plague(d): to give trouble to. 原意は「疫病」(cf. p. 166, l. 30)
[4] **shaving the last few decimal points off interest rates:** つまり，たとえば0.05% (0.0005倍)をゼロにしてしまうこと．
[6] **a classic trap:** i.e. the well-known "liquidity trap"
[9] **the easy assumption . . . is far too optimistic:** この段落と前の段落との間にあった5つの段落をカットした．そこでは，主に日本政府の景気回復策を取りあげ，それらが効を奏さなかった理由が述べられている．
[11] **castigate:** to severely criticize
[14] **the ghosts of the 1930s:** i.e. the haunting fears of economic disaster like the one which occurred in the 1930s.
stalking the earth: cf. p. 89, note [3]
[16] **are paying for their failure to obey the necessary dictates:** are being punished for not obeying the necessary rules
[18] **crony capitalism:** 親族や仲間を優遇する「なれあい資本主義」．
[20] **once the crisis puts its policies in the spotlight:** i.e. once the country faces a crisis, and people start examining the government's policies
[21] **allowed banks to take unsupervised risks yet retain implicit government backing:** 銀行がリスクを冒すのを放置しておきながら，その行動に政府が暗黙の承認を与え続けた．
[26] **the scale of the punishment seems wholly disproportionate:** i.e. the punishment seems [a. disproportionately severe / b. disproportionately light]
[28] **a massive collapse in output and employment:** a shocking fall in production and employment
[32] **parable:** 寓話；たとえ話
some stretch of road: 道路のある区間
[35] **just about:** nearly; virtually
[37] **bald:** i.e. worn out

and so on. The investigators therefore conclude that the problem was not the road but the drivers.

What is wrong with this conclusion? It is doubly biased. First, virtually any car or driver, if subjected to close scrutiny, will turn out to have some flaws. Are these victims clearly more flawed than average? Second, even if they are somewhat worse drivers than normal, the fact that so many of them had accidents here rather than somewhere else suggests that the fault does lie largely with the road, all the same.

To spell it out: Troubled Asian economies have turned out to have many policy and institutional weaknesses, but if America or Europe should get into trouble next year or the year after, we can be sure that in retrospect analysts will find equally damning things to say about Western values and institutions. And it is very hard to make the case that Asian policies were any worse in the 1990s than they had been in previous decades, so why did so much go so wrong so recently?

The answer is that the world became vulnerable to its current travails not because economic policies had not been reformed, but because they had. Around the world countries responded to the very real flaws in post-Depression policy regimes by moving back toward a regime with many of the virtues of pre-Depression free-market capitalism. However, in bringing back the virtues of old-fashioned capitalism, we also brought back some of its vices, most notably a vulnerability both to instability and sustained economic slumps.

Consider four kinds of policy reforms in particular. First is the liberalization of international transactions. In the 1930s and 1940s, experiences like Austria's led to the near-universal adoption of controls on international capital movements, in many cases as part of a general system of exchange control. The original Bretton Woods system was, in fact, crucially dependent on such controls as a way to prevent the "rigidification" of exchange rates by the threat of speculative attack. But over time exchange controls came to be seen not simply as a nuisance but as a source of major abuses, distortions in incentives, and corruption. So first advanced countries, then many developing

THE RETURN OF DEPRESSION ECONOMICS

[3] **biased:** prejudiced; unfair
[4] **if subjected to close scrutiny:** if examined thoroughly
[5] **more flawed:** [a. more to blame / b. more damaged]
[8] **the fault does lie largely with the road, all the same:** the road is nevertheless the main cause of the accidents
[10] **To spell it out:** To say it clearly and explicitly
[11] **policy and institutional weaknesses:** 政策的・制度的欠陥
[13] **in retrospect:** when looking back
[14] **damning things to say:** severe criticisms
[15] **make the case:** to argue or to prove
[18] **vulnerable** [vʌ́lnərəbl]: at risk of being hurt, attacked, etc.
[19] **travail(s):** trouble; suffering
[21] **responded to . . . by moving back . . . :** cf. *Stacy responded to her mother's cruel remark by running out and not returning home until midnight.*
      post-Depression policy regimes: 1920年代の自由放任経済体制が大不況を招いたとして，それ以後，ケインズらの理論を基盤に形作られた，政府の役割を重視する経済体制をさす．
[23] **virtue(s):** a merit (⇔ vice)
[25] **a vulnerability . . . to . . . instability:** 不安定な状態に陥りやすいこと
[28] **liberalization of international transactions:** 国際取引の自由化．たとえば国内業者の保護のために設けていた関税を撤廃すること．
[29] **experiences like Austria's:** オーストリアでは1931年5月，中央銀行(クレディート・アンシュタルト)が倒産，これが世界金融恐慌の発端となった．
[31] **system of exchange control:** 為替管理体制
[32] **Bretton Woods:** アメリカ，ニューハンプシャー州の町．1944年7月に戦後をにらんだ国際金融体制についての会議が開かれ，世界銀行とIMF (International Monetary Fund) の設立，固定相場制(全参加国がドルに対する通貨レートを固定すること)の採用が決定された．この体制は，1973年初頭まで続いた．
      crucially dependent on such controls: 「そのようなレート調整が不可欠なものであった」．ブレトン・ウッズ体制は固定相場制だったが，レートが現実に即さなくなった場合，参加国の協議によって値を調整(control)することになっていた．
[33] **the "rigidification" of exchange rates by the threat of speculative attack:** 投機的な操作(による通貨価値の下落や高騰)を恐れるあまり，(各国通貨間の)為替レートが(現実に即した流動性を失って)一定値に "凝り固まって" しまうこと．
      rigidification < rigid: inflexible; unable to change
[34] **over time:** as time passed; gradually
[35] **nuisance:** something annoying; a bother. *Flies are flies; they are a nuisance.*
[36] **a source of major abuses:** something that leads to serious cases of bad practice
      distortions in incentives: (経済活動を推進する)動機を歪めるもの

countries, moved toward full currency convertibility and free capital movement. But in so doing they left themselves vulnerable once again to destabilizing speculative attacks.

Second is the liberalization of domestic financial markets. In the shadow of the 1930s, almost all countries established tightly regulated, heavily guaranteed banking systems. These systems tended to be safe but inefficient, paying depositors low returns and doing a pretty bad job of transferring savings to their most efficient uses. Over time, a loosening of regulation made financial systems far more competitive and efficient. At the same time, however, it revived the possibility of destabilizing financial panics like the one that almost derailed the U. S. economy in the autumn of 1997.

Third is the reestablishment of price stability. In the postwar era most countries experienced substantial inflation, with a worldwide explosion of prices in the 1970s and early 1980s. This inflation needed to be brought under control and ultimately was. Almost all nations now have achieved remarkably stable prices and credibly established the belief that they will continue to maintain price stability in the future. But it turned out that inflation had some unappreciated advantages. For one thing, countries that found themselves with substantial internal debt could simply inflate that debt down to manageable proportions, as Japan did with bad real estate loans in the 1970s. More important, a country with five percent inflation and eight percent interest rates has much more room to cut rates to fight a recession than a country with stable prices and three percent interest. In other words, advanced countries would be far less vulnerable to liquidity traps had they not been so assiduous about pursuing price stability in the 1980s.

Finally there is the restoration of fiscal discipline. Many countries ran huge budget deficits in the 1970s and 1980s. As a result the 1990s have seen a great push toward fiscal responsibility, with European deficit spending curtailed first by the Maastricht Treaty and now by the post-EMU "stability pact," while the United States finally eliminated its budget deficit. Although pushed by its slump into deficit spending, Japan has

THE RETURN OF DEPRESSION ECONOMICS

[1] **full currency convertibility:**「完全通貨交換制」．どの国の通貨とも制限なく交換できる制度

[4] **In the shadow of the 1930s:** During the period when the dark memories of the 1930s were keenly felt. 1930年代の不況時代には銀行システムが崩壊し，預金者が押し寄せる「取り付け騒ぎ」が世界で頻発した．

[5] **tightly regulated, heavily guaranteed banking systems:** 銀行の融資額や利率にきびしい制限を設け，政府の強いバックアップ体制をしいた銀行制度

[7] **depositors** < deposit: to put (money) in the bank (⇔ withdraw)

[8] **doing a pretty bad job:** being poor or ineffective.　cf. *You're not doing a very good job of convincing me.*
transferring savings to their most efficient uses: 預金者から預かった金を最高の効率で運用できる形にする

[11] **destabilizing financial panics:** sudden waves of fear which spread through the financial community and upset the economy. "destabilizing" は形容詞的用法．

[12] **the one that almost derailed the U.S. economy in the autumn of 1997:** 1997年秋，アジア経済危機 (p. 161 note [12]) に際して，米国金融界で起きたパニックをさす．　**derail:** to throw something off track

[16] **explosion of prices:** a sudden great increase of prices

[19] **credibly established the belief that ... :** convinced people that ....

[21] **inflation had some unappreciated advantages:** i.e. there was a [a. good / b. bad] side to inflation which was [a. well / b. not] recognized.

[22] **substantial internal debt:**（国債など）国内での多額の負債

[23] **inflate that debt down:** インフレーションによって負債額を目減りさせる

[24] **as Japan did with bad real estate loans:** ひどい不動産向け貸付を抱えていた日本がそうしたように

[26] **cut rates to fight a recession:** cf. p. 153, note [4].

[29] **had they not been so assiduous about pursuing price stability:** i.e. if they [a. had worked harder at / b. had been more relaxed about] bringing down inflation.
assiduous [əsídʒuəs]: enthusiastic; persistent

[32] **deficit(s):** ⇔ surplus

[33] **the 1990s have seen a great push toward fiscal responsibility:** i.e. in the 1990s many countries decided to [a. increase / b. limit] expenditure.

[34] **deficit spending:**（国債発行などによる）赤字を伴なう支出
curtail(ed): to cut down; limit

[35] **Maastricht** [máːstrikt] **Treaty:** 1991年12月，オランダのマーストリヒトでEC 11カ国が調印した欧州連合創設に向けての条約．EU (European Union) 議会の強化，中央銀行の設立と通貨統一，共同防衛のための政策協議など，連合に向けての大きな決意を盛り込んでいる．
post-EMU "stability pact": EMU (European Monetary Union) の成立以後，参加諸国は，「安定協定」とも呼びうる取り決めで膨張型の財政を規制している．

attempted whenever possible to reverse course and move back toward balance — and in so doing helped push the economy back into recession.

In short, the reason Depression economics has now re-emerged as a real concern is not that governments did not do the right thing, but that they did. Truly, no good deed goes unpunished.

At the moment there is a sort of odd inconsistency in the attitudes of responsible people toward such issues as capital controls and inflation. Nearly everyone is glad that not all developing countries managed to liberalize their capital accounts before the 1997 crisis hit; in particular, China, thank heavens, still has a nonconvertible capital account. But a Malaysian-type reversion to capital controls is regarded with horror. Similarly, everyone sleeps better knowing that the United States has two percent inflation and five percent interest rates, not stable prices and three percent interest rates — but proposals that Japan should actively seek a target of three or four percent inflation are still an anathema. It is a good thing, in other words, to be there, but not to go there.

Still, it is hard to avoid concluding that sooner or later we will have to turn the clock at least part of the way back: to limit capital flows for countries that are unsuitable for either currency unions or free floating; to reregulate financial markets to some extent; and to seek low but not too low inflation rather than price stability. We must heed the lessons of Depression economics, lest we be forced to relearn them the hard way.

THE RETURN OF DEPRESSION ECONOMICS

[2] **balance:** i.e. balance of revenue and expenditure; zero deficit
[11] **liberalize their capital accounts:**「資本勘定」を自由化する． **capital account:** 借入額，貸与額を含む総資本の明細
[12] **the 1997 crisis:** 1997 年 7 月のタイのバーツ切り下げに端を発し，インドネシア，韓国等，それまで奇跡的と言われた高成長を達成してきた国々の経済を一挙に冷え込ませた「アジア経済危機」．

China, thank heavens, still has a nonconvertible capital account: It is fortunate that the Chinese yuan (元) is still not freely exchanged for other currencies.
[14] **Malaysian-type reversion to capital controls:** マレーシアのマハティール (Mahathir) 首相は，アジア通貨危機の原因を国際的な投機資金グループの陰謀だとして，国際的な資金流出入をシャットアウトする政策をすすめた．
[15] **everyone sleeps better knowing that the United States has two percent inflation and five percent interest rates:** i.e. it is comforting that the current inflation rate in the U.S. is [a. as high as / b. as low as] two percent.
[19] **anathema** [ənǽθəmə]: something that is strongly disliked; a curse

It is a good thing ... to be there, but not to go there: 自然とインフレになるのはよいが，わざわざインフレを作り出そうとするのはよくない，ということ．
[22] **to turn the clock ... back:** i.e. to adopt the (more controlled) policies of the past
[23] **currency unions:**「通貨統合」がヨーロッパで達成され統一通貨 euro が登場して以来，世界の通貨をどのように統合していくかという議論が一段と盛り上がっている．
[24] **free floating:** 規制をなくし自由な浮動に任せること
[26] **heed:** to listen to and learn from
[27] **lest we be:** so that we will not be

SESSION 16

Time in Medieval Europe

David Duncan

WHAT did time mean to a farmer in the Rhine River valley in the year 800? What sort of calendar did, say, a weaver use in central France? Or a fisherman on the often drizzly coast of Northumbria?

Little is known about commoners during a period when even chronicles and official records of kings and nobles are scarce. On a continent of illiterates barely getting by, most people seem to have spent their days hoeing fields, avoiding wild beasts, worrying about crops and the weather, burying the dead, celebrating marriages and local saint's days, and telling stories around hearth fires during the long, cold, deadly winters. They lived, ate their meager portions, bore children, repaired leaks in their thatch roofs, tried to avoid armies if they came into the area, took an excited peek at the lord or king if he came along their road, grudgingly paid taxes, attended mass, followed the orders of the lord's foreman, and died, all in a continuous cycle of days and years that to them had no discernible past or future.

To farmers on the Rhine or weavers in France, who had little control over their environment or their lives, the whole idea of attempting to calculate and measure something as unfathomable and unremitting as time was either blasphemous or laughable. The few written insights into the mind-set of commoners on the subjects of time, calendars, and science in general suggest a great deal of snickering at monks, scholars, and

TIME IN MEDIEVAL EUROPE

極東の島国の帝が新都平安京を造り，海を越えた大国へ留学僧らを送り出したころ，西ヨーロッパでは一人の武帝が，ローマ以来最大の領土を支配していた．フランク王国の王シャルルマーニュである．教皇レオ3世からローマ帝国皇帝の冠を授けられたこの王は，しかし教養の面からはどうだったろう．歴史の本には，「カロリング・ルネッサンスを推進した」と記されている．だが，皇帝自身は読み書きが満足でなかったらしい．貴族・騎士らもほとんどが書物の読めない人種だった．東方に目を向ければ，イスラム世界は商業的・文化的繁栄のまっただなかにあった．アーバース朝に君臨する第5代カリフ，ハールーン・アッラシードは遠い西の国の皇帝に，一度に12時間も計時できるという壮麗な砂時計を贈ったと伝えられている．だが，実際それがどれほど有用だったかは定かでない．というのも，当時のヨーロッパはまだ，計時が意味をもつ社会に入っていなかったからである．ここに収めたのは，暦について，有史以来の歴史を綴ったベストセラーの一節．

[Notes]

[4] **drizzly** < drizzle: 霧雨
Northumbria: ノーサンブリア王国．5世紀から9世紀ごろにかけてアングロ・サクソン人が興したイングランド七王国の一つ．北イングランドに位置し，リンディスファーン島の修道院はイギリス・キリスト教文化の最初の拠点となったが，それもこの時代にはヴァイキングによって破壊されていた．

[5] **commoners:** ordinary people (without noble rank or title).   cf. p. 48, l. 12

[6] **chronicle(s):** 年代記

[7] **On a continent of illiterates barely getting by:** まだ文字文化を持たない人々が細々と生きていた(ヨーロッパ)大陸では

[8] **hoe(ing):** くわで耕す

[10] **local saint's days:** saint's day は，聖人を祭る日．国や地域によって祝う聖人祭が異なることがある．例えば，聖パトリック祭(3月17日)は，主にアイルランドや米国で祝われる．

[12] **ate their meager portions:** ate what little share of food they could get.   **meager:** small (amount); insufficient

[13] **thatch roofs:** 草や藁でふいた屋根

[14] **took an excited peek at:** 胸を躍らせてそっとのぞいた

[15] **grudgingly:** reluctantly; unwillingly

[16] **lord's foreman:** 民衆を直接監督する領主の家来

[21] **unfathomable:** too deep (to measure or understand)

[22] **unremitting:** continuing with the same force; persistent
blasphemous: showing contempt or lack of respect for sacred things

[23] **written insights into the mind-set of commoners on the subjects of time:** 一般庶民が時間というものに対しどんな捉え方をしていたかを見せてくれる書き物

[25] **snickering** < snicker: laugh quietly and disrespectfully.   cf. *snicker-snack* (p. 14, l. 8)

SESSION 16

astrologers bumbling about counting on their fingers and staring at the sky. The Miller in Chaucer's *Canterbury Tales* pokes fun at an astronomer-astrologer, but the verse might also have applied to anyone with their head in the clouds, so to speak:

> *Men sholde nat knowe of Goddes pryvetee.*
> *Ye, blessed be alwey a lewed man*
> *That noght but oonly his bileve kan!*
> *So ferde another clerk with astromye;*
> *He walked in the feeldes for to prye*
> *Upon the sterres, what ther sholde bifalle,*
> *Til he was in a marle-pit yfalle.*

In other words, this "clerk," or scholar of astronomy, did not heed what every "lewed" — unlearned — Christian knew and believed: that "men should not know of God's private affairs." He foolishly studied the moon and stars and was such a dolt, according to the Miller, that he was looking up when he should have been looking down at his feet — and fell in a "marle-pit."

Still, even the simplest Christian presumably had at least a vague knowledge of critical events in Christian history. In fact, for most people this timeline remained far more real than a history of their own era: the sequence of the Creation and events in the Old Testament; and episodes in Christ's life and the lives of the saints. These events needed to be recorded and dated to become valid, and it was this need that motivated time reckoners such as Dionysius and Bede to devise their year-by-year dating schemes in an age when otherwise few people cared about what year it was beyond year 6 or 10 in the reign of their local king or squire.

Several chronological schemes were proposed and used besides Dionysius Exiguus's *anno Domini*. These included the old Roman system of fifteen-year indictions, which had started with the first year of Constantine's reign in 312. Iberians used something called the Era of Spain, which tracked Easter cycles starting with the Roman conquest of Iberia in 38 B.C. Others observed the Era of the Passion, with year 1 dated back to A.D. 33, supposedly the date of Christ's crucifixion and

TIME IN MEDIEVAL EUROPE

[1] **bumbling** < bumble: （口の中で）もぐもぐいう．cf. *mumbling* (p. 104, l. 3)

[2] **Chaucer's *Canterbury Tales*:** ジェフリー・チョーサー Geoffrey Chaucer (1340?–1400) は，英詩の父と称される詩人．その代表作が『カンタベリ物語』(1387–1400) で，これはカンタベリへの巡礼のために集まった様々な階級の人々（騎士，女子修道院長，商人，粉屋など約 30 名）が道中のつれづれに，各自物語を聞かせるという趣向の物語集．引用は粉屋の語る話 (*The Miller's Tale*) から．

poke(s) fun at: あざける，からかう，茶化す

[3] **astronomer-astrologer:** チョーサーの時代には天文学 (astronomy) と占星術 (astrology) は明確に区別されてはいなかった．

[4] **with their head in the clouds:** 夢みたいなことを考えて；空想に耽って

[5] 「粉屋の話」は人妻をめぐる男 3 人の騙し合いを描いた滑稽詩（ファブリオ）．引用されている箇所では，大工を騙すために気がふれたふりをするオックスフォードの学生を見て，占星術・天文学に夢中になり過ぎておかしくなってしまったと大工は思い，同情して言ったせりふ．以下その現代英語訳．

> Men should not know of God's secrets. / Yes, may an unlearned man be always happy / Who knows nothing but his creed! / So fared another clerk with his astronomy, / He walked in the fields to peer / Upon the stars, to see what was to happen, / Till he had fallen into a clay pit.

[15] **dolt:** 愚か者

[18] **Still, even the simplest Christian . . . :** 中世ヨーロッパでは天地創造，キリストの生誕・復活，最後の審判などを題材とした演劇が盛んに行なわれ，一般の民衆もこうしたものを通じて聖書中の記事に親しんでいたと考えられる．

[25] **reckoners** < reckon: to count or calculate

Dionysius [dàiəníʃiəs]: ディオニュシオス・エクシグウス (*c.* 530–?)．ローマの学僧．キリスト生誕の暦年を決定し，いわば人類に西暦をもたらした．

Bede [biːd]: ベーダ (673–735), Baeda [biːdə] とも．"the Venerable Bede"（尊師ベーダ）の通称を持つ，ノーサンブリア王国の聖職者．西暦を使ったイギリス教会史 *Historia ecclesiastica gentis Anglorum* を書いたほか，時間論，暦論についての著作 (*De temporibus, De temporum ratione*) がある．

[28] **squire:** 郷士，地主，地方の名士

[30] **anno Domini:** 西暦，すなわちキリスト生誕年から数え始める年号方式．ラテン語で 'from the year of (our) Lord' の意味．略号 A.D. (cf. B.C.: before Christ)

[31] **fifteen-year indictions:** A.D. 312 年 9 月 1 日を起点とする「15 年紀」．（課税のための資産査定を 15 年ごとに行なったところから．）

[32] **Constantine** [kɔ́nstəntàin / -tìːn]: コンスタンチヌス 1 世は 312 年に西方ローマの支配権を確立．翌年「ミラノの勅令」によってキリスト教を公認．

[35] **the Passion:** キリストの受難

dated back to: "back" とは制定時点から見て，ということ．

[36] **crucifixion:** （キリストの）磔刑，十字架上の死

resurrection. But none was more popular as a possible alternative to the year of our Lord than a timeline based on the date of the Creation as year 1. Bede, for instance, carefully studied what he considered the relevant passages in the Bible and somehow came up with a specific day that he believed God began forming the sky, earth, and water: March 18, 3952 B.C. If Europeans had decided to use Bede's calculation of the Creation, our year 2000 would be 5951 A.C. — after the Creation.

And what about predicting the future? Time in Christianity was, of course, heading someplace: to Christ's second coming and eventually to eternity, events that would occur along the same timeline as past events. This made it tempting for medieval chronologists to try to date not only the beginning of the world, but the end. A century before Charlemagne, one scholar in the royal Frankish court calculated, using poor addition, that the world was 5,928 years old in the year 727. Applying this to the notion that the world was moving through six ages of 1,000 years apiece, this computor decided that the world would end in exactly 72 years.

Bede, following the example of Augustine, condemned such predictions. He insisted that future time belonged to God, "who, as the Everlasting, created times whenever he wanted, knows the end of times, and puts an end to the fluctuating processes of time when he wishes." Still, most people who thought about such things believed that however old the earth might be, the end was near. "The world is growing old," wrote Fredegar, a seventh-century Frankish chronicler who wrote in corrupt Latin. "We live at the end of time."

Medieval chroniclers were constantly looking for portents of the grand finale: plagues, earthquakes, eclipses, battles, and omens of every kind. Mystics looked for signs of the Antichrist's coming, with writers such as the remarkable theologian and poet Hildegard von Bingen offering vivid descriptions of what he would look like: "A beast with monstrous head, black as coal, with flaming eyes, wearing asses' ears and with gaping jaws decorated with iron hooks."

TIME IN MEDIEVAL EUROPE

[1]　**resurrection** [rèzərékʃən]：（キリストの）復活
　　none was more popular as a possible alternative to (A) than (B)：i.e. A was most commonly used, but outside it, B was the most popular.
[3]　**the Creation:** 天地の創造，創世．旧約聖書 (Old Testament) の「創世紀」(Genesis) に記述されている．
[14]　**Charlemagne** [ʃɑ́:ləmèin]：シャルルマーニュ (742–814)．768 年フランク王国の王．800 年ローマ教皇から西ローマ帝国の帝冠を受けカール 1 世となる．
[15]　**using poor addition:** その足し算が今日の目で見て無価値なものだということ．
[18]　**computor:** 現代では computer と書くと機械が想像されるので，それと区別して「計算する人」の意味でこの綴りを用いている．
[20]　**Augustine** [ɔ́:ɡʌ́stən, ɔ́:ɡəsti:n]：初代キリスト教最大の教父アウグスティヌス (354–430)．その説教集は中世を通じてよく読まれた．
[22]　**the Everlasting:** 永遠の存在者である神
[23]　**fluctuating:** cf. *fluctuations* (p. 24, l. 36; p. 142, l. 35)
[27]　**in corrupt Latin:**（正式のラテン語とは異なる）訛ったラテン語で
[29]　**portents:** 兆候，前兆
[30]　**eclipses:** 日（月）食
[31]　**the Antichrist's coming:** 初期キリスト教徒は，キリスト再臨前に反キリスト (Antichrist) が出現してこの世を悪で満たすであろうと恐れた．
[33]　**Hildegard von Bingen:** ビンゲンはドイツ西部ライン河畔の町．その尼僧院長だったヒルデガルト (1098?–1179) は，中世最大の神秘詩人とうたわれ，絵画や音楽にも異才を発揮した．下の挿画は，彼女が天から受けた啓示を修道僧が羊皮紙に書き取っているところ．

Hildegard records a vision on a wax tablet with a stylus.

Amidst this official pessimism certain dates took on meaning at least for a few, such as the coming of the year 1000, though the *anno Domini* system was still not widely followed. Even where it was, Christians did not necessarily *fear* the end. They expected trials and tribulations and a final, horrific apocalypse, as predicted in the Bible. But they also looked forward to what would come after the current age ended and the calendar truly stopped — when Christ would usher in an age of eternal happiness for the elect, which of course included them.

But despite the "vast indifference to time" that permeated Europe during the reign of Charlemagne, already under way were real changes that centuries later would usher in a revolution in the perception of time. For even though Charlemagne saw clocks as curiosities, his keen interest in them and the idea of telling time made a lasting impression on future generations. At the same time a new invention was spreading slowly across the West: the bell. Called *glocka* in German — whence came our word *clock* — bells were used to signal hours and other times of the day. By legend, church bells were invented in the fifth century in the town of Nola in Campania — thus the term "Campanola bells." Another legend credits Pope Sabinianus (pope from 604 to 606) with ordering churches to mark the hours of the day by ringing their bells. Bells probably spread first to monasteries, where monks used hand bells to signal canonical hours. Later tower bells summoned people to mass.

Bells probably had a minimal impact on the average person. Yet they were the first mechanical "clocks" to govern everyday life in Europe, usually rung according to time as measured on a water clock or sundial. Imagine a farmer in a field being told to have an acre plowed by the time the bell tower rang noon, when before he had been told by his lord simply to work until the sun was high. Or think of a clock that signaled the beginning of a mass with an exactitude never before known when hours were measured using the position of the sun in the sky. This was an entirely different way of viewing time, with a measurement of it being assigned a specific value.

TIME IN MEDIEVAL EUROPE

[3] **Even where it was:** Even where the *anno Domini* system was followed
[5] **trials:**「試練」．キリスト教の教えでは(ユダヤ教，イスラム教も同様)，世界の終末に全人類に対し神の裁き (Last Judgment) が下るとされる．
tribulations: great sufferings
apocalypse [əpɔ́kəlips]: 世界の終末．新約聖書「ヨハネの黙示録」(*The Revelation to John*) にきわめて具体的に記されている．

"*And I heard a voice from heaven, as the voice of many waters, and as the voice of a great thunder: and I heard the voice of harpers harping with their harps: And they sung as it were a new song . . . and no man could learn that song but the hundred and forty and four thousand, which were redeemed from the earth.*" (*Revelation* 14: 2–3. King James Version)

[8] **usher in:** to bring in; introduce
[10] **permeated Europe:** could be found in every part of Europe
[11] **under way:** in progress
[17] *glocka*: 現代ドイツ語の Glocke「鐘」に対応する古高ドイツ語 (*c.* 750–*c.* 1050) の形．
whence came our word *clock*: 厳密に言うと，"clock" はドイツ語からではなく(中期)オランダ語からの借入．ドイツ語形も含め，すべての究極の語源は，中世ラテン語の *clocca* (bell)．英語の初出は 1370 年頃．
[20] **Campania:** イタリア南部の州．古代から良質のブロンズの鋳造地．イタリア語では「鐘」のことを campana という．
[21] **credits Pope Sabinianus with . . . :** 〜の功績が教皇サビニアヌスにあると見なす．cf. *Edison is credited with the invention of the light bulb.*
[24] **canonical hours:** 時禱(毎日数回定時に行なわれる祈禱の時間)
[29] **sundial:** cf. l. 34
[36] **a measurement of it being assigned a specific value:** ⇔ "to calculate and measure . . . time was either blasphemous or laughable" (p. 162, l. 21).

SESSION 16

The Holy Roman Emperor Charlemagne died on January 28, 814. His empire died soon after, as his heirs argued and fought and divided his realms among them. With it perished the political order that Charlemagne had briefly imposed. So did the emperor's infatuation with learning, manuscripts, and marvelous timepieces, which it turned out was not shared by his immediate successors. They dismissed the scholars from the court and closed the schools for children opened by the emperor. Still, the age of Charlemagne ignited a spark, with the scholar Alcuin of York and others compiling encyclopedias and collecting manuscripts. It also provided an example and a context for quality, taste, humanistic culture, and sound grammar, which laid a foundation for a slow — very slow — evolution toward an era when dates and calendars would begin to matter to more than just a few monks sitting in their cloisters trying to calculate the age of the world and when the end would come.

But Europe was not where the action was for time reckoning and the calendar anyway in Bede's or Charlemagne's era. Indeed, as Europe slept, developments were under way far to the East, where science was not ignored and a long line of brilliant thinkers were making discoveries that centuries later would penetrate at last the darkness of the West to astonish and inspire men like Roger Bacon, and to once again commence the movement of time.

TIME IN MEDIEVAL EUROPE

[5] **infatuation with learning, manuscripts, and . . . timepieces:** 学問や書物や計時器への心酔．シャルルマーニュが進めた文芸復興が，王の個人的嗜好からきたものにすぎないことを匂わす言い方．cf. *I've never seen a man so infatuated with* (= *crazy about*) *a girl as he is with her.*

[9] **ignited a spark:** i.e. provided a dramatic beginning

[10] **Alcuin** [ǽlkwən]：英国出身の哲学者・神学者・教育者 (735?–804)．ベーダの学問体系を継承，カロリング・ルネサンスを主導した．

[16] **cloister(s):** monastery（修道院）

[18] **where the action was:** the center of activity. *The downtown area is mostly poor neighborhoods; it's not where the action is if you're thinking of going to concerts and things.*

for time reckoning and the calendar anyway: ともかくも時の計測や暦に関してはそうだった

[20] **far to the east:** この段落に続く章では，300年ほど時間をさかのぼって，インドのグプタ王朝の数学と天文学の天才アーリアバータ Aryabhata の話が語られる．

[23] **penetrate:** to enter into; pierce

[24] **Roger Bacon:** (1214?–92?) 英国の修道僧で近代科学の先駆者．当時使われていたシーザー暦では，1年に約11分の遅れが生じることをつきとめた．

SESSION 17
Arresting the Flux of Life

Naomi Rosenblum

WHETHER facing the natural landscape or the urban scene, many photographers other than those investigating motion for scientific reasons found that they, too, were eager to arrest the continuous flux of life, to scrutinize and savor discrete segments of time, and to capture them on glass plates and, later, film. This first became possible with the short-focal-length lenses on stereograph cameras. By 1859, Edward Anthony in New York (*pl. 1*) and Adolphe Braun and Hippolyte Jouvin in Paris (*pl. 2*) among others had begun to make and publish stereograph views of the "fleeting effects" of crowds and traffic on the principal streets of urban centers and at festive events. Acclaimed because they seemed to embody "all life and motion," these views also disclose the distinctiveness of different cultural environments. Stereographs of city streets reveal at a glance the profound dissimilarities between public life in New York and Paris, for example, while others show the contrast between social conditions in industrialized countries and in those being opened to colonization and exploitation.

That this interest in the flux of urban life engaged painters of the time as well as photographers is apparent in canvases by the French Impressionists that seem to capture as if by camera the moving forms of people and traffic in the streets and parks of Paris. Besides a preference for high horizons and blurred figures, similar to that seen in numbers of stereographs of city

ARRESTING THE FLUX OF LIFE

中世ヨーロッパに広まった鐘が，テクノロジーによる時の変容の第一歩だとするなら，その約千年後にひらけた光学像の焼き付け技術は，現代のディジタル映像処理に直結する「過去の物象化」の第一歩だといえる．今から百年ほど前，手軽な写真機の登場によって人間と時との関係にどんな変化がおとずれたのか，写真史の定番教科書 *A World History of Photography* の一節を読んでみよう．

[Notes]
[2] those [photographers who were] **investigating motion for scientific reasons:** たとえば，アメリカの写真家イードウィアード・マイブリッジ Eadweard Muybridge は，「疾走する馬の脚が4本とも全部，同時に地面から離れることがあるか」という論争にけりをつけるために，1872年，馬の連続瞬間撮影を成功させた．その結果，馬の4本の脚は確かに同時に離れる瞬間があるが，それは，それまで信じられていたように馬の脚が前後に開くときではなく，脚が内側に折り込まれるときであることが証明された．マイブリッジが映画の創始者のように言われることがあるのは，こうした連続写真を後に「動物の動きを見る装置」という意味の「ズープラクシスコープ zoopraxiscope」という装置にかけて，一種の「活動写真」の上映に成功したからである．
[4] **to arrest the continuous flux of life:** i.e. to capture a moment of life
scrutinize and savor: to examine closely and enjoy
[5] **discrete segments of time:** 時の流れから切り出された瞬間瞬間
[6] **glass plates and, later, film:** イーストマン社が感光性セルロイドのロールの特許をとったのは1889年のこと．それ以前はガラス板が使われていた．ガラスに臭化カリウムを含む液を塗った wet plate の発明は1847年．臭化銀とゼラチンを使った「乾板」の発明は1878年．ガラス板以前は，1839年に実用化されたダゲレオタイプ(銀板に塗った沃化銀の光化学反応が像を捉える)の時代である．
[7] **stereograph:**「立体写真」．左右に2個のレンズのついたカメラで同時撮影した2枚の写真は，stereoscope に入れて3D像を楽しむ．
[8] **Edward Anthony ... Adolphe Braun ... Hippolyte Jouvin** [ipɔlíːt ʒuvɛ̃]: ここに挙げられた3人のなかでは特にアドルフ・ブラウン(1811–77)の写真が，絵画史に強く影響を与えたといわれている．
[10] **"fleeting effects" of crowds and traffic:** 人や乗り物が「過ぎ去ってゆく感じ」
[12] **Acclaimed:** widely or enthusiastically praised
embody "all life and motion":「生命と運動のすべて」を体現する．当時の批評家の言葉．
[20] **That this interest in the flux of urban life engaged painters ... :** That painters ... were attracted by the flux of urban life

pl. 1 (Above) EDWARD ANTHONY. *New York Street Scene,* 1859. One half of an albumen stereograph. Collection George R. Rinhart.

pl. 2 (Below) HIPPOLYTE JOUVIN. *Porte St. Denis, Paris,* c.1860. Albumen stereograph. Collection Ivan Christ, Paris.

streets and exemplified in Claude Monet's *Boulevard des Capucines* (*pl. 3*) — a view actually painted from Nadar's studio — the Impressionists broke with tradition in their preference for accidental-looking arrangements of figures that appear to be sliced through by the edges of the canvas in the manner of the photographic plate. Certain canvases by these painters also mimic the optical distortions of figure and space visible in stereographs, suggesting that, as Scharf said, "photography must be accorded consideration in any discussion of the character of Impressionist painting." [1] [5] [10]

The appeal of the spontaneous and informal continued unabated during the last decade of the 19th century and resulted in the extraordinary popular interest in small, hand-held single-lens cameras that would simplify the taking of informal pictures. Of all the apparatus developed to fulfill this need, the most sensational was the Kodak camera, first marketed in 1888 by its inventor George Eastman. By separating printing from exposure, this fixed-focus box gave photography mass appeal and created the photo-processing industry. [15]

ARRESTING THE FLUX OF LIFE

[1] **Claude Monet's *Boulevard des Capucines*:** モネ (1840–1926) が仲間と独立展を開き,「印象派」と呼ばれだすのは,「カピュシーヌ大通り」を描いた翌年のこと.

[2] **Nadar:** ナダール (1820–1910) は 1858 年に気球から最初の航空撮影を行なった航空家, 発明家, 芸術家. ドラクロワ, ベルリオーズ, ボードレールなど当時の多くの有名人を生き生きと捉えた肖像写真を撮ったことでも知られている.

[3] **the Impressionists broke with tradition in their preference for accidental-looking arrangements:** 伝統的な絵画では構図が非常に重視されたことに注意.

[7] **mimic the optical distortions of figure and space visible in stereographs:** 立体写真は, ショート・フォーカスのレンズを使うため, 遠近感が極端になる. その効果を真似た印象派の絵画の例としてよく引き合いに出されるのが, ドガの「ディエゴ・マルテッリ像」(1879). この絵の高い視点のために, 机の上に散らかった物が平たく, モデルの男が短足・胴長に見える.

[8] **Scharf:** エアロン・シャーフ (1922–). アメリカの美術・写真史家. 引用は *Art and Photography* (1968) より.

photography must be accorded consideration in any discussion of the character of Impressionist painting: i.e. We should always keep in mind how important the influence of photography was on Impressionist painting. **accord:** to give

[11] **The appeal of the spontaneous and informal:** the attractiveness of not having to plan or arrange things carefully

[12] **unabated:** not reduced or weakened

[16] **the Kodak camera, first marketed in 1888:** A small, light, $25 camera which came loaded with a roll of photographic paper long enough for 100 exposures. When the film had all been exposed, the entire camera was sent to the Kodak factory in Rochester, N.Y., where the exposed strip was developed and printed, a new strip was inserted for $10, and the camera was returned to its owner with the finished prints.

[17] **George Eastman:** この後 1889 年にセルロイドのロールフィルムを開発, 1895 年には pocket Kodak が大当たりし, 1900 年には定価 1 ドルの Brownie box camera を発売する.

ドガ,「ディエゴ・マルテッリ像」(1879)

SESSION 17

pl. 3 CLAUDE MONET. *Boulevard des Capucines, Paris (Les Grands Boulevards),* 1873–74. Oil on canvas. Nelson-Atkins Museum of Art, Kansas City, Mo.; Kenneth A. and Helen F. Spencer Foundation Acquisitions Fund.

The Kodak and the snapshot (Herschel's term to describe instantaneous exposures) were promoted through astute advertising campaigns. Freed from the tedium of darkroom work, large numbers of middle-class amateurs in Europe and the United States used the Kodak to depict family and friends at home and at recreation, to record the ordinary rather than the spectacular. Besides serving as sentimental mementos, these unpretentious images provided later cultural historians with descriptive information about everyday buildings, artifacts, and clothing — indisputable evidence of the popular taste of an era.

Whether by accident or design, snapshots do on occasion portray with satisfying formal vigor moments that seem excised from the seamless flow of life. For one thing, the portability of the instrument enabled the user to view actuality from excitingly different vantage points, as in a 1900 image made by French novelist Émile Zola from the Eiffel Tower looking down (*pl. 4*). In its organization of space it presented an intriguing pattern of architectural members and human figures, foreshadowing the fascination with spatial enigmas that would be explored more fully by photographers in the 1910s and '20s. In a different vein, the small camera made possible the refreshing directness visible in images of small-town life by Horace Engle (*pl. 5*), an American engineer who used a Gray Stirn Concealed Vest camera before turning to the Kodak. Because the camera was so easy to use, a photographer stationed behind a window

[1]　**Herschel:** ジョン・ハーシェル (1792–1871) は，1839 年にガラスに溶剤を塗った感光版での撮影に成功，1842 年青写真を発明し，「フォトグラフ」「ネガティブ」「ポジティブ」の用語を一般化させた．

[2]　**astute advertising campaigns:** Kodak's famous sales pitch was: "You Press the Button, We Do the Rest." **astute:** clever; shrewd; crafty

[3]　**tedium of darkroom work:** slow, tiresome work of developing and printing

[7]　**mementos:** things to remember past moments by

[8]　**unpretentious:** not showing off; simple and true

[11]　**Whether by accident or design:** Whether it was planned or mere luck
　　　do on occasion portray: sometimes actually make a good picture of (moments...)

[12]　**with satisfying formal vigor:** 見る者を満足させるガッシリとした描写力で

[13]　**excised from:** cut out from

[14]　**view actuality from excitingly different vantage points:** see things from new and interesting points of view.　**vantgage point:** cf. p. 9, note [37]

[16]　**Émile Zola:** エミール・ゾラ (1840–1902)

[17]　**an intriguing pattern of architectural members:** 鋼材のなす魅力的なパターン．これについては松浦寿輝著『エッフェル塔試論』(筑摩書房)が，多数の写真・設計図入りで解きあかしている．**intriguing:** interesting; fascinating.　**members:** parts

[18]　**foreshadowing the fascination with spatial enigmas:** 空間というものの不思議への関心が，この時代，すでに表われていたということ．

[20]　**In a different vein:** 別な面では

[23]　**a Gray Stirn Concealed Vest camera:** Gray Stirn plate と呼ばれる丸い感光版を用いた，チョッキに隠せる小型カメラ．別名，ボタンホール・カメラ．

pl. 4 EMILE ZOLA. *A Restaurant, Taken from the First Floor or Staircase of the Eiffel Tower, Paris,* 1900. Gelatin silver print. Collection Dr. François Emile Zola, Gif-sur-Yvette, France.

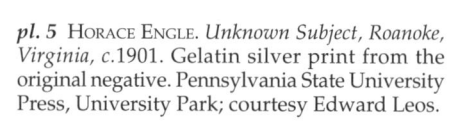

pl. 5 HORACE ENGLE. *Unknown Subject, Roanoke, Virginia,* c.1901. Gelatin silver print from the original negative. Pennsylvania State University Press, University Park; courtesy Edward Leos.

or door, as Engle sometimes was, might intuitively manage light and form to explore private gestures and expressions that almost certainly would be withheld were his presence known. This urge to ensnare ephemeral time, so to speak, also foreshadowed developments of the late 1920s when the sophisticated small Leica camera made "candid" street photography a serious pursuit among photojournalists. Viewed in sequence rather than singly, snapshots sometimes suggest an underlying theme or the emotional texture of an event in the manner of later photojournalistic picture stories and might be considered forerunners in this sense, too.

Though the Kodak in itself was limited in scope, its spontaneity appealed to many serious photographers, who armed themselves with a more sensitive apparatus of a similar nature — the hand camera — to produce the kind of imagery that for want of a better term has come to be called documentation. Turning to the quotidian life of cities and villages for inspiration, artists used the hand camera as a sketchbook, Pictorialists tried to evoke the urban tempo, and still others

[1]　**intuitively manage light and form:** 光とフォルムを直感的(瞬間的)に把握する
[3]　**were his presence known:** if his presence were known
[4]　**urge to ensnare ephemeral time:** たちまち過ぎ去ってしまう時をつかまえようという衝動
[6]　**Leica** [láikə]: ドイツのライカ社から1925年に出た35ミリフイルム使用のカメラは，シャッター速度とフィルム送りの速さに秀でていた．
　　　"candid": 写真に収まる偽りのないありのままの現実をさす言葉．
[10]　**later photojournalistic picture stories:** 1930年にドイツの写真雑誌の編集長となったシュテファン・ローラントは，それまでの1枚ずつの写真掲載に代えて，何枚かの写真を組み合わせることで，出来事をよりドラマチックに物語る方法を発展させた．
[11]　**forerunners in this sense, too:** スナップショットの登場は，単にフォトジャーナリズムの興隆につながる流れをつくり出したというだけでなく ("foreshadowed developments of the late 1920s," ll. 4–5)，出来事を感情をこめて写す方向性を切りひらいたとも言える，ということ．
[12]　**spontaneity** [spɔ̀ntiníːəti]: < spontaneous (p. 174, l. 11)
[16]　**for want of a better term:** cf. "for lack of any other, I had to use the word 'burn'" (p. 114, l. 37)
[17]　**quotidian** [kwoutídiən] **life:** everyday life
[18]　**artists:** ここでは特に画家をさしている．
[19]　**Pictorialists:** 芸術的意志をもって絵画的写真 (pictorial photography) を撮ろうとする写真家たち．スナップショットが氾濫するなかで，1899年アルフレッド・スティーグリッツ (cf. p. 183, note [7]) は，『スクリブナーズ』誌上に「絵画的写真」と題する文章を発表し，写真における絵画主義 Pictorialism の芸術性を主張した．
　　　evoke the urban tempo: 都会のテンポを喚起する

found it a disarming device with which to conquer the anonymity of modern life. Serious workers rather than snapshooters, this new breed of image-maker sought to express a personal vision that embraced the special qualities of the time and place in which they lived.

Street life began to attract hand camera enthusiasts (and some using larger equipment, as well) partly because it offered an uncommon panorama of picturesque subjects. Previously, photographers in search of visual antidotes for the depressing uniformity of life in industrialized societies had either ventured abroad to exotic lands or had searched out quaint pastoral villages as yet untouched by industrial activity. They also had photographed the city's poor and ethnic minorities for their picturesqueness. As urbanization advanced, documentarians, Pictorialists, hand-camera enthusiasts, and even some who worked with large-format cameras were drawn by the animated and vigorous street life in the city to depict with less artifice the variety of peoples and experiences to be found in urban slum and working-class neighborhoods.

As urbanization advanced, it swept away the distinctive physical and social characteristics of the culture of the past, substituting undifferentiated built environments and standardized patterns of dress and behavior. Hand-camera users endeavored to reaffirm individuality and arrest time in the face of the encroaching depersonalization of existence. The French photographer Lartigue was exceptional in that he was given a hand camera in 1901 at the age of seven and continued to use it throughout his lifetime to chronicle the unexpected. His early work portrayed the idiosyncratic behavior of his zany upper-class family whose wealth and quest for modernity impelled them to try out all the latest inventions and devices of the time, from electric razors to automobiles to flying machines. The young Lartigue's intuitive sensitivity to line, strong contrast, and spatial ambiguity, as seen in a view made in the Bois de Boulogne in 1911 (*pl. 6*), evokes the insouciance of affluent Europeans before the first World War.

Other photographers sought out moments of extreme

ARRESTING THE FLUX OF LIFE

[1] **disarming device with which to conquer the anonymity of modern life:**「現代生活の無名性を克服して心を穏やかにする器械」．生活の「顔」を写し出すハンドカメラの心理的・社会的機能への言及．cf. ll. 20–25

[2] **Serious workers rather than snapshooters:** 主語は this new breed of image-maker (この新手の映像作成者たち)．一種の分詞構文だが，文頭に Being を置かないのがふつう．

[8] **picturesque:**「絵になる」．アマチュア写真家が街に出て被写体を探すときのキーワードとも言うべきもの．

[9] **visual antidotes:**「視る解毒剤」

[11] **exotic lands:** ピクトリアル・フォトと呼ばれるもののほとんどは，霧にけぶったような雰囲気や，「異国情緒」を表現するものだった．口絵参照．
quaint pastoral villages: 過ぎし時代を感じさせる牧歌的な村

[13] **ethnic minorities:** 少数民族(ここでの典型的なイメージは，都市の一角にかたまって生きる，独特の習俗をもった移民たち．)

[16] **animated and vigorous:** 生き生きして活気のある

[17] **with less artifice:** i.e. more casually or spontaneously

[22] **substituting:** replacing them with
undifferentiated built environments: 似たり寄ったりの作られた環境

[24] **in the face of the encroaching depersonalization of existence:** 生の非個性化の動きに対抗して．**encroaching:** gradually advancing or invading

[26] **Lartigue:** ジャック・アンリ・ラルティーグ (1894–1986)

[28] **chronicle the unexpected:** 思いがけない風物の歴史をつづる

[29] **idiosyncratic:** peculiar; eccentric
zany [zéini]: こっけいな；突飛な行動に走る

[30] **impelled:** forced, strongly prompted

[31] **try out:** 試してみる，試用する

[32] **flying machines:** 初期の飛行機．1903 年にライト兄弟が史上初の飛行に成功してから第一次大戦で飛行機が活躍しはじめるまでの時代においては，民間の試作機はまだ airplane と呼べるようなものではなかった．

[34] **spatial ambiguity:**「空間のあいまいさ」．犬をつれた婦人の格好やしぐさがどこか公園とは別の空間を思わせることを評したことば
Bois de Boulogne [bwa də bulɔŋ]: パリの西部にあるブローニュの森

[35] **insouciance** [insúːsiəns; Fr. ɛ̃susjɑ̃ːs]: 苦労のない暮らしぶり
affluent: wealthy

181

SESSION 17

pl. 6 JACQUES HENRI LARTIGUE. *Avenue du Bois de Boulogne,* January 15, 1911. Gelatin silver print. © Association Lartigue/SPADEM/VEGA.

pl. 7 HORACE W. NICHOLLS. *The Fortune Teller,* 1910. Gelatin silver print. Royal Photographic Society, Bath, England.

contrast of class and dress, as in *Fortune Teller* (*pl. 7*) by Horace W. Nicholls, a professional photojournalist who recorded the self-indulgent behavior of the British upper class before World War I. Others celebrated moments of uncommon exhilaration, a mood that informs *Handstande* (*pl. 8*) by Heinrich Zille, a graphic artist who used photography in his portrayal of working-class life in Berlin around 1900. Still others, Stieglitz among them, looked for intimations of tenderness and compassion to contrast with the coldness and impersonality of the city, exemplified in *The Terminal* (*pl. 9*) and other works made soon after Stieglitz returned to New York from Germany in 1890.

But not all early photographers saw the city as a threat. Indeed, in the United States at the turn of the century, photographers were specifically urged to open their eyes to the "picturesqueness" of the city, to depict its bridges and structures, to leave the "main thoroughfares" and descend to the slums where an animated street life might be seen. In part, this plea reflected the conviction held by Realist painters, illustrators, pictorial and documentary photographers, joined by social reformers, educators, and novelists, that the social life of the nation was nurtured in the cities, that cities held a promise of excitement in their freedom from conformity and ignorance.

[1]

[5]

[10]

[15]

[20]

ARRESTING THE FLUX OF LIFE

[3] **self-indulgent:** seeking excessively to satisfy one's own desires.　cf. *a self-indulgent film* (one in which the director has concerned himself too much with his own particular feelings or interests)

[4] **exhilaration:** うきうきした気分，はずんだ心

[5] *Handstande*:《独》逆立ち．英語では handstand．動詞で言うなら，stand on one's hands.

[7] **Stieglitz:** アメリカの写真家アルフレッド・スティーグリッツ (1864–1946) は写真は芸術なりというメッセージを打ち立てて圧倒的な影響力を持った．「終着駅」("The Terminal" 1893) について，ニューホールの『写真の歴史』は，「一瞬の光景の記録以上の何か，つまり冬のニューヨークの本質それ自体を捉えている」と評している．

[16] **"main thoroughfares":** 目抜き通りが走る派手やかな地区

[18] **this plea:** スラムを含め，都市をその活力において肯定的に捉えようという「訴え」．

the conviction:「確信」の内容は 20 行目と 21 行目の that 以下．

[21] **nurtured:** nourished; developed

[22] **freedom from conformity:** ability to live as one chooses

[**freedom from**] **ignorance:** access to information

pl. 8 Heinrich Zille. *Handstande*, c.1900. Gelatin silver print. Schirmer/Mosel, Munich.

pl. 9 Alfred Stieglitz. *The Terminal, New York*, 1892. Gravure print. From *Camera Work*, 1911, No. 36. Museum of Modern Art, New York; Gift of Georgia O'Keeffe.

The idea gained ground, too, that a more objective kind of photography had its own value, capturing the facts for their own sake. Stieglitz, in whose magazine the advice appeared, confessed in 1897 that after opposing the hand camera for years, he (and other Pictorialist photographers) had come to regard it as an important means of evoking the character of contemporary life. His suggestion that those using the hand camera study their surroundings and "await the moment when everything is in balance" seems to have forecast a way of seeing that 30 years later became known as the "decisive moment." Whether undertaken consciously or not, the endeavor to assert the prodigal human spirit by capturing the fortuitous moment long remained one of the leitmotifs of 20th-century small-camera photography.

[1]

[5]

[10]

[1] **gained ground:** 広く受け入れられた，広まった (became prevalent)
a more objective kind of photography had its own value: 事実を事実として既成の価値や美意識にしばられずに写す (capturing the facts for their own sake) という，もっと客観的な写真の撮り方も大切だ(という考え)．それは Pictorialism の衰退を意味した．
[8] **await the moment when everything is in balance:**「すべてが釣り合うまで待つ」ということは，線の具合にしても光の具合にしても，あらかじめ考えていた理想的な状態に最も近づくまで待つということ．スティーグリッツは1897年の記事のなかで，「冬――五番街」という作品を撮影する際に吹雪のニューヨークの町角で3時間もシャッター・チャンスを待って立ちつくしたことを語り，あらかじめ理想的な構図を決めておくことの重要性を強調した．
[9] **forecast:** to tell (about something) in advance
[10] **decisive moment:**「決定的瞬間」．1930年代から活躍したフランスの写真家アンリ・カルティエ=ブレッソンが，ちょっとした眼差し，なにげない身振りなどから，人間らしい感情が表出される瞬間を指して用いた言葉．彼が50年代に出した写真集『決定的瞬間』は，"human interest"（人間らしさへの関心）を標榜した戦後の写真家たちの活動の要約でもある．
[11] **the endeavor to assert the prodigal human spirit:** 人間の魂が型にはめることのできない豊かなものであることを示す試み．
[12] **the fortuitous moment:** 偶然の瞬間
[13] **leitmotif(s)** [làitmoutíːf]: a dominant theme

参考・引用文献

オットー・ステルツァー著，福井信雄・池田香代子訳『写真と芸術――接触・影響・成果』(フィルムアート社，1974)

アラン・トラクテンバーグ著，生井英考・石井康史訳『アメリカ写真を読む』(白水社，1996)

イアン・ジェフリー著，伊藤俊治・石井康史訳『写真の歴史――表現の変遷をたどる』(岩波書店，1987)

ジゼル・フロイント著・佐復秀樹訳『写真と社会――メディアのポリティーク』(お茶の水書房，1986)

ヴァルター・ベンヤミン著・久保哲司訳『図説写真小史』(ちくま学芸文庫，1998)

SESSION 18
Our Myriad-Dressed Shakespeare

Shoichiro Kawai

IN *Saturday Night Fever* (1977), a Brooklyn teenager and local disco king (John Travolta) naïvely says to his girlfriend, '*Romeo and Juliet*, yeah? I read that at high school. That's Shakespeare, right?' Of course he is right, but the girl looks disgusted, as if she had heard something completely idiotic. Scornfully she says, 'No, it's Zeffirelli!'

Franco Zeffirelli's *Romeo and Juliet* (1968) is a fascinating film version of the play featuring the young, sprightly Olivia Hussey as Juliet. Travolta's girlfriend apparently doesn't know who wrote the original play. But we cannot dismiss her simply as ignorant, considering that Zeffirelli's film — no doubt one of the most famous films based on Shakespeare — has been enjoyed by millions of people around the world, while very few stage productions of the play will be remembered equally well.

When it comes to enjoying classic plays today, it does not really matter whether you know exactly what the original production was like. Nobody knows much about, say, the original Hamlet performed by Richard Burbage at the Globe around 1601. On the other hand, we have seen many different Hamlets on stage and screen, such as Laurence Olivier's pale, indecisive, and philosophical Hamlet in his film (1948) and Mel Gibson's active and vigorous one (1990). There is even Arnold Schwarzenegger's muscular Hamlet in *The Last Action Hero* (1993), who throws the villainous king out of the window and puts an instant end to this lengthy play — and the accumula-

OUR MYRIAD-DRESSED SHAKESPEARE

　ほぼ400年，多くの国々で上演されてきたシェイクスピアの戯曲．それがいつまで経っても「伝統芸能」に堕さないのは，つねに新しい解釈が加えられ，新しい演出が施されてきたからにほかならない．ここで読むのは，駒場の教師が書いた，シェイクスピア・リメイクの歴史とその意義を論じる文章．タイトルは，コールリッジの有名な賛辞 'our myriad-minded Shakespeare' (p. 188, ll. 13–14) を踏まえている．

[Notes]

[1]　*Saturday Night Fever*: 70年代後半のディスコブームに乗って一世を風靡した映画．土曜の夜のディスコを生き甲斐にしている若者が，恋を通して成長していくお話．

[7]　**Franco Zeffirelli's** *Romeo and Juliet*: フランコ・ゼフィレッリ (1922–　) は舞台及び映画監督．『ロミオとジュリエット』以外にも，『じゃじゃ馬ならし』(1967)，『ハムレット』(1990) などのシェイクスピア作品を映画化している．

[8]　**the young, sprightly Olivia Hussey:** 1951年生まれのオリヴィア・ハッセーは当時16歳，その清楚な美しさで観客を魅了した．

[17]　**the original Hamlet performed by Richard Burbage:** バーベッジ (c. 1567–1619) はシェイクスピアの時代の代表的な俳優で，ハムレットのほかリア王，オセロなども彼が最初に演じたといわれる．

[18]　**the Globe:** シェイクスピアの属する宮内大臣一座によって，1599年ロンドンのテムズ川南岸に建てられた円形劇場．1989年にグローブ座とその近隣のローズ座の土台の一部が発見され，グローブ座は20角形であったことが明らかになった．屋根のない吹き抜け構造，3000名近い収容人数だったとされる．シェイクスピアの作品はほとんどここで上演された．1613年，『ヘンリー八世』を上演中，大砲からの火が藁に引火して火事となり焼失．翌年再建されたが，清教徒革命の嵐のなかで1642年劇場閉鎖．2年後に取り壊された．

[20]　**Laurence Olivier's pale, indecisive, and philosophical Hamlet:** ロシアの文豪ツルゲーネフは，ハムレットを優柔不断型，ドン・キホーテを猪突猛進型と規定したが，名優ローレンス・オリヴィエ (1907–89) 演じる憂いにみちたハムレットも，このツルゲーネフ流解釈に通じるものといえよう．

[21]　**Mel Gibson's active and vigorous one:** 前述ゼフィレッリの監督による，1990年版ハムレット．

SESSION 18

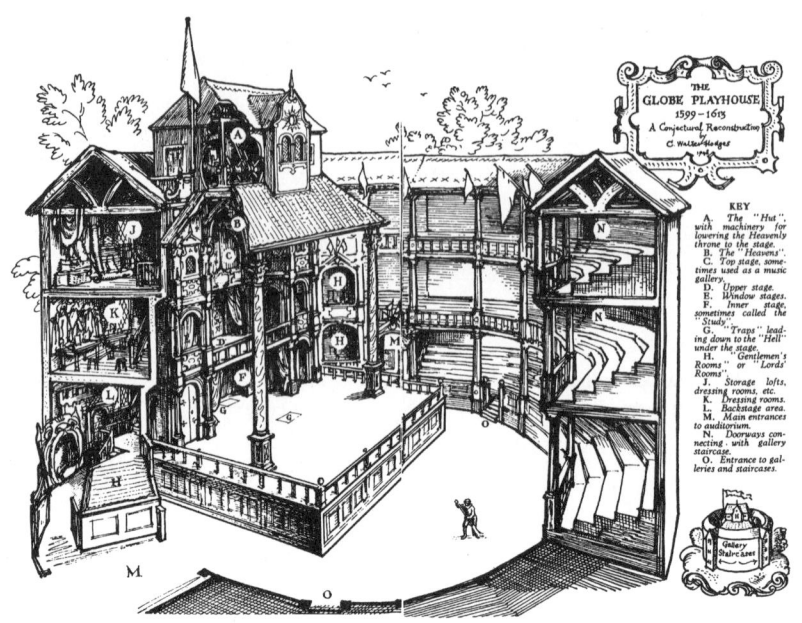

A modern reconstruction of the Globe

tion of these kaleidoscopic Hamlets is what makes the play truly classic. There is no way to decide which one is the closest to the original, for each of the various productions claims to be a unique, 'original' rendition of the play. Classic plays remain classics not because they are valuable cultural relics but because they take root in the imagination of each new generation. They have lived in people's minds for centuries and become part of our culture.

Today, Shakespearean productions are numerous. Every year sees *A Midsummer Night's Dream, Macbeth, Hamlet, Romeo and Juliet,* etc., etc., performed all over the world. His fellow playwright Ben Jonson prophetically said that Shakespeare is meant not only for one age but 'for all time', and indeed 'our myriad-minded Shakespeare', as Samuel Taylor Coleridge puts it, is still attracting millions of people to modern theatres. Moreover, ever since Jan Kott published *Shakespeare Our Contemporary* (1964), it has become quite common to regard the Bard as belonging to our own age. Because the purpose of a play is, as Hamlet says, 'to hold as 'twere the mirror up to nature' so as to

[1]　**kaleidoscopic:** 万華鏡のよう(に多彩)な
[4]　**'original':** i.e. [a. really the closest to the original / b. new]
[5]　**relics:** 遺物
[10]　*A Midsummer Night's Dream*: 媚薬の誤用(?)がもたらすドタバタを描いた恋愛喜劇．イギリスの短い夏を彩る野外演劇では定番中の定番．1595 年ごろ執筆．
[12]　**Ben Jonson:** シェイクスピア同時代のライバル劇作家 (1572–1637)．その初期の作品『セジェイナス』*Sejanus* (1603) の初演には，前述のバーベッジのみならずシェイクスピア自身も俳優として参加した．
[14]　**myriad-minded:** 無数の心を持った
　　　Samuel Taylor Coleridge: 19 世紀前半イギリスの代表的文人 (1772–1834)．
[16]　**Jan Kott:** ヤン・コット (1914–2001) はポーランド人批評家．
[17]　**the Bard:**「ザ・歌人」といったところ．シェイクスピアのこと．The Bard of Avon [éivən] とも．
[19]　**'to hold as 'twere the mirror up to nature ... the very age':**『ハムレット』第 3 幕第 2 場で，義父クローディアスの悪事を暴くために劇中劇を催そうとしているハムレットが，役者たちに与える指示のなかの科白．

　　　'the purpose of playing, whose end, both at the first and now, was and is, to hold as 'twere the mirror up to nature: to show virtue her feature, scorn her own image, and the very age and body of the time his form and pressure.' (III. ii. 20–24)
　　　「芝居というものは，昔もいまも，いわば自然にたいして鏡をかかげ，善はその美点を，悪はその愚かさを示し，時代の様相をあるがままにくっきりとうつし出すことを目指しているのだ」(小田島雄志訳，白水社 U ブックス)．

　　　as 'twere: as it were

SESSION 18

The only existing drawing of an Elizabethan theatre (the Swan Playhouse)

show the image of 'the very age', a modern production of Shakespeare's plays naturally serves as a mirror to reflect our own age. We watch Shakespeare's plays to see ourselves. Thus we see Hamlets wearing sunglasses and Romeos in jeans and T-shirts. You might think that such peculiar sights would make Shakespeare turn in his grave, but we have to remember how much the *real* world has changed since his plays were performed in front of an audience clothed in ruffs, doublets and hose.

One of the earliest modern-dress Hamlets was produced by Barry Jackson in 1925. Since then, there have been countless modern-dress productions of Shakespeare's plays, such as Trevor Nunn's *Timon of Athens* (1991), in which Timon in a dinner jacket is surrounded by news reporters with microphones and TV cameras. Not only the costume but the whole setting is often adapted to our age. The musical *West Side Story* (1957) changes the old Verona of *Romeo and Juliet* into modern New York. Such free interpretations and adaptations, if they work, do lead the audience to a richer understanding of the play.

Today Shakespeare is found everywhere. Attend the opera, and you will find many Shakespearean adaptations such as Verdi's *Otello*. Read a modern play and you may find it based on *Hamlet*, like Tom Stoppard's *Rosencrantz and Guildenstern Are*

OUR MYRIAD-DRESSED SHAKESPEARE

[6] **turn in his grave:** 日本語で言えば「草葉の蔭で嘆く」といったところ．
[8] **ruffs, doublets and hose:** ひだえり，胴衣，タイツ．いずれもシェイクスピアの時代の代表的な衣服．
[10] **Barry Jackson:** Birmingham Repertory Theatre を 1913 年に創設した演出家 (1879–1961)．Royal Shakespeare Theatre の前身 Shakespeare Memorial Theatre の演出家(在職 1945–48)でもあった．
[12] **Trevor Nunn:** 1968–86 年 Royal Shakespeare Company の芸術総監督 (artistic director) を務める (1940–   )．『キャッツ』(1981) や『スターライト・エクスプレス』(1984) などミュージカルの演出も手がける．日本でも『レ・ミゼラブル』などの演出で知られる．
Timon of Athens:『アテネのタイモン』．前 5 世紀アテネの貴族タイモンの没落人生を扱った悲劇．
[15] *West Side Story . . . changes the old Verona . . . into modern New York*:『ロミオとジュリエット』をミュージカルに「翻訳」した『ウェスト・サイド物語』(作曲レナード・バーンスタイン)では，イタリアの都市ヴェローナの名門モンタギュー家とキャピュレット家の対立が，マンハッタンに住む二不良少年グループ(一方は地元育ち，一方はプエルトリコ系移民)の対立に置き換えられ，ジュリエットたちが愛を語りあうキャピュレット家のバルコニーは，トニーとマリアが愛を謳いあげる安アパートの非常階段に置き換えられている．
[17] **work:** うまくいく
[21] **Verdi's *Otello*:** シェイクスピア四大悲劇のひとつ *Othello* の歌劇バージョン．同じくシェイクスピア劇に基づく『ファルスタッフ』(1893) とともに，イタリアの作曲家ヴェルディ (1813–1901) 晩年の力作 (1887)．
[22] **Tom Stoppard's *Rosencrantz and Guildenstern Are Dead*:** ローゼンクランツとギルデンスターンは『ハムレット』の脇役で，王クローディアスからハムレットの行動をスパイするよう命じられ，逆にハムレットの策略によって殺されてしまう．トム・ストッパード (1937–   ) は 1966 年，この哀れといえば哀れな二人の脇役を中心に据えた不条理な戯曲を書いた．

SESSION 18

Dead. Go to the ballet or a concert hall, and you may see *Romeo and Juliet* by Sergey Prokofiev, or hear incidental music such as Mendelssohn's *A Midsummer Night's Dream*. Even a cult sci-fi movie like *Forbidden Planet* is based on *The Tempest*. You really have to 'Brush Up Your Shakespeare' to live in this world, as the famous song goes in the musical *Kiss Me Kate*, itself based on *The Taming of the Shrew*.

Modernization of Shakespeare is not new. The first attempts were made in the Restoration period (1660–85), when many adaptations of Shakespeare's plays were staged to suit the taste of the time. In the Victorian period (1837–1901), however, the pendulum swung back and people tried to produce Shakespeare's plays authentically. In fact, historical correctness became such a fetish to the Victorians that even Shakespeare's own anachronisms were corrected. For example, in *Julius Caesar*, a clock (a thirteenth-century invention) strikes, and Casca is pulled by the sleeve — obviously he is wearing not a toga but an Elizabethan jacket. Shakespeare had quite a liberal attitude to history — a fact that seems to justify twentieth-century directors' even bolder approaches in costuming.

Adaptations aside, when we watch variously costumed Shakespearean plays, we understand how wide the scope of our approach to the classics is. They have been produced in huge skirts in Victorian style, in the black suits and hats of Chicago gangsters, in Napoleonic hats and boots, in Japanese samurai kimonos, and even in pyjamas. In Elizabethan times, on the other hand, clothing was so rich in signs and symbols that it had a special dramatic function. The characters' social identities could be recognised by what they wore. A cap signified a merchant; a blue coat and flat-cap an apprentice; and a hat, doublet, hose, and cloak a gentleman. A woman's black velvet gown indicated that the wearer belonged to a wealthy family, while materials such as russet were a sign of poverty. Certain colours like purple were not supposed to be worn by lower-class people. This sartorial sign system clearly reflected the Elizabethan social hierarchy, although contemporary dramatists were well aware that a person's worth lay not in

OUR MYRIAD-DRESSED SHAKESPEARE

[1] ***Romeo and Juliet* by Sergey Prokofiev**: ロシアの作曲家セルゲイ・プロコフィエフ (1891-1953) による，今日もっとも頻繁に上演されるシェイクスピア・バレエ (1936).
[2] **incidental music**:「付随音楽」．今日でいう BGM より強く作品にかかわる．
[3] **a cult sci-fi** [sáifái] **movie**: カルト的な人気を持つ SF 映画
[4] **... is based on *The Tempest***: シェイクスピアの『テンペスト』の舞台は新大陸アメリカがモデルだが，『禁断の惑星』(1956) ではそれが，紀元 2200 年の惑星アルテア 4 に置き換えられている．『テンペスト』の映画化としてはほかに，映像の魔術師ピーター・グリーナウェイによる，ハイテク技術を駆使した『プロスペローの本』(1991) が印象的．
[5] **'Brush Up Your Shakespeare'**: brush up は 'Brush up your English' というふうに，「～に磨きをかける，～を勉強し直す」といった意味．'Brush Up Your Shakespeare' は有名なポピュラー音楽作曲家コール・ポーターの作で，次行で言及されるミュージカル『キス・ミー・ケイト』(1948) の劇中歌．
[6] **the musical *Kiss Me Kate***: 1953 年の映画版もあり．
[7] ***The Taming of the Shrew***:『じゃじゃ馬ならし』．じゃじゃ馬娘 Katherina が従順な妻になるまでを描いた喜劇．
[9] **the Restoration period**: 王政復古期．清教徒革命が崩壊し，王政が復帰した時期を指す．明治維新も the Meiji Restoration と呼ばれる．
[11] **the Victorian period**: ヴィクトリア女王が半世紀以上 (1837-1901) にわたって統治した，大英帝国がもっとも強大な勢力を誇った時代．
[12] **pendulum**: 振り子
[13] **authentically**: [a. accurately / b. imaginatively]
[14] **fetish**: something people are obsessed about; an object of unreasonable attention
[15] **in *Julius Caesar*, a clock (a thirteenth-century invention) strikes**:「本物」のシーザー（カエサル）が生きたのは，むろん紀元前 1 世紀のこと．
[16] **Casca**: シーザーを暗殺した一味の一人．
[17] **toga**: 古代ローマ市民が着用した，ゆったりした上着．袖はないので引きようがない．
[21] **Adaptations aside**: Apart from adaptations
[30] **apprentice**: 徒弟，見習い奉公人
[31] **gentleman**: 単に「紳士」ではなく，騎士 (knight) の下，郷士 (yeoman) より上の階級を指す呼称．
[33] **russet** [rʌ́sit]: 赤褐色（黄褐色）の粗い手織の布地
[35] **sartorial** [sɑ̀:tɔ́:riəl]: 衣装の
[36] **contemporary dramatists**: 我々から見た現代ではなく，シェイクスピアと同時代の劇作家たち，ということ．

mere appearance. The disguise plot is an element in about seventy percent of extant Elizabethan plays, and audiences loved to see disguised characters prove that their substance had little to do with their appearance.

Today, costume is regarded as only one element of the whole theatrical experience, but for Elizabethan theatre companies, it was certainly as important a resource as the play scripts themselves. When a theatre burned, the first two things to be rescued were costumes and play scripts, for costumes were unbelievably expensive. The accounts of Edward Allen, leading actor of Shakespeare's rival company the Admiral's Men, record £20 10s. 6d. for his 'black velvet cloak with sleeves embro[i]dered all with silver and gold', which is more than a third of what Shakespeare paid for his house in Stratford-upon-Avon. We can naturally assume that costume itself was considered a spectacle on stage, astonishing and delighting the audience with its exquisite material, elaborate embroidery and sparkling accessories. We have to remember that Shakespeare (1564–1616) lived in an age when England was rising to become a world power, and that costume symbolised economic strength and authority. Rich, finely clad merchants stalked along the streets and noblemen proudly exhibited their splendid garments even on the stage, where they occasionally sat, close to the performing actors, not so much to see as to be seen. The glamour and glitter of the age was mirrored by the gorgeous costumes which adorned the stage.

A true *reconstruction* of Elizabethan staging would never be possible today, because our cultural codes are literally centuries away from those in the Elizabethan period. Even if modern producers meticulously followed Elizabethan stage conventions and clothed their actors in ruffs and doublets, many of the symbolic meanings of the costumes would be lost on modern spectators. Moreover, the theatre experience in the Elizabethan period was totally different from today. We sit comfortably in a high-tech theatre with colossal sets and amazing lighting effects. The Elizabethans, on the other hand, usually had to either keep standing or sit on hard wooden seats

[2] **extant:** still existing
[3] **their substance:** what they really are (as opposed to what they seem to be). シェイクスピアより少し前の1590年代には，the Admiral's Men という劇団 (l. 11) による「変装もの」が大ヒットした．
[12] **£20 10s. 6d:** twenty pounds, ten shillings and six pence. かつてイギリスの通貨は1ポンドが20シリング，1シリングが12ペンスだった(現在ではシリングは使われず，1ポンドが100ペンス)．
[13] **embro[i]dered:** 刺繍の入った．[　] (brackets) は引用文を訂正したり補足したりするときに使う記号．
[17] **exquisite** [ikskwízət, ékskwizət]**:** fine; very beautiful
　　 elaborate: worked out with great care; detailed
[19] **an age when England was rising to become a world power:** 1558年に即位したエリザベス一世が，スペインの無敵艦隊を撃破したのが1588年．1600年には東インド会社も設立され，イギリスは対外的にますます勢力を広げていく．
[21] **clad:** dressed
　　 stalked: walked proudly (cf. p. 88, l. 3). 日本語になった「ストーカー」は p. 98, l. 15 の意味から．
[23] **garments:** clothes
[25] **glitter:** splendour
[30] **meticulously:** carefully; precisely (cf. p. 94, l. 32)
[35] **colossal** [kəlósəl]**:** huge; enormous (cf. p. 26, l. 12)

in a public playhouse which had no roof, no artificial light, no stage setting, no proscenium arch, no cloak-room, and even no toilet.

Shakespeare's Globe Theatre has now been rebuilt, as faithfully as possible, on almost the exact spot where the original Globe once stood. It offers a fascinating glimpse of playgoing in Elizabethan times, when many of the audience (the 'groundlings') had to stand under the open sky to watch. But however faithful to the original building, the Globe can only be a site for *our* interpretations and *our* performances of Shakespeare. It is not a time machine which could transport us into Shakespeare's England, or bring the 'real' Shakespeare into the twenty-first century.

Appropriation therefore continues. In Japan, too, appropriating Shakespeare has produced interesting results. Among others, Akira Kurosawa's films — *Throne of Blood* (1957) based on *Macbeth* and *Ran* (1985) based on *King Lear* — are internationally acclaimed, not least because they perfectly integrate Shakespeare into Japanese historical settings. After watching the visual feast of *Ran*, perhaps you might be tempted to say, '*King Lear*, yeah? I watched it on video. That's Kurosawa, right?'

[1] **no stage setting:** 舞台装置はいっさいなかったので，シェイクスピアの芝居では，誰かが死んでも役者は衆人環視のなかで舞台を去らねばならず，かならず「こいつを手厚く葬ってやろう」などと言ってほかの役者たちが引きずっていく．夜明けの美しさなども照明効果で伝えることはできず，勢い，言葉をふんだんに費やすことでその美しさを喚起することになる．

[2] **proscenium** [prousíːniəm] **arch:** 額縁舞台の額縁．舞台の前面に設けられた，そこからカーテンが降りてくるアーチ．

[14] **Appropriation:** taking something for one's own use; adaptation

[16] *Throne of Blood* ... **based on** *Macbeth*: 『蜘蛛巣城』．マクベスにあたる主人公鷲津武時を三船敏郎が，冷血なマクベス夫人にあたるその妻浅茅を山田五十鈴が演じる．

[17] *Ran* ... **based on** *King Lear*: 『乱』．リア王に対応する悲劇の君主一文字秀虎を，仲代達矢が演じる．『蜘蛛巣城』ともに，時代は戦国時代．

[20] **the visual feast of** *Ran*: 制作費 26 億円といわれる『乱』は派手なスペクタクルでも知られる．

SESSION 19

The Jurassic According to Hollywood

Stephen Jay Gould

THE deepest messages often lie in apparent trivialities — for example, in dialogue regarded as too insignificant to scrutinize for error or inconsistency. For me, the most revealing moment in *Jurassic Park* occurs early in the film, as paleontologist Alan Grant discourses to his assistants on the genealogical relationships of dinosaurs and birds, as illustrated by a skeleton, just unearthed, of the small dinosaur *Velociraptor*. Grant correctly points to several anatomical features that suggest a link — hollow bones and a birdlike pelvis, for example. He then ends his discourse with the supposed clincher: "Even the word *raptor* means 'bird of prey.'"

Consider the absurdity of this last pronouncement. First, Grant is flat wrong. *Raptor*, from the Latin *rapere* ("to seize," or "to take by force"), is an old English word, traced to the early seventeenth century and first applied to humans, not birds, in its literal meaning. Later zoologists borrowed it as a technical name for large carnivorous birds.

More important, Grant's error lies in confusing a human construction — and an arbitrary one at that — with an empirical reality. The word is not the thing; the representation not the reality. The bones of *Velociraptor* speak of relationship with birds; the name that we bestowed on the creature is only our fabrication.

All records of history must present biases, yet factual reality remains our partially attainable goal. (You will never get prac-

198

THE JURASSIC ACCORDING TO HOLLYWOOD

映画が事実をそのまま伝えるものでないことは誰でも知っている．だが我々は，歴史上のさまざまな事件や過去について，そのイメージを実は映画から得ていることが案外多くないだろうか．チャップリンの映画を見れば1930年代の大恐慌時代をなんとなく知ったような気になるし，人類の誕生をめぐるイメージは，どうしても『2001年宇宙の旅』の映像などに影響されてしまう．だがむろん，それらの映画は，多分に歪曲の産物である．では，コンピュータ・グラフィックスが大受けした『ジュラシック・パーク』(1993)の描くジュラ紀はどうか？　人気生物学者スティーブン・ジェイ・グールドが診断する．

[Notes]

[1]   **apparent trivialities:** things that seem unimportant
[3]   **scrutinize:** to examine carefully
[5]   **paleontologist** [pæ̀liɑntɑ́lədʒist]: scientist who deals with fossils and ancient animal life
    discourse(s): to lecture; explain
[6]   **genealogical** < genealogy: 系統学
[7]   **unearthed:** dug out of the ground
[8]   *Velociraptor* [vəlùsəræptə]: *"veloci-"* comes from a Latin word meaning "speed."
    anatomical features: 体のつくりの特徴
[11]   **clincher:** (議論にけりをつける)決めの文句．supposed (〜のつもりの)がついているのは，事実誤認のためにまるで「決まって」いないから．
    bird of prey: bird that feeds on other birds and animals
[12]   **pronouncement:** (strong) statement
[13]   **flat wrong:** simply, utterly, completely wrong
[16]   **technical name:** 学名
[17]   **carnivorous:** flesh-eating
[18]   **human construction:** i.e. [a. a building / b. an idea]
[19]   **and an arbitrary one at that:** それも必然性のないものを．*I had to take care of a child, and a noisy one at that!*
    empirical: 観察に基づく; 経験(知覚)される
[20]   **The word is not the thing; the representation not the reality:** The name is not the thing named; the sign not the thing it stands for と言っても同じ．記号とそれが表わすものとが arbitrary な関係 (cf. p. 63, note [18]) にあることを述べている．
[22]   **bestowed on:** gave
    our fabrication: something we made up
[24]   **must present biases:** [a. cannot be / b. must be] completely true to reality
[25]   **get . . . to espouse:** convince . . . to support; talk . . . into believing

ticing scientists like me to espouse postmodernist relativism in pure form; we spend too much time engaged in the daily and excruciatingly tedious tasks of cage cleaning and sample preparation to believe that knowledge is nothing but social construction.) Eyewitness testimony has its biases; written text embodies more severe prejudices. But films intended for popular audiences include more fact-distorting conventions (often quite honorable and necessary) than any other medium. If we could keep the two personas separate — Ingrid Bergman as Joan of Arc vs. the enigmatic and probably schizophrenic Maid of Orléans — then cinematic distortion would not be problematical. However, when a movie image, with all the conventions that falsify history, becomes our primary representation of a person — as has happened again and again and again — then we face a troubling situation.

Let me say that, in my view, *Jurassic Park* deserved all its substantial success. The special effects of living dinosaurs, in particular, are spectacular. I was awestruck when I learned that actor Sam Neill (as Alan Grant) and the two children reacted to nothing on the film's set and that the stunning herd of charging *Gallimimus* dinosaurs were computer images added later!

I could list a compendium of factual errors from a professional paleontologist's viewpoint, starting with the observation that most dinosaurs depicted in *Jurassic Park* date from the later Cretaceous period. Instead, I would rather concentrate on the film's two "great" errors, for these faults share two properties that operate on a sufficiently grand scale to preclude pettiness:

1. **Insufficient recognition of nature's complexity.** If anyone on this planet remains unaware of *Jurassic Park*'s plot line, let me epitomize: Entrepreneur sets up theme park of living dinosaurs. He extracts dinosaur DNA from blood preserved inside mosquitoes trapped and fossilized in amber (and thus shielded from decay over a minimum of sixty-five million years, since the extinction of dinosaurs). His scientists amplify the DNA, put together complete sequences, inject the code into eggs, and induce embryological development. Dino-

[1]   **postmodernist relativism:** ポストモダン思想が得意とする相対主義．cf. note [4]; p. 207, note [12]
[3]   **excruciatingly tedious:** painfully boring
[4]   **knowledge is nothing but social construction:** 知は社会的に構成されるものにすぎない．つまり時代や文化を超えた絶対的に正しい知を手にすることはできないということ．
[5]   **written text embodies more severe prejudices:** i.e. it is more difficult to communicate things as they are when we use the medium of writing.
        films intended for popular audiences: popular entertainment films
[7]   **fact-distorting conventions:** 事実を歪曲する約束ごと
[8]   **honorable:** respectable; fine
[9]   **persona(s)** [pəːsóunə]: character
        Ingrid Bergman: イングリッド・バーグマン(1915–82)．スウェーデン出身の女優．Humphrey Bogart と共演した *Casablanca* (1942) は，ハリウッド史上最もポピュラーな映画のひとつ．
        Joan of Arc: ジャンヌ・ダルク (Jeanne d'Arc, 1412–31) の英語での呼び名．バーグマン主演の映画 *Joan of Arc* は 1948 年制作．
[10]   **the enigmatic and probably schizophrenic Maid of Orléans:** refers to the [a. film version of / b. actual, historical] Joan of Arc. **enigmatic:** mysterious. **schizophrenic** [skìtsoufrénik]: 分裂症の
[17]   **substantial success:** great success (especially in terms of money)
[22]   **list a compendium of . . . :** 〜を一覧にして示す
[25]   **Cretaceous** [kritéiʃəs] **period:** 白亜紀．ジュラ紀に引き続く中生代最後の時代．1 億 4000 万年前〜6500 万年前．
[27]   **preclude pettiness:** 些細な言いがかりにはならない
[30]   **epitomize:** to summarize
        Entrepreneur [ùːntrprənóː]: a person who organizes and operates a business venture（起業家）
[32]   **trapped and fossilized in amber:** 樹脂にはまったまま琥珀中の化石となった
[33]   **over a minimum of . . . :** i.e. at least for . . .
[36]   **induce embryological development:** i.e. cause the eggs to start multiplying their cells and develop as embryos. cf. p. 205, notes [1] [2]

saurs of many species are thus revivified (females only, as a protection against uncontrolled breeding). The park's defenses do not work for various reasons rooted in human scheming and technical malfeasance, and mayhem of all sorts results.

The scenario is clever (it had been discussed as fantasy by several scientists before Michael Crichton wrote his book). However, we should understand why such revivification is impossible — for non-acknowledgment of this reason promotes one of the worst stereotypes about science and its role in our culture.

We should distinguish between two very different claims for "impossibility" often made by scientists. The first (impossible to reach the moon, impossible to split the atom) records lack of imagination and only embarrasses those prognosticators who spoke too definitely. But another species of impossibility — the true and permanent disappearance of historical records — seems ineluctable because the only conceivable data have not survived. If, for some reason, I wanted a list of every rebel crucified with Spartacus along the Appian Way (wasn't Kirk Douglas great in that scene?), I could not acquire such a record because it doesn't now exist (and probably never did). Historical items are not formed predictably under laws of nature; they are contingent configurations that, if lost, cannot be reconstituted.

Dinosaur DNA falls into the category of Spartacus's list, not into the domain of predictably reconstructible consequences of nature's laws. Someday we may (one dubious report says we already have) recover short fragments of dinosaur DNA. (One complete gene, for example, has been recovered from a twenty-million-year-old magnolia leaf.) But remember that an entire organism contains thousands of different genes all necessary for revivification. DNA is a very fragile and decomposable compound: coding sequences can survive for geological ages only in the most favorable circumstances, and I see little prospect that anything close to a complete set of dinosaur genes could be preserved under any conditions. Moreover, the situation is even more hopeless — even if a complete set of genes could be

THE JURASSIC ACCORDING TO HOLLYWOOD

[1]   **revivified:** brought back to life
as a protection against uncontrolled breeding: so that the dinosaurs wouldn't start mating uncontrollably

[3]   **human scheming:** 人間の(意図的な)たくらみ

[4]   **technical malfeasance** [mælfíːzəns]: 技術的なミス
mayhem: great disorder

[6]   **Michael Crichton** [kráitn]: American fiction writer of enormous popularity (1942–). The movie *Jurassic Park*, like *Disclosures*, *Rising Sun*, and several more, is based on his best-seller of the same title.

[8]   **non-acknowledgment of this reason promotes ... stereotypes about science:** as long as we are ignorant of this reason, our view of science remains oversimplified and false

[13]   **records lack of imagination:** i.e. only appears "impossible" to those who lack imagination

[14]   **those prognosticators who spoke too definitely:** people who talked too confidently about the future, saying things like "We can *never* reach the moon."
prognosticators < prognosticate: to predict; foretell

[17]   **ineluctable** [iniláktəbl]: inevitable; unavoidable

[19]   **crucified:** 磔の刑にされた. cf. *crucifixion* (p. 164, l. 36)
the Appian Way: アッピア街道. ローマからイタリア半島南部へ至る古代の道.

[20]   **Kirk Douglas:** スタンリー・キューブリック監督の *Spartacus* (1960) では，古代ローマの奴隷反乱を率いた英雄スパルタカスを熱演.

[22]   **Historical items are not formed predictably under laws of nature:** By contrast, most items of classical sciences (how objects fall, how chemical reactions proceed under certain conditions, etc.) are predictable. cf. *The Universe of English II*, SESSION 15, "What Science Can and Cannot Predict"

[23]   **contingent configurations:** 偶発的に生起するもの. **configuration:** (出来事の)パターン

[24]   **reconstituted:** reconstructed; recovered

[25]   **falls into the category of:** belongs together with

[27]   **dubious** [djúːbiəs]: doubtful; unreliable

[30]   **magnolia:** モクレンやコブシなどの仲間の総称. アメリカ南部を代表する花のひとつ.

[32]   **a very fragile and decomposable compound:** a chemical structure that easily breaks apart

[33]   **coding sequences:** DNAのことを，そのはたらきから捉えた言い替え.
for geological ages: i.e. for tens (and hundreds) of millions of years

[34]   **I see little prospect ... :** i.e. the author thinks that such an event is [a. likely / b. unlikely] to happen.

reconstituted, an embryo still could not form, for development requires the proper environment in a maternal egg. Embryology cannot proceed without a complex set of maternal gene products already in place within the egg. So the scientists of *Jurassic Park* would not only require the complete dinosaur code but also have to know the maternal genes needed to produce proper proteins and enzymes within the egg — thus heaping impossibility upon impossibility.

Michael Crichton understood these limitations perfectly well. John Hammond, the godfather of *Jurassic Park*, admits that his scientists couldn't reconstitute an entire dinosaur code, so they patched in some frog DNA to supply the missing pieces. This lame solution (to a real problem) embodies the worst stereotype of science as a reductionist enterprise — just mix the right ingredients (or the best surrogates) and the desired entity will emerge. But organisms are not simple sums of (imperfect) parts. You cannot dump in eighty percent of the required pieces, then add twenty percent of things close enough, and emerge with a functioning totality (frogs aren't even genealogically near dinosaurs — why not use birds?).

We must debunk the silly idea that scientists are wizards who break totalities into little bits of chemistry and physics and then know the essence of the thing itself, thereby gaining the power to build it anew from basic constituents — shades of Hollywood's Frankenstein myth. Complex, whole organisms have emergent properties that arise non-additively (to use the technical term) from interactions among their parts and cannot be predicted or built by simply stringing the bits together. We cannot decompose intelligence (or anything else) into percentages of nature and nurture; we must study organisms at their own level, in all their multifariousness and interactive complexity.

2. Stereotypes of science and history. Hollywood seems to know only one theme in treating the power of science — hubris, otherwise rendered (in old-style language) as "man must not go where God (or nature's laws) did not intend." The movies, throughout scores of versions, have distorted Mary

THE JURASSIC ACCORDING TO HOLLYWOOD

[1] **embryo** [émbriòu]: 胚（卵や種子の中で発生を始めたばかりの幼生物）
[2] **Embryology** [èmbriálədʒi]: ここでは「発生学」ではなく「発生」の意味．
[3] **maternal gene products:** 卵子から作られる遺伝物質
[7] **enzyme(s)** [énzaim]: 酵素
[10] **godfather:** マフィアのボスだけでなく，組織や企画の支柱的人物を広く指す．原意は「代父」（生まれた子の洗礼式に立ち会い，名を与え保証人となる）．
[12] **patch(ed) in:** 継ぎ当てする
This lame solution . . . embodies the worst stereotype of . . . : こんな安易な解決策が持ち出されるところに，以下のようなひどい思いこみが見て取れるということ．**lame:** weak; clumsy
[14] **reductionist:**「還元主義的な」．reductionism: a tendency to explain complex phenomena or structures by simple principles (see ll. 21–)
[15] **surrogate(s)** [sə́:rəgèit, sʌ́rəgət]: 代理のもの
[17] **You cannot dump in . . . and emerge with ～ :** You cannot get ～ by just throwing in . . .
[19] **a functioning totality:** i.e. a living organism
[21] **debunk:** to expose the falseness of
[24] **constituents:** 構成要素
shades: influences
Hollywood's Frankenstein myth: フランケンシュタイン博士の怪物は，死体の部分を縫い合わせ，雷の高電圧によって作ったもの．ハリウッドでは1931年の『フランケンシュタイン』の大ヒット以来，科学の生み出した怪物が破滅をもたらすという筋の映画が多数作られてきた．
[26] **emergent properties:**「創発性」と訳される．本文で説明されているが，ある条件下でナトリウムに塩素を加えれば食塩ができるというような足し算方式で事が進むのではない，というところにこの概念のポイントがある．
[27] **cannot be predicted . . . :** 主語は25行目の organisms.
[29] **decompose intelligence . . . into percentages of nature and nurture:** 知性というものを，何パーセントが生まれつき (nature) で，何パーセントが教育の結果 (nurture) だというふうに分解して考える
[31] **multifariousness:** great variety
[35] **hubris** [hjú:brəs]: 不遜，傲慢
otherwise rendered: put another way
"man must not go where God . . . did not intend": たとえば1958年制作の *The Fly*（『蠅男の恐怖』）という映画では，発明した物質電送機でみずからを電送した科学者が，まぎれていた蠅と合体した姿になってしまう．妻から "It's frightening; it's like playing God" と警告されていたにもかかわらず．
[37] **scores of:** 何十もの (a score = twenty)
Mary Shelley's moral tale: Mary Shelley (1797–1851) wrote the story in her teens, which later was published as *Frankenstein, or the Modern Prometheus* (1818).

205

Shelley's moral tale about the responsibility of creators toward their "offspring" into a story of technology transgressing the boundaries of its legitimate operation (not a word can be found in Shelley about the dangers of science or technology; nor did she discourse on what God did or did not license us to do).

Given the weight of such an overbearing tradition, the film of *Jurassic Park* inevitably took this same hackneyed course: The theme-park proprietors shouldn't have remade the dinosaurs because such a project violates nature's intended course — and human malefactors must therefore pay the price.

We are all used to the claim, so prominent in postmodern criticism, that history (or any knowledge) cannot be fully objective but must be socially constructed. History — whether presented in books, on the stage, or in films — is subject to yet another distinct and profound form of bias in representation: literary bias, based on dramatic conventions about story plots that work to move our souls and pique our fascination. We cannot hope for even a vaguely accurate portrayal of the nub of history in film so long as movies must obey the literary conventions of ordinary plotting. But must film be so unimaginative? Could we not, following my opening theme in this essay, find a way to uncover the bones of history and not rely upon human conventions about the names?

- [1] **the responsibility of creators toward their "offspring":** シェリーの原作でのフランケンシュタイン博士は，怪物が完成したとたんにそれに対する愛情を失ってしまう無責任な人間．
- [2] **transgress(ing):** to go beyond
- [3] **boundaries of its legitimate operation:** 適正な活動範囲
- [5] **license:** to allow; permit
- [7] **hackneyed:** overfamiliar through overuse
- [10] **malefactor(s)** [mǽləfæktə]: evil-doer
- [11] **prominent:** [a. common / b. rare]
- [12] **history . . . must be socially constructed:** 歴史というものは，過去のありのままの事実ではなく，それを語る人たちが自分たちの生きる社会の中で意味をもつように作ったものだとする考え方．
- [16] **dramatic conventions:** ドラマを盛り上げるための約束ごと
- [17] **pique:** to provoke; stimulate
- [18] **the nub of history:** the core truth of history. 22行目の the bones of history と同義．
- [22] **the bones of history . . . human conventions about the names:** 冒頭で述べられた，（科学的調査によって発掘される）「事実」と，（人間の作りものである）「名前」との対比がここでもう一度想起される．

SESSION 20
The New Age of Man

Malcolm Gladwell

THE traditional scientific approach to the problem of aging has been to accept our biological limits and try to rearrange the lives and the care of the elderly to make old age more manageable. Our efforts have been largely palliative — to put elevators in buildings, to make public spaces accessible to wheelchairs, to devise better treatments for cataracts, to perform coronary-bypass operations to cut down on chest pain, and even, in the case of one of the more imaginative projects sponsored by the Centers for Disease Control, to try to make fluid-filled pads for elderly hips and thus protect against the fractures that are such a common form of disability in the old. The motto of the Gerontological Society of America has been "Add life to years, not years to life," which is a statement not just of intention but of apparent fact. For a long time, no one thought you *could* add years to life. Mice were thought to live about two years, dogs about fifteen years, and human beings at most a hundred years — all according to some immutable genetic clock — and any scientists who made spectacular claims of reversing the aging process were treated with skepticism.

The new field of aging is quite different. It is not a tuneup so much as an engine overhaul. There is Rose, with his Methuselah flies, and in just the past decade, there has arisen a whole field of scientists using evolutionary and genetic techniques to create entirely new long-lived strains of lower organisms.

THE NEW AGE OF MAN

Why do we grow old? Modern answers to this ancient question can be divided into genetic and non-genetic theories. Genetic theories argue that the life-span of an organism is genetically determined, like size or weight. The 'somatic mutation' theory, for example, claims that when cells divide, a small proportion of them mutate. The more often cell division occurs, the larger this proportion of abnormal cells becomes, leading to the damage we call aging. Non-genetic theories, on the other hand, look to 'wear and tear' or the accumulation of waste products to explain aging. But if aging is genetic, and if we are now beginning to understand and control genetic mechanisms, does that mean that we will soon be able to control aging? And if we do suddenly gain that long-dreamed-of power, what will we do with it?

[Notes]
[4] **palliative:** helping to [a. soothe symptoms / b. cure the disease]
[6] **cataract(s):** 白内障 (cf. p. 29, note [13])
[7] **coronary-bypass operations:**「冠状動脈バイパス手術」．冠状動脈 (coronary artery) の血流が阻害されたときに，よそからとってきた血管を心臓とつなげてこれに代える．
cut down on: to lessen; ease
[9] **the Centers for Disease Control:**（アメリカの）疾病管理センター
[11] **fracture(s):** breaking of a bone.　cf. Box on p. 151
[12] **Gerontological** < gerontology: the science of aging (and biological, psychological and sociological phenomena related to old age)
[15] *could*: そんなことはとても無理だという気持ちが，強勢に反映されている．
[18] **immutable:** unchangeable
[21] **tuneup:** a minor adjustment of an engine
[22] **There is Rose, with his Methuselah flies ...:** カリフォルニア大学アーヴァイン校のマイケル・ローズ教授は，英国サセックス大学の院生時代以来 20 年以上にわたって，ミバエ (fruit flies) の個体群から最晩産の子だけを選り抜くという "evolutionary" な方法で，長寿のハエを作る研究に成果を挙げている．Methuselah [məθjúzlə] は聖書の創世記 5: 27 に登場する 969 歳まで生きた長命者で，ノアの祖父．長命であったジョージ・バーナード・ショーは長大な戯曲『メトセラへ返れ』(*Back to Methuselah*)（1921 年出版，1922 年アメリカ初演，1923 年イギリス初演）で，Eden の園から西暦 31920 年までを扱い，長寿によって優れた社会が築けると主張し，あまりにも目先のことしか考えない政治のあり方を批判した．
[25] **long-lived strains of lower organisms:** 長命の（遺伝子を受け継ぐ）下等生物の種族

209

In 1996, two researchers at Montreal's McGill University published a paper in the journal *Science* showing how they genetically altered worms to live almost seven times as long as is normal. Kenyon showed me one of her mutant worms moving across a microscope slide as gracefully and vigorously at eight weeks as a normal worm moves at two weeks. Recently, too, an entirely separate field has arisen that analyzes aging at the cellular level and looks to treat and possibly cure many of the conditions and diseases of old age by focussing on the mysterious role played by the strips of DNA that cap the ends of our chromosomes. There are now serious researchers — not just science-fiction writers or crackpots — who think that we are close to curing cancer and other diseases of old age, and there are some who are convinced that the day is not far off when science may be able to extend the human life span by twenty or fifty, or even a hundred, years. To this new crop of researchers of aging — those who look at the extension of life at a cellular evolutionary level — growing old now seems less an immutable fact of human existence than a chronic disease that can be delayed and treated and manipulated as if it were diabetes or high cholesterol.

Hutchinson-Gilford syndrome is a rare, probably genetic disease that causes the interval between childhood and old age to shrink from the normal fifty or sixty years to just over a decade. There are fewer than thirty children with this accelerated aging, or progeria, around the world.

These progeric children suggest aging has its own mechanism, and here something known as telomere theory offers an elegant and fascinating explanation. Among the cells that make up human skin are the fibroblasts, which float in a sea of collagen, the substance that makes skin thick and resilient. Each fibroblast is a tiny repair kit, which works to keep skin healthy. If you suffer sun damage or a cut, your fibroblasts will make a substance called collagenase, which breaks down the damaged collagen and clears it away. If necessary, your fibroblasts will divide, to replace the damaged cells, and then they will pump out new collagen, so that what is known as the matrix can

THE NEW AGE OF MAN

[4]　**Kenyon:** カリフォルニア大学サンフランシスコ校の研究者シンシア・ケニオン．線虫綱の微生物を使った彼女の研究が，ローズの研究とともに，この記事の最初の部分(本テキストではカット)で紹介されていた．
[8]　**cellular** [séljulə]: < cell
[11]　**chromosome(s):** 染色体
[12]　**crackpot(s):** an eccentric person with strange ideas
[16]　**new crop of researchers:** a new generation of researchers
[19]　**chronic disease:** 慢性病．**chronic:** lasting a long time (⇔ acute)
[20]　**diabetes** [dàiəbíːtiːz]: 糖尿病．cf. diabetic [dàiəbétik]: 糖尿病患者
[21]　**cholesterol** [kəléstəròul]: コレステロール
[26]　**progeria** [proudʒíəriə]: 早老症．*See Box below.*
[28]　**telomere:** telo（末端）+ mere（部）．次頁で説明される．
[30]　**fibroblast(s):** 結合組織形成細胞．fibro（繊維）+ blast（噴出）
[31]　**collagen:** 日本語では「コラーゲン」だが，英語の発音は [kúlədʒən]．
　　　resilient: not easily damaged
[34]　**collagenase** [kúlədʒənèiz]: 日本語では「コラゲナーゼ」．
[37]　**what is known as the matrix:** "matrix" はいろいろな分野でいろいろな意味に使われる言葉だが，根本的な意味は「母」または「産」．この文脈に対応する日本語は「細胞間質」または「基質」．

Progeria

　Signs of infant progeria, the Hutchinson-Gilford syndrome, appear at about age one, after an evidently normal infancy. Affected individuals seldom exceed the size of a normal 5-year-old, although they have the physical appearance of 60-year-old adults by the time they are 10. Many of the superficial aspects of aging, such as baldness, thinning of the skin, prominence of blood vessels of the scalp, and vascular（血管関連の）diseases, occur. Sex organs remain small and underdeveloped. A few individuals with progeria are mentally retarded, but most have normal intelligence and may even be precocious. By age 10, extensive arteriosclerosis（動脈硬化）and heart disease have developed, and most patients die before they reach 30; the median age of death is 13. A hereditary basis has been suspected, but there is no evidence to support the suspicion, and the cause remains a mystery.　　　　　　　(from *Britannica*)

return to normal. This is a remarkably efficient operation. But it comes with one limitation. Inside a fibroblast, on the end of each of its chromosomes, there is a telomere, which researchers propose is a sort of timing device. Every time a fibroblast divides and the chromosomes inside the cell split up in order to form two new cells, the telomere gets a little shorter. The telomeres of a ten-year-old, for example, are, on average, longer than those of a twenty-year-old, which, in turn, are longer than those of a forty-year-old. After a fibroblast has divided about fifty times — which will take the average person into middle age — the telomere is shortened to a "critical length," and the timer goes off. A cell with a critically shortened telomere cannot divide any further, and so the whole repair operation that is used to keep skin thick and healthy is thrown out of whack. It's not that skin cells die; rather, it's as if they had become senile.

Progerics get heart disease, on this theory, because the cells that line their arteries start running out of telomeres and the arterial walls start to harden. Their movements get creaky because the cartilage that lines their joints begins to break down. In the same way, AIDS may kill by prematurely aging the white blood cells which fight infection. Telomere therapy could, if successful, give patients a rejuvenated immune system.

At this point, the idea that telomeres regulate the aging of cells is only a theory. Although there is plenty of highly suggestive evidence in its favor, it hasn't been definitively proved. If — or once — it is, however, it is not hard to see how revolutionary it will be. The original wear-and-tear idea of aging was essentially defeatist: it suggested that aging was inevitable, because it seemed so clearly linked to the passage of time. But telomeres suggest quite the opposite. In fact, telomeres make it much easier to believe that by tinkering with the body's machinery we can substantially prolong life, for if there are genetic changes capable of shortening telomeres in progerics, then shouldn't there also be changes capable of making them longer in the rest of us?

But such research also raises all kinds of hard questions, some

- [12] **the timer goes off:** cf. When an alarms clock goes off, it [a. starts ringing / b. stops ringing].
- [14] **out of whack:** out of order
- [16] **senile** [síːnail]**:** old and disabled
- [17] **the cells that line their arteries:** 動脈の内壁をなす細胞． cf. "brake-linings", p. 102, l. 21
- [19] **get creaky:** become slow or painful. cf. *Rusty machinery makes a creaking noise when it moves.* See p. 19, note [4]
- [20] **cartilage that lines their joints:** 動脈の節をつなぐ軟骨
- [21] **prematurely aging the white blood cells:** 白血球の早期老化をもたらす
- [23] **rejuvenated:** renewed
- [26] **evidence in its favor:** evidence that supports the telomere theory
- [28] **wear-and-tear idea of aging:** the idea that aging is caused unavoidably by accumulating damage
- [29] **defeatist:** 敗北主義的；宿命論的
- [32] **tinker(ing) with . . . :** 〜をいじりまわす
- [37] **such research:** reserches ではなく単数形をとっているのは，その種の研究全体を集合的に捉えているため．

of which may not be obvious at first. There is, for instance, a possibility that advances in medicine will lead people to live longer but without commensurate improvements in health. In other words, science may succeed in pushing the average life expectancy from seventy-five years to ninety-five, but the diseases that used to leave us sick and disabled at eighty-two or eighty-three may still hit at eighty-two or eighty-three — the result being that we would live in a nursing home for the last twelve years of our lives instead of the last two years. Epidemiologists call this possibility the "expansion of morbidity," and it has commanded more and more attention in recent years. Today, many kinds of medical improvements that we have devised are, after all, no longer aimed at saving people from dying at twenty-five or thirty of tuberculosis or smallpox, and so enabling them to enjoy another forty or fifty years of healthy life. Those diseases have been cured. Most attempts to improve longevity today focus on the diseases that primarily afflict the old — cancer, heart disease, stroke, arthritis — which means it is now much more likely that saving people from one disease may only result in their getting sicker and sicker with another.

Another way to look at this matter is from the standpoint of cost. If we were to cure cancer, and give six months of inactive life to the average seventy-year-old woman, that's six months with a nurse or in a home that society is going to have to pay for. The financial implications of this are huge.

When Jonathan Swift wrote *Gulliver's Travels*, in the early eighteenth century, a series of apparent scientific and medical breakthroughs had created a new optimism about the prospects of extending life. The Venetian architect Luigi Cornaro's work on how to live long, *Discourses on the Temperate Life*, was reprinted in fifty editions in England through the eighteenth and nineteenth centuries. The English philosopher Francis Bacon laid out, to great acclaim, his theories for improving longevity, calling it medicine's "most noble" objective. The pioneering British doctor William Harvey autopsied a poor

THE NEW AGE OF MAN

[3]   **without commensurate improvements in health:** それに見合った健康の増進なしに
[4]   **life expectancy:** 寿命
[10]   **Epidemiologists** < epidemiology: 疫学 (the study of *epidemics*, or outbreaks of disease that affect large numbers of people)
   "expansion of morbidity":（「寿命の延び」ならぬ）「病弱状態の延び」
[11]   **commanded . . . attention:** forced people to pay attention
[14]   **tuberculosis** [tjubə̀:kjulóusis]: 略称 TB. 最近ふたたび患者数が増加している結核は20世紀前半まで死因の上位を占めていた.
   smallpox: 天然痘. 1980年5月にWHO (World Health Organization) は地球上からの天然痘根絶を宣言した.
[18]   **stroke:** 脳卒中
   arthritis [a:θráitəs]: 関節炎
[29]   **breakthrough(s):** a sudden advance or discovery
   a new optimism about the prospects of extending life: 寿命を延ばすことができそうだという新しい期待感
[30]   **Luigi Cornaro:** ヴェネツィアの貴族で建築家のコルナーロ (1475–1566) は, 40歳で自らの不健康を痛感し, 厳密な食事制限によって長寿を全うしたという. 83歳のとき『節制生活論』*Discourses on the Temperate Life* を出版.
[33]   **Francis Bacon:** フランシス・ベーコン (1561–1626). *Novum Organum* (1620) でアリストテレスの演繹論に対抗する経験主義的な知の方法を展開.
[34]   **laid out, to great acclaim, his theories:** presented his theories and received great praise for them
[36]   **William Harvey:** ウィリアム・ハーヴェイ (1578–1657). 血液循環を発見したことで有名なイギリスの医師.
   autopsied < autopsy [ɔ́:tɑpsi]: 死体解剖検査

farmer named Thomas Parr in 1635 and announced that he was a hundred and fifty-two years and nine months old at death — a finding (later discredited) that lent Parr such celebrity that he was buried in Westminster Abbey, close to where Charles Darwin was later buried. This was the attitude that Swift was satirizing when he had Gulliver, upon first hearing of the Struldbruggs, rhapsodize over the possibility of immortality. Swift's concern was not just that people seemed to want to live forever; it was that they still desired to live longer, even in the face of evidence that longer life only brought increased infirmity. What Swift recognized was that this desire was basically irrational: that men were so afraid of death that they constructed an "unreasonable" fantasy of what living longer would mean — unreasonable because it supposed a "perpetuity of Youth, Health and Vigour" when the real question was "not whether a Man would chuse to be always in the Prime of Youth, attended with Prosperity and Health, but how he would pass a perpetual Life under all the usual Disadvantages which old Age brings along with it."

There are ways around the problem that Swift outlined, of course. Telomere therapy combined with medical interventions that address some of the other mechanisms of aging might be a good start toward extending life without extending disability. But this is all very speculative and all very far off. For the moment, the battle against aging is characterized by an unrestrained enthusiasm that sounds an awful lot like Gulliver when he first heard about the Struldbruggs. Then he actually met the Struldbruggs, the living exemplars of what longer life really was, and his fantasies about defeating death were laid to rest. He looked immortality in the eye and turned away: "They were the most mortifying sight I had ever beheld."

THE NEW AGE OF MAN

[3] **discredited:** found to be false
lent . . . celebrity: gave . . . fame
[4] **Westminster Abbey:** ウェストミンスター寺院(歴代国王の戴冠式や葬儀，また偉大な市民の国葬が行なわれる教会)
[6] **satirizing:** [a. ridiculing / b. supporting]
[7] **Struldbruggs** [strʌ́ldbrʌ̀gz]:『ガリヴァー旅行記』の正式な題名は *Travels into Several Remote Nations of the World, by Lemuel Gulliver.* 有名な小人の国 Lilliput のほか，巨人の国 Brobdingnag, 現実離れした学者の国 Laputa, 不幸な不死者 Struldbruggs の国，理性的な馬 Houyhnhnm [húinəm] の国，獣人 Yahoo の国を，風刺をこめて描き出す．
rhapsodize: to talk very enthusiastically
[10] **infirmity:** weakness; loss of health (especially by age)
[14] **perpetuity** [pə:pətjú:əti] < perpetual [pə:pétʃuəl]: everlasting
[16] **chuse:** choose の古い綴り
Prime of Youth:「若さの頂点」．16〜18 世紀ごろの英語はドイツ語のように名詞のはじまりを大文字にすることもよくあった．
[20] **ways around the problem:** ways to avoid the problem
[22] **address:** to deal with
[24] **all very speculative:** not based on facts; purely theoretical
far off: i.e. [a. far in the future / b. far from the truth]
[29] **laid to rest:** buried; dead and gone
[30] **looked immortality in the eye:**「不死の眼をのぞき込む」とは，不死というものの実の姿をまざまざと見ること
[31] **mortifying:** displeasing の意味で広く使われるが，原意は deadening.

SESSION 21
The Thrill of Fear

Walter Kendrick

IT has often been said that human beings are the only [1]
species who know they must die, who can conjure up the
event as if it were happening now and react accordingly.
Animals fear death, but the fear seems to come on them only
when death immediately threatens. They do not brood upon it. [5]

A nineteenth-century doctor reports a case of an insane woman who was terrified by the imagined spectacle of her body rotting away. This reminds us that human beings can also imagine being dead, a very different thing from death and perhaps a more frightening one. Deprived of soul, spirit, force, [10] whatever you may call it (this fear requires no religion), human flesh is meat and it goes meat's way. Few seventeenth-century preachers would have balked at summoning up the madwoman's vision in their congregations' minds. Then, as in all prior Christian centuries, the lesson was plain and familiar: [15] Put your faith in flesh and you'll end up feeding worms; put your faith in spirit, subdue the ephemeral flesh, and you'll transcend the grave.

Well into the eighteenth century such lessons went on being preached, but they sharply dwindled after 1750, and I know of [20] no one who preaches in that style now. By the late nineteenth century, the idea that the flesh will rot seemed as horrifying as ever, to mad and sane alike. The idea, however, had long since lost its religious usefulness; though it could still frighten, it no longer admonished. Indeed, decorum hardly admitted notions [25]

THE THRILL OF FEAR

「死からの逃避」というテーマは，もちろん医学の領域に限った話ではない．過激で暴力的な映像の氾濫する時代に生きる私たちは，一種の娯楽として死の観念と戯れることは多くても，その一方でリアルな「死」を身の周りから完全に追放し，それをまた当然のことと考えていないだろうか．過去の時代，人々は「死」とどのようにつき合ってきたか，そしてそれがどのように変化してきたのか——以下の文章の出典 *The Thrill of Fear* は，"250 Years of Scary Entertainment" という副題のホラー通史である．

[Notes]
[2]　**conjure up the event:** i.e. imagine the moment of death
[5]　**brood** [bru:d]**:** to meditate; worry
[9]　**being dead, a very different thing from death:** Throughout the essay, "death" (the *event* of dying) is set in contrast with "deadness" (the *state* of "being dead").
[11]　**this fear requires no religion:** i.e. it makes no difference whether you call death the loss of soul or spirit (which are religious terms), or of force (which is a non-religious term).
[12]　**goes meat's way:** rots as meat does
　　　Few seventeenth-century preachers would have balked at summoning up . . . : i.e. it was [a. common / b. uncommon] for seventeenth-century preachers to use frightening images of being dead. **balked at:** hesitated
[14]　**congregations:** 会衆，信徒
[15]　**Christian centuries:**「新興宗教」としてのキリスト教はイエスの時代からあったが，国家の容認・保護を通して支配的な社会勢力となるのは4世紀から．cf. p. 165, note [32]
[16]　**Put your faith in flesh:**「肉に信仰を置く」とは，具体的には肉体的・五感的な欲望に生きること．
[17]　**ephemeral:** i.e. lasting only while you live in this world; momentary (⇔ eternal)
　　　transcend the grave: i.e. overcome physical death
[20]　**sharply dwindled:** rapidly became rare
[25]　**admonished:** warned (i.e. served as a lesson)
　　　decorum hardly admitted notions of deadness into public discourse: i.e. the subject of deadness became a taboo in polite situations. **decorum:** polite behavior

of deadness into public discourse. Fond as they were of funerals and all the panoply of mourning, the Victorians exhibited a thoroughly modern squeamishness in regard to the symptoms of being dead. They continued a development that began at the end of the seventeenth century and has not ceased — hiding deadness away, cosmeticizing corpses, denying ever more strenuously that anything nasty happens to the body after death. The gaudy American funeral industry that Evelyn Waugh lampooned in *The Loved One* (1948) and Jessica Mitford lambasted in *The American Way of Death* (1963) is only the most grotesque by-product of a long, slow, immensely complex process of deliberate forgetting.

It may seem paradoxical that death itself, especially violent death, has remained immune to the taboo against deadness. In their newspapers, melodramas, and popular fiction, the Victorians exhibited the same fervent interest in the varieties of dying that their Elizabethan and Jacobean ancestors had gratified at bloody stage plays and public executions. We have inherited that interest, and we cultivate it, if possible, with even greater fervor. But our interest fades once the deed is done; what happens to the corpse thereafter belongs in a different zone, a shadowy one, where we, like the Victorians, would prefer not to tread. Those Elizabethans and Jacobeans (and the generations before them) exhibited a very different attitude, one that must strike a modern observer as callous, revolting, utterly incomprehensible, or perhaps all three. Before the eighteenth century, though decay was horrible enough to induce repentance, it was not strange; it did not bring on the peculiarly modern sensation of terror at the very idea of being dead.

The roots of any such large-scale change are impossible to locate with precision. Our recoil from deadness may be just one aspect of the overall tidying up that has been going on in Western culture for the last two hundred years. Frequent baths, efficient disposal of garbage and excrement, the banishing from ordinary view of all things that smell bad — these and many other apparently hygienic practices have reached a high degree of thoroughness in the most advanced Western nations,

THE THRILL OF FEAR

[1] **Fond as they were of funerals:** Though they liked funerals
[2] **panoply of mourning:** 喪を表わす一連の装い，飾りつけ
[3] **exhibited ... squeamishness in regard to the symptoms of being dead:** i.e. the Victorians [a. were tolerant about / b. would have turned away in disgust from] anything that suggested deadness.
[6] **cosmeticizing corpses:** 死体に化粧をほどこすこと
[7] **ever more strenuously:** with ever greater effort. **nasty:** unpleasant
[8] **gaudy:** けばけばしい
[9] **Evelyn Waugh** [wɔː]: 20世紀前半の英国を代表する小説家のひとり (1903–66). **lampoon(ed):** to satirize; ridicule
The Loved One: 「宗教と芸術の理想的融合の場」と人から勧められてウォーが訪れたハリウッドの共同墓地をモデルに，アメリカ葬儀産業を徹底的に皮肉った小説．（タイトルの「愛しい人」とは「故人」を指すきまり文句．）
[10] *The American Way of Death*: 20世紀アメリカの葬儀産業がいかなる手口で「高価」な葬式を押しつけるかを暴いた，ジャーナリスト Mitford による糾弾 (lambasting) の書．
[12] **deliberate forgetting:** （deadness を）心の中から意図的に消し去ること．
[14] **immune to:** unchanged by
[16] **fervent interest in the varieties of dying:** 1888年，売春婦連続殺人犯 Jack the Ripper が当時のマスコミに大々的にとり上げられたのはその一例．事件は迷宮入りし，多くの小説の種を提供した．**fervent:** passionate; enthusiastic
[17] **Elizabethan and Jacobean ancestors:** シェイクスピアが登場したエリザベス朝 (1558–1603) とそれに続くジェームズ朝 (1603–25) はイギリス演劇の隆盛期で，John Webster ら，血の惨劇を描くのを得意とする劇作家が多く登場した．
[18] **public executions:** 広場などで見世物として行なわれた処刑
[19] **cultivate it:** to make it grow
[20] **once the deed is done:** i.e. once people are killed
[23] **tread** [tred]: 踏み込む
[25] **must strike a modern observer as callous:** must make today's people feel that Elizabethan and Jacobean people were very cruel. **callous:** unfeeling
[27] **induce repentance:** 宗教的な悔悟の気持ちを引き起こす
[28] **bring on:** to cause
peculiarly: distinctly
[29] **terror at the very idea of ... :** ～を思うだけで生じる恐怖
[31] **locate with precision:** to say precisely where (the roots are)
recoil: reaction of [a. fear / b. fascination]
[32] **tidying up:** cleaning up (of unpleasant things)
[34] **excrement** [ékskrəmənt]: 排泄物．cf. *feces* (p. 46, l. 26)
[36] **apparently hygienic practices:** 衛生のためと思われている慣行．たとえば現在のような形の水洗便所が発明されたのは18世紀末のこと．

221

and the sequestering of the dead may merely have moved alongside them. This is probably progress; certainly no one would wish any of it undone. But progress, as Sigmund Freud was fond of pointing out, exacts costs that often work unseen. By the end of the eighteenth century, deadness had entered the realm it still inhabits: Being dead had joined the ranks of what Freud, in a famous 1919 essay, called "The 'Uncanny.'"

Freud's point works better in German: *Das Unheimliche* literally means "the un-home-like" and suits itself well to Freud's definition as "that class of the frightening which leads back to what is known of old and long familiar." It may also, however, be something "that ought to have remained secret and hidden but comes to light." As might be expected, Freud proceeds to discover a good deal of castration anxiety in the business, along with survivals of primitive beliefs and emotions. With these tried-and-true formulas he manages to answer a number of questions. Yet he never quite smooths out the apparent discrepancy between those two possible meanings of *das Unheimliche*. Nor does he satisfactorily explain a classic occasion for the feeling, though he cites it more than once: "doubts whether an apparently animate being is really alive; or conversely, whether a lifeless object might not be in fact animate."

"Since almost all of us still think as savages do on this topic," says Freud (evidently not including himself in that majority), "it is no matter for surprise that the primitive fear of the dead is still so strong within us." Perhaps so, but older cultures feared the dead as vengeful spirits, not as rotten, reeking things. And that old fear was grounded in belief; it could be met and mastered by rituals designed for the purpose. Modern fear of deadness gets no solace from worn-out platitudes about heaven and the afterlife. We may believe that we'll end up sitting on clouds, strumming harps; we may cherish some subtler notion of the soul's survival, or none at all. Whatever happens to the soul, it cannot save the body, which will turn to clay and can be seen already moving in that direction before death. Nothing can console this modern fear — which is why, on the whole,

THE THRILL OF FEAR

[1] **sequestering:** removal; hiding
have moved alongside them: i.e. have become a similar kind of activity
[3] **wish any of it undone:** i.e. wish to go back to the years before the "tidying up"
[4] **exacts:** demands; requires
costs that often work unseen: はっきりと意識されないところで作用することの多い悪影響
[7] **"The 'Uncanny'":**「無気味なもの」. the Unconscious, the Ego など精神分析学の用語はよく大文字で表記される．The が大文字になり，二重引用符がついているのは，論文のタイトルだから．
[8] **works better:** is more effective
Das Unheimliche: *Unheimliche* の発音は「ウンハイムリッヒ」に近い．
[10] **class:** 類；集合
which leads back to ... long familiar: フロイトはこの「無気味なもの」を，個人が自分の幼年期の記憶に戻ることと，原始時代（人類全体の幼年期）の記憶に戻ることとに重ねあわせて考えた．
[11] **of old:** 昔から
[14] **castration anxiety:** 去勢不安．"As might be expected" という句がついているのは，フロイト心理学では，現実の心の動きや行動を，無意識の世界で働く性的な欲動や恐怖で説明するのが常だから．
the business:「無気味なもの」のはたらき全体を漠然とさす．
[16] **tried-and-true formulas:** うまくいくことが立証済みの議論の進め方
[18] **discrepancy:** disagreement; gap
those two possible meanings: この頁の 10～13 行目，次の頁の 5～6 行目参照．
[19] **classic occasion for the feeling:** a typical case where the feeling of the "Uncanny" arises. cf. "a classic trap" (p. 154, l. 6)
[26] **it is no matter for surprise that . . . :** it is not surprising at all that . . .
[28] **vengeful spirits:** 怨念をもった霊
reeking: making a strong smell. cf. p. 82, l. 3
[29] **that old fear:** fear of the dead as [a. vengeful spirits / b. rotten, reeking things]
was grounded in belief:（無意識へと抑圧されるのでなく）信仰の中に正当な位置を与えられていた
be met and mastered by rituals: 儀式を通して克服される
[31] **solace** [súləs]: なぐさめ (consoling)
worn-out platitudes about heaven and the afterlife: 死んだら天国に行けるとか，来世が待っているとかいった，言い古されたセリフ
[33] **subtler:** more refined; more sophisticated
[35] **turn to clay:**「土に還る」

we prefer not to discuss the subject.

Yet, of course, we know it well. We can picture what goes on underground, in those gleaming, satin-lined caskets, especially if we've never seen it. Such secret knowledge renders the subject un-home-like in both of Freud's senses: familiar and strange, hidden and blatant, all at once. And the fear it inspires is focused on just the instance of the uncanny that Freud cited without exploring it: the line, if there is one, between being alive and being dead. When the loved one dies and is buried or cremated, we wish that only her ethereal aspect would survive — her soul perhaps, her memory certainly. At the same time, we remember that she lingers on in a more material form, even if it's only a handful of dust. And we may well be made uneasy by the mysterious kinship between the human being she once was and the hidden thing some part of her is now. Maybe the difference between being alive and being dead is not so absolute as our wishes would make it. Maybe the dead retain more of life than we care to acknowledge; there may be more of death in life than we can think of without a shudder.

At the end of the twentieth century, these are literally unspeakable matters. We have been born into a late stage of a process, more than two centuries old, that has almost totally removed the after-effects of death from most Western experience, leaving them to cavort in the imagination. We do not discuss the frailty and ultimate dissolution of our flesh, and when the fact leaps at us, as the AIDS epidemic has made it do, it elicits redoubled horror thanks to the entrenched strength of our denial. Even as we deny that our flesh must decay, however, we surround ourselves with fictional images of the very fate we strive to hear nothing about.

It looks paradoxical at best — psychotic at worst — that one might go from an hour on the Nautilus machines or in an aerobics class, where the body is urged to the acme of aliveness, directly to a screening of *Night of the Living Dead*, which pits animated corpses against the living and lets the corpses win. If this were the fourteenth century, the spectacle of death's ravages would admonish pride of life. The admonition might

THE THRILL OF FEAR

- [3] **gleaming, satin-lined caskets:** キラキラ光る，サテン地張りの(高級な)棺
- [6] **blatant** [bléitənt]**:** conspicuous; highly visible
  all at once: [a. all of a sudden / b. all at the same time]
- [8] **if there is one:** 本当にそんな境界線があるのかどうか定かでないのだが，という含み．
- [10] **cremate(d):** cf. p. 114, l. 36
  ethereal: immaterial; spiritual
- [12] **lingers on:** remains
- [14] **kinship:** [a. closeness / b. difference]
- [15] **the hidden thing some part of her is now:** i.e. her corpse. thing の後に関係詞 that を補って読む．
- [18] **more of life than we care to acknowledge:** われわれが認めたくないくらいの量の「生」．死んでも消えてなくならないものの多さを言っている．
- [20] **literally unspeakable:** unspeakable という言葉は，単に「おぞましい」くらいの意味で使われることが多い．ここではそうではなく，文字どおりに unspeakable だということ．
- [23] **after-effects of death:** 死後の作用
- [24] **cavort:** to dance or act freely and wildly
- [25] **frailty:** もろさ，はかなさ
  dissolution: 消滅 (< dissolve: 溶ける)
- [26] **when the fact leaps at us:** when we are strongly reminded of the fact. **leap:** to jump
- [27] **elicit(s):** to bring out
  thanks to the entrenched strength of our denial: because we stubbornly deny it; because we refuse to bring it out in the open
- [28] **Even as . . . :** 〜しながらも(その一方で)
- [31] **. . . at best, . . . at worst:** よく言えば〜，悪く言えば〜
- [32] **Nautilus machines:** (その社名がフィットネス器具の代名詞となるほどポピュラーな)フィットネス器具
- [33] **acme of aliveness:** height of life
- [34] **screening:** 上映
  Night of the Living Dead: ジョージ・ロメロが 1968 年に作ったホラー映画の古典．
  pits animated corpses against . . . : has zombies fight against . . .
- [37] **admonish pride of life:** i.e. tell people to be [a. more / b. less] proud of being alive

go unheeded — people might go on living pridefully, as they evidently did after the plague had claimed a third of Europe — but there would at least be a coherent relation between the two experiences. In the late twentieth century, there seems to be none. Pride of life has carried the day; death's ravages are bearable now only because they have been processed to enhance that pride instead of mortifying it. From Count Chocula and the cutesy rituals of Halloween to the most vomit-provoking splatter film, scary entertainments can entertain only because even as they apparently violate the taboo against showing the after-effects of death, they transform them into affirmations of the body's impregnability.

In this way, the horror of death and dying is rendered safe; it is turned into a celebration of being permanently alive, forever immune to decay. Death and dying are made to provide pleasure — not of an intellectual sort or even exactly an emotional one, but the gut thrill of deep breaths, shouts, and half-serious clutches at the viewer in the next seat. Fear of deadness has become a reliable reservoir of muscular innervation that can be tapped at any time, without much inventiveness or, it seems, any anxiety that it will ever run dry. The cleverest horror films may offer political commentary, even social criticism, thereby winning the approval of those who would otherwise never glance at a horror movie. But such things are extras; they're far from necessary, and they sometimes threaten to impede horror's fundamental errand — to assure the viewer that his flesh will always remain firm and intact, that for all this display of rot and carnage, there is nothing to fear.

[1] **go unheeded:** to be ignored. cf. *heed* (p. 160, l. 26)
[2] **the plague had claimed a third of Europe:** 14世紀半ばにクリミア半島で発生した黒死病はヨーロッパ全土に広がり，人口の3人に1人が犠牲となったと言われる．
[3] **the two experiences:** i.e. the experience of the "acme of aliveness" or the pride of life on the one hand, and the "spectacle of death's ravages" on the other
[5] **has carried the day:** has won
[6] **they have been processed:** i.e. their meaning has been transformed
[7] **mortifying it:** making it humble; putting it to shame.   cf. p. 216, l. 31
Count Chocula: ドラキュラ伯爵 (Count Dracula) をもじった漫画的人物を箱に描いたチョコレート味のシリアル
[8] **cutesy rituals of Halloween:** かわいらしく仕立てたハロウィーンの儀式．もともとは死者の霊との交わりの催しだったハロウィーンも，骸骨の服を着たり，カボチャの提灯を作ったりして楽しむお祭りになってしまった．
[11] **affirmations of the body's impregnability:** i.e. denial of "the frailty and ultimate dissolution of our flesh"（前頁25行目）．**impregnability:** invulnerability（無敵さ）
[17] **gut thrill:** 体の底から感じるスリル
[19] **a reliable reservoir of muscular innervation that can be tapped at any time:** 「いつでも確実にたくわえを引き出せる筋感覚神経反応の貯水池」．すなわちホラー映画を見れば必ずゾクゾクする恐怖感 (gut thrill) が味わえるということ．
[21] **run dry:** 干し上がる（貯水池の比喩のつづき）．
The cleverest horror films may offer political commentary, even social criticism: たとえば *Night of the Living Dead* では，ゾンビに侵入される家の中での男女間・人種間の葛藤が描かれ，またメディアの空しさといった問題も扱われている．
[25] **impede:** to hinder; make less effective
[26] **errand:** mission; task
[28] **carnage:** slaughter; killing and wounding

SESSION 22

The Buckeyball: A Diamond Maker's Dream

Robert M. Hazen

HIGH-PRESSURE research now consumes the lives of countless scientists and engineers, who know there are many breakthroughs still to be made. Some researchers are consumed by the quest for metallic hydrogen, while others continue to investigate minerals of the earth's deep interior. Chemists now search for valuable new materials, while physicists use pressure to probe the properties of matter. And for thousands of scientists, diamonds and other exotic forms of carbon still prove an irresistible lure.

Even after forty years of routine high-pressure synthesis, the diamond adventure is far from over. In the early 1990s an extraordinary discovery was made that has elated scientists and engineers and that may give rise to remarkable new high-tech products.

Just when it seemed that we had learned nearly all there was to know about diamond making — when synthesis of large, isotopically pure diamond crystals and vapor-deposited diamond films was redefining our mastery of carbon — scientists made a fantastic breakthrough, discovering a totally new way to make diamonds under pressure. The new approach was catalyzed by a discovery so remarkable and unexpected that it may take decades for scientists to sort out all of its implications.

In all the centuries of focused research on carbon and its compounds, nothing has caught scientists more off guard or has had a more immediate impact than the discovery of the

THE BUCKEYBALL

胸躍る科学礼賛の話が一つくらいあってもいい——というわけで，現代の高圧圧搾技術の生み出す魅惑の世界を紹介する文章を1本選んでみた．出典は *The New Alchemists*（現代の錬金術師たち）という題の高圧技術の歴史をつづった本．著者は地球科学者で，*Science Matters: Achieving Scientific Literacy* などの著書で科学教育の推進を提起している．

[Notes]

[1]　**consumes the lives of:** occupies the hours of; absorbs the whole energy of. cf. *time-consuming*

[3]　**breakthroughs:** cf. p. 214, l. 29

[5]　**investigate minerals of the earth's deep interior:** 直接の観測は不可能だが，3000°C 100万気圧という状況下での実験を通して，核とマントル境界のようすを科学的に推測する等の研究が続いている．

[7]　**probe** [proub]**:** to explore; investigate

[9]　**prove an irresistible lure:** are felt to be extremely attractive

[12]　**elate(d):** to delight

[13]　**give rise to ...:** lead to the invention of ...; bring ... into being

[15]　**all there was to know about ...:** everything that can be known about ...

[17]　**isotopically pure diamond crystals:**「同位体的に純粋な」というのは，原子量14の炭素同位元素を含まず，原子量12の炭素原子だけでできているということ．**isotopes:** atoms that have the same atomic number (same number of protons), but which contain a different number of neutrons

　　　vapor-deposited diamond films: "(chemical) vapor deposition" とは，超低圧下で加熱し気化させた炭素原子をゆっくり冷却しながら，3つではなく4つの原子と隣接するように (p. 233の図参照) 結晶化していく方法．この方法で作られるフィルム（薄片）状のダイヤは，優れた半導体としての活用が期待されている．

[18]　**redefining our mastery of carbon:** enabling us to control and make use of carbon in new ways. *Jimi Hendrix redefined rock music with his screeching guitar.*

[20]　**catalyze(d):** to make happen more quickly or easily; trigger. cf. *catalyst* [kǽtəlɔst]: 触媒，*catalysis* [kətǽləsis]: 触媒作用

[22]　**sort out all of its implications:** その発見のもつ多岐にわたる意味合いをすべて整理して把握する

[23]　**compound(s)** [kάmpaund]**:** a chemical compound（化合物）

[24]　**nothing has caught scientists more off guard:** nothing came as a bigger surprise. *Larry's question caught his mother off guard; for a moment she was speechless.*

229

buckeyball. For centuries carbon was known in only two basic forms — graphite and diamond. Now there are three.

Surprisingly, the serendipitous path to the new type of carbon began with studies of starlight. For more than half a century astronomers had puzzled over the distinctive light-absorbing properties of interstellar dust, which suggested the presence of clumps of carbon atoms — soot formed in the vicinity of stars. Several groups of scientists tried to simulate interstellar dust in their laboratories, vaporizing graphite in an effort to match the astronomers' spectra.

The first clear evidence of a new form of carbon came on September 4, 1985, when Harold W. Kroto of Sussex University, in collaboration with a group at Rice University led by Richard E. Smalley, discovered an unexpected concentration of molecules in their synthetic soot that weighed exactly 720 atomic mass units, corresponding to the weight of a cluster of sixty carbon atoms. An intense few days of study led them to conclude that these C_{60} molecules represented a particularly stable form of carbon that adopted the spherical form of a soccer ball, which is constructed from thirty-two panels — twelve pentagons and twenty hexagons that meet at sixty vertices. The distinctive alternation of these pentagonal and hexagonal rings, characteristic of the geodesic architecture of R. Buckminster Fuller, led Kroto's and Smalley's groups to name the new molecule buckminster-fullerene. Soon everyone was calling them buckyballs for short.

Once scientists knew what to look for, they found that C_{60} clusters are ubiquitous. Under hundreds of different synthesis conditions researchers observed complex mixtures of C_{60} and various other carbon-rich molecules, including ordinary graphite. They found that while the sixty-carbon form is usually most abundant, there are also many other enclosed carbon molecules. The football-shaped C_{70} cluster is particularly common, but a staggering variety of fullerenes, from C_{32} to C_{600}, have also been identified.

From 1985 to 1990 many teams of chemists around the world studied the new carbon, but all were frustrated by their inabil-

THE BUCKEYBALL

[2] **graphite and diamond:** In diamond, carbon atoms are each surrounded by a pyramid of four other carbons, creating the strongest atomic network found in nature. In graphite, each carbon is strongly bonded to three neighbors in layers, while bonds between layers are relatively weak. (See Figure on p. 233)
[3] **serendipitous** [sèrəndípətəs]: タナボタ式に得られた
[6] **interstellar dust:** 宇宙塵.　**interstellar:** (located) between the stars
[7] **in the vicinity of:** in the space around; near
[9] **vaporizing graphite in an effort to match the astronomers' spectra:** 黒鉛を気化したものを分光解析して，宇宙観測から得られたスペクトルと同じものができていないか調べる
[16] **atomic mass unit(s):** 原子質量単位．略 AMU．炭素 12 の質量の 1/12 が単位．
[21] **twelve pentagons and twenty hexagons . . . :** この立体は，正 12 面体 (12 の合同な正 5 角形からなる) の 20 の頂点を，断面が正 6 角形になるように切り落としたものと見ることができる．口絵参照．
[22] **vertices** [vớ:təsì:z] < vertex: 頂点
　　　distinctive alternation: 鮮やかに交互して並んでいるさま
[23] **geodesic architecture of R. Buckminster Fuller:** アメリカの工学デザイナー・バックミンスター・フラー (1895–1983) の作った「ジオデシック・ドーム」は，新しい居住哲学をあらわすものとして，1950 年代以来大きな脚光を浴びてきた．直線構造材の組み方にはいくつものパターンがある．下図参照．
[28] **ubiquitous** [jubíkwətəs]: everywhere
[33] **The football-shaped C_{70} cluster:** 楕円体をなす炭素原子の結合体 C_{70}
[34] **staggering:** astonishing.　**stagger:** to sway unsteadily

A Fuller dome

ity to purify the stuff. Richard Smalley and his colleague Robert Curl wrote, "We could not collect more than a few tens of thousands of these special molecules. This amount was plenty to detect and probe with the sophisticated techniques available in our laboratory, but there was not enough to see, touch or smell.... All we had to do was make more of them — billions and billions more."

German scientist Wolfgang Kratschmer and his graduate student Konstantinos Fostiropoulos isolated pure buckeyballs at last on May 18, 1990, when they discovered that C_{60} dissolves in benzene, an ordinary liquid solvent. By washing their soot in the colorless liquid, the two scientists from the Max Planck Institute for Nuclear Physics in Heidelberg were able to produce a beautiful magenta solution of buckeyballs. Kratschmer immediately telephoned their longtime collaborator in fullerene research, Donald Huffman at the University of Arizona in Tucson.

Huffman vividly recalls the day. "Within minutes I was able to verify the solubility," he wrote. "Then came the ultimate 'Eureka' experience in my life as a solid-state physicist. With graduate student Lowell Lamb, I allowed a small drop of the red benzene solution to dry on a slide. Under the microscope [thousands of] beautiful little hexagonal platelets of apparently pure carbon were revealed — a brand new form of solid carbon." For the first time, humans could watch and study crystals of the unexpected substance.

In a matter of days they had learned to produce buckeyballs in quantity. The easiest way was to heat graphite in helium gas to produce a soot rich in C_{60} and other molecules, then to isolate the fullerenes with benzene. One of the earliest production devices at Arizona employed an old beer keg as the helium chamber. With their unique supplies of fullerenes, the Heidelberg and Arizona groups could finally measure many of the buckeyball's properties for the first time. The extraordinary results were presented to the world at a conference in Germany in early September and were published in their article "Solid C_{60}: A New Form of Carbon," which appeared in

THE BUCKEYBALL

[14] **magenta solution:** 紫紅色の溶液
[17] **Tuscon:** [tú:sn]
[19] **verify the solubility:** confirm that C_{60} is soluble [sáljəbl].
[20] **'Eureka':** According to legend, Archimedes jumped out of his bath and shouted "Eureka!" ("I have found it!") when he realized that the volume of an irregular object could be found by measuring how much water it displaces.
solid-state physicist: 固体物理学者
[23] **platelet(s):** ふつう血小板 (blood platelet) をさす.

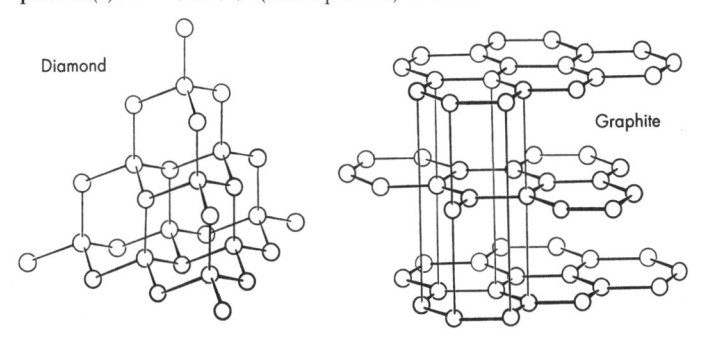

Diamond

Graphite

What Puts the Sparkle in a Diamond?

Light travels at 300,000 kilometers per second. Yes — in a vacuum. In water and ice, light slows to about 70% of that, and ordinary window glass slows it down even more. Special lead-rich glass (such as you might find in a decorative chandelier or crystal decanter) slows light down to almost half its vacuum speed, because the added lead has lots of electrons that get in the way.

Diamonds can put the brakes on light like no other colorless substance we know. Diamond is simply crammed with electrons — no substance you have ever seen has its atoms more densely packed — and light struggles through it at less than 130,000 kilometers per second. Diamond can "freeze" light even more than ice.

It's the same density of structure in a diamond which bends and reflects light more dramatically than any other clear substance. Light enters a faceted diamond from all sides, but it may bounce back and forth several times before it finds a straight path out. All this changing direction has very dramatic effects, because so-called white light actually contains all the colors of the rainbow. Each color bends and reflects inside the diamond at slightly different angles, and the farther the light travels, the more the colors separate. It's this magical separation of colors that puts the enchanting — and expensive — sparkle in a diamond.

(R. M. Hazen, adapted)

the September 27, 1990, issue of *Nature*.

An explosion of buckeyball research followed the September revelations. The stuff was easy to make, was easy to study, and possessed extraordinary chemical and physical properties. By mid-1991 thousands of scientists had jumped on the buckeyball bandwagon and hundreds of articles had appeared in record time. Pure C_{60}, it was found, is an electrical insulator, but add a little bit of potassium and it becomes a semiconductor. Add a little more and it becomes a superconductor. Buckeyballs mixed with other elements have achieved superconductivity at an amazing forty-five degrees above absolute zero — a record surpassed only by the so-called high-temperature copper superconductors. Buckeyballs are the most resilient of molecules: propel them at a diamond target at speeds of 20,000 miles per hour — a speed that would blast other molecules to pieces on impact — and they simply bounce off, undamaged. Some varieties of buckeyballs even become magnetic at low temperature, a phenomenon unique among carbon-based materials.

The buckeyball's chemistry is every bit as amazing as its physical properties. While the sixty-carbon cluster is physically tough, it is also quite reactive. Scientists at Rice University have synthesized buckeycages that enclose individual atoms or groups of atoms inside the carbon sphere. Chemists at Berkeley have created bunnyballs, which have a pair of earlike molecules branching off the main sphere. Northwestern University workers found that a layer of buckeyballs dramatically increases the speed of vapor deposition of diamonds — perhaps by a factor of ten. Chemists envision dozens of fullerene variants: $C_{60}H_{60}$ fuzzyballs with a hydrogen coating; $C_{60}F_{60}$ teflonballs that are predicted to have unusual lubricant properties; and fullerene hairyballs with elongated molecules that festoon the outside of the C_{60} sphere. Materials scientists have also synthesized a rich variety of buckeytubes, long cylinders of carbon atoms that produce incredibly strong fibers with the potential to revolutionize the field of lightweight construction.

When *Science* named buckeyballs its 1991 Molecule of the

THE BUCKEYBALL

[3] revelation(s): disclosure. 学会発表と論文掲載をやや大げさに言った言葉.
[5] jump(ed) on the . . . bandwagon: join others (in doing something currently popular)
[7] in record time: in the shortest time ever. cf. *a record level of unemployment*
insulator: 絶縁体. cf. semiconductor, superconductor
[8] potassium [pətǽsiəm]: カリウム. cf. sodium [sóudiəm]: ナトリウム
[14] resilient [rizíljənt]: resistent to damage; able to recover quickly. *She is resilient to stress.*
speeds: 複数になっているのは「だいたいその範囲の」という含みがあるため.
[15] 20,000 miles per hour: approximately 9 kilometers per second
[18] unique: i.e. among carbon-based materials, *only* buckyballs become magnetic
[20] every bit as amazing as . . . : no less amazing than . . .   *Susan is every bit as intelligent as you are.*
[21] physically tough: i.e. resilient; difficult to damage
[22] reactive: i.e. chemically reactive; ready to combine with other atoms and molecules
[28] increases . . . by a factor of ten: make . . . ten times as fast
vapor deposition of diamonds: cf. p. 229, note [17]
[30] $C_{60}H_{60}$ fuzzyballs: buckeyball の 60 の頂点のそれぞれについている水素原子を「ケバ」に見立てた言い方.
$C_{60}F_{60}$ teflonballs: テフロンの分子構造は $F_2C=CF_2$. これを fullerene の型につないでいければ作れるはず.
[31] lubricant [lú:brikənt] properties: 摩擦のなさ；(テフロン加工したフライパンのような)スベスベの特性.
[32] fullerene hairyballs with elongated molecules that festoon the outside of the C_{60} sphere: どんなものか想像してみよう. elongated: 細長く伸びた. festoon: (花や葉をリボンなどとつないで作る)花綱(で飾る).
[33] Materials scientists: テクノロジーへの応用のためさまざまな物質の研究と開発を進める「材料科学者」.
[37] its 1991 Molecule of the Year: cf. *The Singer of the Century Award in the Female Jazz section goes to Billie Holiday.*

Year, the study of fullerenes was barely a year old, yet the round form of carbon stood poised to transform materials science. Almost buried in this avalanche of discovery was a short letter in *Nature* by Argentinean scientist Manuel Nufiez Regueiro and his co-workers Pierre Monceau and Jean-Louis Hodeau at Grenoble, France, who had performed the simplest of diamond-anvil cell experiments on buckeyballs. Having squeezed buckminsterfullerene to a modest 200,000 atmospheres, they had observed the transformation of the black material to a clear, yellowish solid. It was diamond — diamond formed at room temperature.

Many chemists predict that buckeyballs will soon be available for a few dollars per pound. If so, it may well usher in a new era of diamond making. Fast, cheap, no complicated heating requirements, just a simple squeezer to synthesize pounds of diamonds — buckeyballs could become a diamond maker's dream.

The high-pressure adventure continues at an ever more intense pace, as research teams in a score of countries explore matter at extreme conditions. In the eighty years since Percy Bridgman first broke the 2,000-atmosphere mark in his makeshift laboratory, the range of routine research pressures has increased a thousandfold, and new records are set every few years. We have only just begun to discover the astonishing variety of new materials that pressure can provide — super-hard abrasives, dense deep-earth minerals, exotic crystalline forms of ordinary liquids, and perhaps even metallic hydrogen, all created in the past quarter century. What new wonders await us? What unimagined substances will change our lives?

[2] **stood poised to transform ...**: i.e. was about to transform ... 宙に浮いたバッキーボールが奇跡を行なっているといったイメージ.
[3] **avalanche** [ǽvəlæntʃ]: a sudden great rush
[6] **diamond-anvil cell:** 2個のダイアモンド片を使って数万から数百万気圧の圧力をかける装置. 下図参照
[19] **a score of countries:** some twenty countries
[21] **makeshift:** 間に合わせの
[22] **has increased a thousandfold:** has become a thousand times greater
[25] **superhard abrasives:** 超硬質研磨材
[26] **exotic crystalline forms:** 不思議な形の結晶
[27] **perhaps even metallic hydrogen:** ダイアモンド・アンヴィルで水素を圧縮する実験は長い歴史をもち，本文が書かれた1993年には，金属水素の成功は間近いと考えられていたが，生成した固体水素は2.5メガバールの圧力で崩れ，金属化には成功しなかった．1996年，液体水素に気体銃で圧力をかける実験で，金属水素ができていることが確認された．

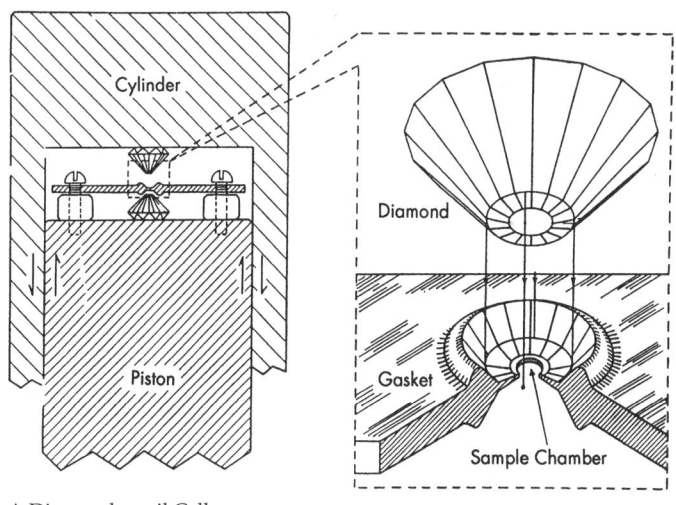

A Diamond-anvil Cell

a/b 選択の答

SESSION 1
    p. 7　[30]——— a
SESSION 2
    p. 13　[8]——— a
    p. 19　[30]——— a
    p. 21　[1]——— a
SEESION 4
    p. 33　[16]——— b
    p. 41　[20]——— b
    　　　　[25]——— b
    　　　　[26]——— a
SESSION 5
    p. 45　[14]——— b
    　　　　[30]——— b
    p. 47　[13]——— a, b
SESSION 7
    p. 69　[15]——— a
    p. 71　[10]——— b
SESSION 8
    p. 75　[24]——— a
    p. 81　[28]——— b
SESSION 9
    p. 85　[3]——— a
SESSION 10
    p. 97　[9]——— a
    p. 99　[2]——— b
    p. 101 [16]——— a, b
SESSION 12
    p. 123 [3]——— b
    　　　　[27]——— a
    p. 125 [20]——— b
    p. 127 [8]——— b

SESSION 14
    p. 145 [17]——— b
SESSION 15
    p. 153 [4]——— a, a, a
    p. 155 [26]——— a
    p. 157 [5]——— a
    p. 159 [21]——— a, b
    　　　　[29]——— b
    　　　　[33]——— b
    p. 161 [15]——— a
SESSION 18
    p. 189 [4]——— b
    p. 193 [13]——— a
SESSION 19
    p. 199 [18]——— b
    　　　　[24]——— a
    p. 201 [10]——— b
    p. 203 [34]——— b
    p. 207 [11]——— a
SESSION 20
    p. 209 [4]——— a
    p. 213 [12]——— a
    p. 217 [6]——— a
    　　　　[24]——— a
SESSION 21
    p. 219 [12]——— a
    p. 221 [3]——— b
    　　　　[31]——— a
    p. 223 [29]——— a
    p. 225 [6]——— b
    　　　　[14]——— a
    　　　　[37]——— b

Memorandum

Memorandum

Memorandum

Memorandum

Memorandum

Memorandum

The Expanding Universe of English II
2000 年 3 月 22 日　初　　版
2008 年 2 月 28 日　第 8 刷
［検印廃止］
編　者　東京大学教養学部英語部会
発行所　財団法人 東京大学出版会
代表者　岡本和夫

113–8654　東京都文京区本郷 7　東大構内
電話：03–3811–8814・FAX: 03–3812–6958
振替：00160–6–59964

印刷所　研究社印刷株式会社
製本所　株式会社島崎製本

© 2000 Department of English, The University of Tokyo, Komaba
ISBN 978–4–13–082104–9 Printed in Japan

R〈日本複写権センター委託出版物〉
本書の全部または一部を無断で複写複製(コピー)することは，
著作権法上での例外を除き，禁じられています．本書からの複
写を希望される場合は，日本複写権センター (03–3401–2382) に
ご連絡ください．

東京大学が発信する新しい教養英語テキスト
On Campus
東京大学教養学部英語部会 編
B5 判・194 頁 / 定価（本体価格 1700 円 + 税）

Campus Wide
東京大学教養学部英語部会 編
B5 判・202 頁 / 定価（本体価格 1700 円 + 税）

The Universe of English II
東京大学教養学部英語部会 編
ベストセラーになった東大駒場の1年生用統一テキストが全章新しくなった．最新の英文で語られる知の宇宙と，味わい深い短編小説世界を豊富な注に導かれて散策する「教養英語」の新・定番テキスト．

［テキストのみ］菊判・240 頁 / 定価（本体価格 1900 円 + 税）
［テキスト + 4CD］菊判・函入 / 定価（本体価格 3800 円 + 税）

「もう一つの別な宇宙」……？
The Parallel Universe of English
佐藤良明・柴田元幸 編
ともに翻訳家にしてエッセイストとして知られる二人が選りすぐったポップなアンソロジー．小津映画からバービーまで，日米の文化をいまどきの英語で読む15編．
A5 判・208 頁 / 定価（本体価格 1800 円 + 税）